We all can see the technology storm coming, but the church has adapted to technological storms in every era. My hope is that we can not only adapt this time but even *thrive* in coming years in what might be our greatest challenge so far. David Swisher's book, *Early Warning*, offers church leaders a clear, hope-filled guide for navigating technological disruption with both wisdom and courage as we "lead proactively rather than reactively" as he advises. After reading Swisher's work, I hope we can all feel like we've got an "early warning system in place...." As he says, "You can not only thrive, but even offer your congregation hope and peace in the midst of the storm." The tech analysis and practical ministry experience combined in *Early Warning* promises to show church leaders how to face disruption faithfully, and without fear.

—**David Drury** is the founder of more than a dozen organizations and church plants and is the author of a dozen published books found at DavidDrury.com

I've watched David Swisher guide educators and ministry leaders through technological disruption for years, and *Early Warning* distills that rare wisdom into essential reading for pastors. His chapters on VR and metaverse ministry opened my eyes to mission fields I'd walked through and been unsure of. The care he puts into talking about potential pitfalls as well as opportunities for every topic is something that will challenge your assumptions and equip you to lead faithfully through the digital disruptions already reshaping ministry.

—**Andy Mage**, Creative Pastor, Lux Digital Church

David Swisher's *Early Warning* is a wonderfully interesting, insightful, and wise look at the technologies of our times, with historical insights, biblical frameworks, and sober analysis. Ministry leaders would do well to read and discuss it.

—**Quentin Schultze**, PhD, author of *Habits of the High-Tech Heart: Living Virtuously in the Information Age*

Swisher has written a book of practical wisdom that will help all leaders navigate the emerging features of our technological culture with biblical fidelity, theological sensitivity, and missional ingenuity. He avoids the traps of unreflective optimism and unwarranted pessimism by steering a wise path through the risks and opportunities of current innovations for the future of the church. What we are given is not just a primer on developing technologies, nor merely advice on how to incorporate them into ministry settings, but a compendium of principles that help us discern the signs of the times and respond with faithful confidence.

—**Phillip R. Meadows**, Sundo Kim Professor of Evangelism and Practical Theology, Asbury Theological Seminary

David is a great storyteller with a talent for weaving church history with modern-day scenarios that drive home important ideas and cement them into reality. If you're feeling uncertain about technology in the church, this book is your guide. Prepare to be inspired and equipped.

—**Mike Jones**, MFA, Assistant Director, IWU Future Learning Lab

Rapid change happens. Change raises questions. What is happening? Can I live with it? Is it to be shunned or embraced? AI and other technological changes are rapidly transforming society, churches, the economy, research, writing, and mundane daily tasks. To what future should leaders lead? Swisher provides a remarkably useful tome that demystifies the origins and development of diverse technologies, discusses applicability, and offers constructive guidance for leaders and organizations: look for the new opportunities! The volume is multi-disciplinary: historical, theological, technological; an important contribution to cultural history. It is informative, provocative, and a fun read!

—**David Bundy**, Manchester Wesley Research Centre

Early Warning is more than a book—it's a lifeline, a lightning rod, and a lighthouse. David Swisher doesn't just help us "weather the storm" of technological disruption; he trains us to become storm chasers for Christ. With the eyes of a historian, the heart of a pastor, and the imagination of a futurist, Swisher offers not gadgets and gimmicks but guidance and grace.

This book is not about running from disruption but running toward it with faith, courage, and hope. Swisher shows that the storms of AI, blockchain, the metaverse, and autonomous tech are not threats to be feared but thresholds to be crossed—opportunities to reimagine ministry for a new generation. If you want to help your people not just survive disruption but sing in the storm, this is the book you've been waiting for. David Swisher is the early warning system the church desperately needs.

—**Leonard Sweet**, prolific author (e.g. *The Star Still Beckons*), professor, preacher, publisher, proprietor

Dr. David Swisher has a deep and palpable love for the local church. His focus on mission drives him to help churches use technology to enhance their work to make the world a more just and beautiful place. That passion for mission along with expertise in technology and change makes this work a must read for leaders seeking to be good stewards of the organizations they lead.

—**Joel Liechty**, Kairos University

Dr. David Swisher's many years of professional experience and hands-on use of technology in varied and diverse settings makes him a prime resource for this type of book. His historical perspective gives important foundational insights along with scripture reference. Yet to me, one of the most powerful aspects of this book is its interesting vignettes that really make the information come alive with realistic examples and pragmatic descriptions of effective technological use. This is a much-needed book for anyone that wants to lead with insightful wisdom in a world dominated by fast-paced and ongoing technological change.

—**Brent A. Anders**, PhD., University Lecturer and Researcher, Director of the Sovorel Center for Teaching & Learning

I had the honor of working with David at Tabor College. He knows his stuff when it comes to educational technology. *Early Warning* proves it.

—**Jules Glanzer**, President Emeritus Tabor College

Today, the church is faced with a technological storm of immense proportions. We struggle to understand, much less how to engage, this multifaceted challenge. Fortunately, we now have a reliable guide in David Swisher, who brings his extensive background in emerging technology and Christian ministry to gift us with this outstanding book. If, like me, you know little about the myriad technologies found on the internet, you will learn much from David's clear presentation. But more than that, his theologically sound insights help us navigate the pitfalls and embrace the opportunities for ministry in these new technologies. This is an enormously helpful book, and I cannot recommend it enough!

—**Henry H. Knight III**, Emeritus Professor of Wesleyan Studies and Evangelism, Saint Paul School of Theology, Leawood, Kansas

As a district superintendent working with more than 100 churches, I am pleased to endorse Dr. David Swisher's insightful book on navigating disruptive technology innovation for pastors and ministry leaders. This timely resource offers a compelling and practical guide for integrating technological advancements into ministry with wisdom and purpose. Dr. Swisher skillfully blends deep understanding, actionable strategies, and a heartfelt commitment to ministry, providing church leaders with a clear framework to address the challenges and opportunities of our rapidly evolving landscape. I strongly recommend this book to ministry professionals seeking to lead their congregations with confidence and foresight in an age of technological transformation.

—**Mark Gorveatte**, District Superintendent, Crossroads District of the Wesleyan Church

EARLY WARNING

FULL-SIZE COLOR IMAGES

Since space constraints and the nature of black and white printing limit the size and quality of images, full-size color images (with additional notes) are available for all of the pictures included in this book at: https://tinyurl.com/EW-Images

EARLY WARNING

HOW TO
LEAD WITH WISDOM
IN TIMES OF
TECHNOLOGICAL
DISRUPTION

David J. Swisher

invite
PRESS
Plano, Texas

CONTENTS

"HE'S THE TECH GUY."

When I first met David Swisher, one of our colleagues introduced us with this description. I quickly learned this was a vast understatement.

Yes, David knew how to solve computer and network problems in the office. But as time went on, I quickly realized David himself was far more wide-ranging and multifaceted than the label "tech guy." His knowledge and skills transcend such simple categories.

I learned that we had both been shaped by the same doctoral program, which gave us common ground even before we realized it. Both of us had studied Semiotics and Future Studies with Dr. Leonard Sweet and had been radically shaped by our experience. This doctoral program was unlike any in the country and combined history, philosophy, and theology with contemporary analysis and the study of future trends. It wasn't simply an academic pursuit—it became a way of seeing the world differently, of reading both culture and scripture with fresh eyes. That's something David has carried forward in his life and his writing.

Over the years, my friendship and partnership with David have gone far beyond the office. We've walked together through ideas that, at the time, felt experimental but turned out to be formative. From his developing the Technology for Ministry course at Tabor College, which helped students see technology not just as tools but as part of their ministry calling, to our collaboration with Leonard Sweet on the Future Studies course within the Tabor College Ministry Entrepreneurship and Innovation MA program, to co-hosting an AI Showcase at Indiana Wesleyan University with our faculty, where we explored how artificial intelligence is reshaping teaching, research, and the academic landscape, I've watched the themes in this book take shape in real time. What you hold in your hands is the fruit of those years of exploration.

In these pages David tackles technologies both familiar and surprising: AI, livestreaming, VR, even autonomous vehicles. What makes his approach so valuable is the way he frames each issue through history and theology, then helps leaders imagine how to live and lead faithfully in light of it. Because whether we embrace them or resist them, these technologies will shape all of us.

Something you won't learn in these pages is David's passion for the Trans-Siberian Orchestra's Christmas storytelling performances—a spectacle of holiday music, thundering electric guitars, lights and pyrotechnics. That same sense of wonder, creativity, and energy infuses David's work. He doesn't just present information; he turns it into spectacle, bringing it alive.

David is like a Chagall window—multifaceted, unique, and always surprising. That surprising range shows up in the many sides of his life.

What you'll discover as you read is David is so much more than a tech guy. His range of interests will come clear as you turn the pages. He is a master cake decorator. He understands at a deep level the world of cryptocurrency, the metaverse, and the future. He brings a historian's eye to current issues. He is also deeply rooted theologically and presents this material in a way that is honest to scripture and tradition.

I've watched David engage with ideas that many would shy away from, not because he enjoys controversy, but because he takes seriously the call to love God with our minds. He does not settle for easy answers, and he invites readers into that same kind of wrestling. That's what makes this book so valuable.

But let me be clear: this isn't just a book about gadgets or innovation, nor is it only about ministry challenges. It is about ministry at the intersection of disruption and faithfulness. David writes as someone who has lived in that tension and who understands that technology is not merely a set of tools, but a cultural force shaping the way we see the world, relate to one another, and live out our calling. That's why I believe pastors and ministry leaders need to read this book now: not to become experts in the digital world, but to lead wisely, faithfully, and with hope in an age of constant change.

Be prepared: this book will leave no stone unturned, and you'll end it wiser and better informed, with a fair bit of pyrotechnics thrown in. But more than that, you'll find yourself challenged to think, to question, and perhaps to see God's world with new eyes.

My encouragement as you begin is to approach these pages with openness. Don't just read for information, but with imagination. Whether you are navigating AI, social media, or digital ministry, let David's insights challenge you, even unsettle you at times, but also encourage you. This book is a pastoral invitation to lead with wisdom, courage, and hope in the midst of disruption. And I can't imagine a better voice to guide you in that journey than my friend, Dr. David Swisher.

Rick Bartlett, DMin
August 2025

DEDICATION

This book is dedicated to all of the pastors and ministry leaders currently ministering in difficult and challenging roles, especially those serving smaller churches in rural areas:

I know that you genuinely want to serve your community, follow Jesus wholeheartedly, and truly make a transformative difference in people's lives. I see you, and I've been there. I want you to know that your work is not in vain. People do listen, learn, and grow, even though it's often slow-going and unrewarding, even when the signs of progress seldom materialize. It takes time, but it's still worth it. Also, you are not alone. Even when it feels like you are, God still has a remnant of thousands like you who remain faithful and serve wholeheartedly. God knows your heart and your service.

I hope that this book encourages you and gives you useful insights and practical perspectives to better understand the technology that so easily overwhelms, so that you can use it instead for ministry progress. These technologies may be slower to arrive where you serve and your community will likely be slower to embrace or even engage with them. However, understanding what's coming and knowing the people you serve will help prepare you to lead with wisdom.

ACKNOWLEDGEMENTS

No book (or any creative writing project for that matter) is ever written in a vacuum; each one stands on the support and encouragement of many people. This book is no exception.

First and foremost, I'm grateful for my wife, Nicole, and my kids – Lydia, Josh, Jeremiah, and Susannah. They believed in me and stood by me throughout this project, nurturing, supporting, and encouraging me, as well as enduring all the odd hours and writing times. They handled so many things while I was secluded at my desk researching and writing, and they put up with my incessant sharing of ideas and thoughts before they were fully formed.

I would also be remiss if I didn't mention Bernard Holmes and Gordon MacDonald. My Discipleship professor and mentor, Dr. Holmes didn't just teach the subject—he lived it. I was blessed to meet with him and a group of guys every Tuesday morning for discipleship throughout my college experience. He introduced me to Gordon MacDonald's *Ordering Your Private World*, which was a pivotal influence on my spiritual formation while studying for ministry, followed by *Renewing Your Spiritual Passion*, which shaped me even further.

Later, while pastoring in rural Kansas, I discovered MacDonald's *Who Stole My Church?* and led my congregation through it as a study. That book provided a theological framework for innovation in ministry, opened my eyes to the people and generational dynamics involved, and gave us a safe, story-driven way to explore church change. Its blending of church history with future possibilities has significantly influenced my approach to ministry innovation. I had forgotten just how formative it was until I recently asked my Ministry Leadership students at Kingswood University to study it as well. Reflections of MacDonald's approach and influence are scattered throughout this book.

This book also benefitted greatly from the many insight-filled conversations I enjoyed over the years with Phil Meadows and Brannon Hancock at the Wesleyan Theological Society annual meetings. Those conversations challenged my thinking, sharpened my ideas, and encouraged me. They also assured me that what I was working on was a much-needed perspective that would make a valuable contribution.

This book would not exist had it not been for the incredible support, encouragement, and insatiable intellectual curiosity of my education and ministry innovation colleague and friend, Rick Bartlett, who not only gave me the opportunity to develop a previously unheard-of course in *Technology for Ministry*, but who also spent considerable time ideating, dreaming, planning, and encouraging me as I took those initial ideas and began considering a book.

I still remember the day that Len Wilson met with the students in my *Technology for Ministry* class, providing insight, relevance, and practical guidance to these entrepreneurial, innovation-minded students. Years later, Len is now my friend and publisher, and I couldn't be more thrilled. After he helped me re-think the way I approached this book (more on that in the concluding chapter), several of those same students gave insightful feedback on my initial outlines and planning draft: Kit Berry, Kurt McDonald, and Shelly Westfall.

My friend and ministry encourager, Josh Engle, was also an incredible sounding board and constant source of encouragement as I explored various angles, and continually refined my approach. An extended conversation with Lori Wagner was a gamechanger; that dialogue helped shape the trajectory. She focused my efforts in a way that finally felt viable, and her encouragement and feedback convinced me it could not only be done, but that it would also be a valuable contribution to future ministers and church leaders.

Several colleagues of mine from Indiana Wesleyan University, all of whom are now long-time friends, were absolutely instrumental in shaping my thoughts, as well as exploring technology, innovation, and AI with me: Tiffany Snyder, Mike Jones, Annie Els, and again Rick Bartlett. They pushed me, challenged me, affirmed me, ideated with me, and encouraged me – and you, my reader, are the beneficiary. Our innovation road trip to Phoenix really opened all of our minds to the possibilities and potential before us.

In addition to these colleagues, this book has been significantly enhanced thanks to my friendship and ongoing dialogues with Jason Moore, T'Neil Walea, and Sandra Metzger. From hearty affirmations to challenging pushback, from passing along new tips and techniques to discussions of new innovations, and even late-night chats with Jason about writing and publishing procedures as well as AI challenges, these three kept the learning and inspiration alive that drove me to bring to life what you see in these pages.

Furthermore, my pastor, Scott Rhyno; my District Superintendent, Mark Gorveatte; and my denominational G.S., Wayne Schmidt; and my former pastors, John & Danielle Freed, have all supported and encouraged my research and writing and look forward to this book's release. They *'get'* why it matters.

I am also grateful to my colleagues in ministry who gave feedback on specific chapters: Brent Anders, Danielle Freed, John Howell, Harrison Painter, Frank Poncé, Elizabeth Rhyno, Scott Rhyno, Corey Seales, Joni Sedberry, and T'Neil Walea. Each offered helpful insights, suggestions, revisions, and improvements that made the finished book far better than it would have been otherwise.

Lastly, my editor at Invite Press, Ariana Weberg, artfully found the beauty in what I did well and helpfully articulated areas where it needed improvement. She urged me to revise some challenging sections and formatting that greatly improved clarity and flow, which ultimately made this book so much better.

There are many more who had a hand in shaping it, whose voices weren't felt editorially but whose influence still mattered. I can't possibly name all of them, but please know that I appreciate you, and this book is better because of it.

For everyone mentioned here (as well as those I've undoubtedly missed), I thank you.

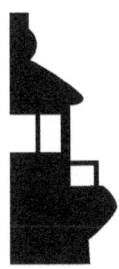

HOW GENERATIVE AI FACTORED INTO THIS BOOK

Since I am an AI trainer and consultant, and have worked with generative AI for several years now—regularly training faculty and ministry leaders on it—you may be wondering how I used it in this book.

I value the power and potential of generative AI, but I am also a firm believer that an author's words should be their own. This book represents my voice, my convictions, and my experiences. Every chapter has been prayerfully written, personally reviewed, and carefully edited by me. If you hear my "voice" in these pages, that's because it truly is mine.

That said, I want to be transparent that generative AI was a significant collaboration partner throughout the ideation and drafting process. I used it in much the same way as I would a trusted research assistant, conversation partner, or brainstorming colleague.

Specifically, I used AI to:

- Identify specific examples of emerging technologies and example ministry use cases

- Generate potential metaphors, illustrations, and teaching angles to spark my own thinking

- Help shape the fictional but plausible ministry vignettes by combining realistic contexts and pastoral roles

- Iterate ideas until they resonated with my goals for accuracy, tone, and pastoral applicability, and

- Review drafts for clarity, coherence, or missed connections

In every case, I provided the context, carefully articulated the prompts, judiciously evaluated the results, and then intentionally rewrote, reshaped, or discarded what did not align with my vision. No sentence appears here without my deliberate choice to include it. In that sense, AI has been less a ghostwriter and more a storm-spotter—a tool that helped me scan the horizon more quickly and with greater clarity, but one that still required my judgment, discernment, and voice to interpret what I felt mattered.

I disclose this not because I fear AI's involvement undermines the integrity of my work, but because I believe honesty builds trust. Just as pastors and ministry leaders must thoughtfully discern how to use these tools in their own contexts, I want you to know how I have done so in this book: Responsibly, ethically, and transparently, with the firm conviction that the minister should always be in the driver's seat, listening first and foremost to God's voice. After all, technology should be our servant, not a master.

PLAUSIBLE INTERSECTIONS OF MINISTRY WITH TECHNOLOGY

(About the Ministry Context Vignettes)

When new technology emerges, it is often difficult to understand how it might be utilized or what it could look like in practice, especially when the concepts and applications are entirely new. For this reason, in each chapter I have included a plausible scenario describing a hypothetical minister's experiences in a realistic context as they engage with the new technology. I do this to showcase how the technology can be used in a ministry context and to illustrate the questions it raises.

Each scenario is fictional, yet modeled after real churches and ministry contexts I am familiar with or have learned about through conversations with ministry friends. However, no specific church, ministry, or context is identified directly, and none are real. Instead, each scenario is an amalgamation of multiple ministers and contexts, with all names, places, roles, and details being hypothetical.

To develop these scenarios, I engaged in substantial ideation with generative AI, carefully guiding its output while infusing my own background and experiences into the process. As a tribute to those on the frontlines and the cutting edge, I have named the primary ministers in each scenario after real ministry technology leaders whose innovation and leadership I admire.

Introduction

CHASING THE STORMS

Leading Ministries Well Through Disruptive Technology Innovation

"When He got into the boat, His disciples followed Him. And behold, a violent storm developed on the sea, so that the boat was being covered by the waves; but Jesus Himself was asleep. And they came to Him and woke Him, saying, "Save us, Lord; we are perishing!" He said to them, "Why are you afraid, you men of little faith?" Then He got up and rebuked the winds and the sea, and it became perfectly calm. The men were amazed, and said, "What kind of a man is this, that even the winds and the sea obey Him?" Matthew 8:23-27 (NASB)

Storms have always fascinated me. I love to sit on my porch or in the safety of a shelter and watch as powerful storms roll in. The sheer power and forces that are unleashed are incredible to watch – the visual displays of lightning, the audible roar of thunder, the pelting of rain or hail, and whatever else the storm dishes out. I find it awe-inspiring, and it reminds me of the incredible power, beauty, and creativity of the God I serve.

But it's another thing altogether to be caught in a storm unprepared. Without the safety of a shelter or a screened-in covered porch to watch from a safe vantage point, those same storms can be terrifying, unnerving, & relentlessly chaotic. It's easy in those circumstances for fear to creep in and worries to emerge. After all, storms can wreak havoc, cause substantial property damage, and even harm human life too...as well as create a disruptive impact on electricity and power, wireless access, and travel networks.

Growing up in the Midwest, I've experienced my fair share of storms, including the awe-inspiring and yet highly-dangerous variety which regularly inhabit "Tornado Alley" (my home region). I have ministry friends who vividly remember the massive EF5 tornado that cleared a swath through Moore, Oklahoma in 2013 and ravaged their neighborhoods and churches. I pastored a church in Topeka, Kansas which had been in the direct path of the famous EF5 tornado of 1966, one which plowed a nearly 900-ft wide path of destruction for 21 miles;[1] the church miraculously escaped destruction because it sat on the leeward side of Burnett's Mound, enabling the tornado to hop over the building.

While pastoring in Abilene, Kansas, we saw firsthand the devastation of a violent EF4 tornado which plowed through nearby Chapman, KS in 2016...a tornado which stayed on the ground for 90 minutes, leaving a 26-mile long swath of destruction that leveled entire neighborhoods. While doing missions work in Guatemala and the Philippines, I witnessed gale-force winds which pummeled the region from tropical storms. And more recently here in Indiana, I saw firsthand the destruction caused by an EF2 tornado which tore through the heart of nearby Pendleton, Indiana in 2019 and brought the city to a standstill for days.

I've grown up with tornado safety drills being a regular part of school schedules: Moving to the interior hallways and tucking our heads into our knees as normal preparation for tornado warnings. And I've sheltered with my own family as tornado sirens sounded dozens of times. Around here, tornados and destructive storms are common enough events that when people buy and rent homes, they pay close attention to what these homes offer for tornado shelters, basements, and storm protection measures.

What you might find surprising, though, is that I have always been fascinated by the storm chasers...those courageous (or crazy?) individuals who rush TO centers of peak tornado activity when everyone else is sheltering or leaving. After all, storms fascinate me. But on top of that, I'm a video and multimedia creator, and the idea of documenting a massive tornado up close and in person on video (or better yet, seeing it from the inside) would be the ultimate adventure for me. Of course, my parents and teachers always insisted that we stay deep in the heart of the protective interior of the building, and once I became a father, keeping my children protected was an undisputed priority. So as much as I loved weather forecasting and tracking significant storms, I never got the opportunity to go chase one myself. However, I've often dreamed about what that experience might be like, and I've watched multiple documentaries about how these storm chasers detect emerging systems, predict where and how they'll strike, spot funnel clouds as they emerge, capture tornadoes when they touch down, and measure the aftermath.

Those brave souls who can do that have contributed extensive knowledge in order to increase the amount of warning time we get...and that ultimately saves lives. And then of course there's one of my all-time favorite movies:

---

1.   Topeka Capital-Journal, "A History of Twisters: Tornadoes in Kansas since 1950," *cjonline*, Data archive, Tornado archive, https://data.cjonline.com/tornado-archive/

Twister (1996), starring Bill Paxton and Helen Hunt. The plotline centers around a group of storm chasers led by Jo, a weather scientist now in her 40s, who as a child saw her father perish in a tornado and today leads a team trying to research tornadoes to develop and deploy an early warning system. Reuniting with her ex, they study a huge outbreak of multiple tornadoes, attempting to launch diagnostic instruments to get scientific data and measurements, and ultimately find themselves with a terrifying front-row seat to several tornadoes closer than most people have ever dared to go. The movie's certainly not PG, though; it's scary and frightening because although storms like these may be awe-inspiring, they are also very dangerous. And the more recent reboot of it only ups the ante with even more danger, extreme storms, and special effects.

So why do people like these storm chasers invest so much time and energy in understanding how storms like these emerge, where they form, which way they'll go, and how bad they'll be? They know that the better we understand how the storms develop (and where, and when), the greater the amount of advance warning so that people can take cover in order to survive. After all, **if you know what's coming and how it will impact you, you can prepare for it, and ultimately thrive**. Early warnings are extremely beneficial. When you're caught unprepared, the storms cause tremendous damage and collateral impact, and struggling to recover becomes a time-consuming priority. However, when you're prepared, you can be an alert first responder offering life-giving hope to people who are devastated by the storms.

This, in a nutshell, is what I'm hoping to accomplish in this book. The COVID-19 pandemic of 2020 forced upon us a massive disruption on multiple fronts…a storm of epic proportions whose effects we are still feeling today. As a technology coordinator and experienced Zoom administrator who was already very comfortable with online worship and teaching, I spent every waking hour for several months straight helping pastors and ministry leaders transition their worship services into online and livestreamed experiences. I developed lots of lists and handouts and technology training resources to help my fellow pastors survive that storm. But as much as we would have liked to have a respite following the pandemic's end, unfortunately, the disruptive forces are nowhere near over.

The rapidly-shifting cultural forces brought on by changing demographics, coupled with the initial necessity and then later opportunity of online and later viewing of services has led to a new reality where far fewer people attend church live or in person, and that challenges the norms of how we disciple and evangelize…as well as how we measure attendance or "success." And in the midst of all this, the growth in online networking and proliferation in online & livestreamed ministries has given rise to new forms of church expression through virtual reality and the metaverse, which challenges our preconceptions and forces us reconsider how necessary buildings are, even re-evaluating what "church" necessarily looks like. There has been tremendous growth in the digital church as well as VR, metaverse, and avatar-based church expressions.

At the same time, many of my colleagues, and so many pastors and church leaders are now seeing the rapid dissemination of generative AI now becoming readily available in conversational language to the average person, and they are reeling from that impact, too…trying to figure out what it is, as well as determine whether it's harmful or helpful, what's acceptable, and how best to lead our congregations wisely through these murky waters.

And if that wasn't enough, many of the technologies which were merely on the fringe a few years ago (such as cryptocurrency, blockchain, NFTs, and DAOs) are now part of common parlance and are poised to re-shape some of our traditional understandings of church administrative structure, governance, and financing within the next few years. I am also aware of multiple disruptive technology innovations which are rapidly coming down the pike (such as autonomous vehicles, delivery, & passenger service) which will undoubtedly have a huge impact on how we live, work, do business, and interact with each other… and these will undoubtedly impact how we do church in years to come.

It can be overwhelming and debilitating for the leader who's unprepared for what's coming. But when you've got an early warning system in place to know what's coming, you can not only thrive, but even offer your congregation hope and peace in the midst of the storm. That informed context of an early warning system is what this book offers.

My heart goes out to all the pastors who are navigating these challenging days, and my aim in this book is to give you hope and courage, as well as insights and practical advice, on how you can not only survive this storm, but understand what's coming and thrive in the midst of it. Like the "tribe of Isaachar" from Bible times[2] (those who understood the times and knew what Israel should do), I see myself as a "storm chaser" who's analyzing the disruptive technologies and their impact so that I can equip you to use the adversity and challenges these storms bring to open the doors of opportunity for an even brighter future.

How do I know this is possible? I've been doing it for several decades! I've been in ministry now for 39 years, and for the vast majority of that I've been bi-vocational, working with technology, typically in some kind of role involving classroom technology, multimedia, and instructional design & technology.

---

2.   1 Chronicles 12:32.

In fact, for the last 2 decades, I've worked in higher education, managing and implementing technology innovation, and I've been a regional leader and chair of an organization which hosts conferences and professional development on these emerging technologies and their impact. My job has literally been to stay abreast of all the emerging technologies which are likely to impact us, experiment with them, and learn best practices for them, and then prepare university leaders and faculty to use them well. It's what I do for a living.

And then I take all the ideas and concepts I've learned in the academy and translate them for church and ministry leaders. Some people are called to be pastors, teachers, or missionaries, but MY calling is to ministry technology. My passion is helping the Church learn how to wisely utilize and embrace technology for ministry, evaluate it theologically and pragmatically, and help its leaders know how to use it effectively. In fact, I even formed a theological society a few years ago to do that, and my ministry friends and denominational leaders all know that this is my specialty. It's what I do.

So as we set out on this storm-chasing adventure together, I want to reassure you that you're not alone. God understands what challenges you're facing from all this disruptive technology, and He's not surprised by any of it, nor is He caught off guard. Also, many respected church leaders throughout history have been through what you're going through, and we can learn a lot from them (in fact, many of them are known to us today *because* of the stormy challenges they faced).

Furthermore, I've been down this road before, and I know this field of ministry technology extremely well. I understand these disruptive technology innovations which are coming, too, and although I am well aware of the all-too-present challenges and risks, I also see the long-range potential and opportunities before us in this emerging technology disruption.

And I'm looking forward to helping you thrive amidst these storms. Strap in! It will be an incredible ride.

> *"With Christ in my vessel, I can smile at the storms,*
> *as we go sailing home."*
>
> ~ **Popular Children's Bible action song**

PANDEMIC PANIC

Technology After Livestream

The COVID-19 pandemic forced massive changes in the way we conduct church, moving most churches online and necessitating innovation & creative outreach. These were long overdue changes which helped the Church to think creatively and engage strategically. What has emerged in the aftermath, however, is a paradigm shift in attendance patterns – the decline of in-person, rise of online-only & flex attendance, & DVR'ing of services (watching later rather than live).

I remember the early days of the COVID-19 pandemic all too well. At the time, I was the leader of the camera production team at Waterline Church (Fishers, IN), and we had already been recording and uploading our services to YouTube for a few years. In 2018, we started experimenting with streaming our services on Facebook Live, first with a weekly "Lunch Break Live" (informal hangout with the pastors) and then that fall, our first livestreamed services. So when the pandemic hit, thankfully we already had about 15 months' worth of experience behind us. In hindsight, we can see how God providentially had been preparing us to understand and use the technology well so that we could confidently assist other ministry leaders as they, too, made the transition.[1]

But, oh, my! How quickly things changed. In the spring of 2020, soon after the WHO declared it a global pandemic, the CDC announced "social distancing" guidelines, and there was talk of cancelling services (or making them virtual-only) for a few weeks to "flatten the curve." Many state governments banned large gatherings for a time, often including religious services, and suddenly a huge swath of the Church throughout the Western world was

---

1. In full disclosure, it was also providential that I had learned about and experienced multi-camera live productions through Community Access Television (Salina, KS) and through my work with commencement ceremonies and our hosting of Steve Fossett's record-setting GlobalFlyer adventures at Kansas State Polytechnic (K-State's Salina campus), and then I later served as an active volunteer on the camera/production team at Newspring Church (Wichita, KS), helping to run our livestreamed – and later aired on TV – services.

scrambling to figure out how to take what had nearly always been in-person worship and teaching and make it available to parishioners online.

As the weeks turned into months, we quickly began to realize that this wasn't just a temporary situation, but was instead a new reality that we were going to have to figure out, without knowing how long it would last. Initially many pastors just recorded their sermons or devotional insights and uploaded them or shared links to them. Some just sent out transcripts, or audio-only files (after all, at first, it was just a matter of getting the *content* of the messages out, not about replicating the worship & teaching experience online). But as the lockdowns continued and it became clear it would last much longer than anyone anticipated, pastors everywhere began trying to find better ways.

Some pastors organized drive-in services at church facilities: Stay in your cars, but tune in to the worship and sermon via shortwave radio. Some turned to familiar platforms like Facebook or YouTube, using smartphones to broadcast the worship and sermon. Lacking experience with video production, the quality and experience for many was all over the map (but for the most part, sub-par and not very engaging, at best.)

Then came more questions...and more issues:

- How do we do **communion**? (especially when it had been a really long time since we last had one). Many experimented with drive-by communion, or pastoral blessing of the elements which were then mailed out or available for pickup.
- Can we do **baptism** socially distanced?
- How do we have **meetings** (like Sunday School, committees, and board meetings) online? Or **discipleship**?

Enter Zoom. Most of us heard about Zoom and quickly experimented with this new technology platform that could make live videoconferencing with others work well with minimal equipment and technology required.

It was one of the Church's darkest and most difficult time periods. And yet it was simultaneously one of her brightest. Why? Because the pandemic and its lockdowns forced us to get creative to fulfill our mission and purpose. And THAT is where the Church excels! After all, ***creativity and innovation are at the very heart and soul of our Creator God***. As difficult and challenging as those days were, as physically and emotionally exhausting as they were, I am absolutely certain that God smiled proudly when He saw the Church rise up to meet the challenge in creative and innovative ways.

LEARNING FROM RECENT HISTORY

Although the global pandemic and the government mandated lockdowns *felt* largely unprecedented (in fact, we used that word a lot during the first year or so of it), it certainly wasn't the first time in church history that the Church wrestled with major health crises coupled with government overreach and uncertain futures. Here are just a few notable examples:

Plague of Cyprian (250-270 AD) – Shortly after the New Testament period, this plague, which was named after St. Cyprian (bishop of Carthage), who described it as signaling the end of the world. It has often assumed to have been smallpox, but given Cyprian's description, it was more likely a viral hemorrhagic fever like Ebola.[2] Cyprian organized relief efforts and urged Christians to care for the sick, fostering a strong sense of community and service…and these efforts led to many conversions.[3]

Black Death (1347 – 1351) – The Bubonic Plague (also known as the "Black Death") arrived in Europe through trade routes and killed an estimated 25 million people…about a third of the population of the continent.[4] Unfortunately, this one was NOT a positive example of the Church's involvement: The Church struggled to provide an adequate and organized response, with many clergy dying or fleeing.[5] Ultimately, this led to a loss of faith in the Church's authority, which paved the way for multiple religious reforms.[6]

Spanish Flu (1918 – 1919) – Soon after the turn of the century, this H1N1 influenza virus infected about a third of the world's population, which led to approximately 50 million deaths worldwide. Many church services were canceled, and churches were often turned into hospitals. Governments imposed mask mandates and banned large gatherings, which included religious services.[7] [8]

---

2.   Glenn Sunshine (2020, July 01), "The Church's Response to Pandemics Throughout History and the Lessons for Today," *Mission Frontiers Magazine*, accessed Sept. 28, 2024 from https://www.missionfrontiers.org/issue/article/the-churchs-response-to-pandemics-throughout-history-and-the-lessons-for-to

3.   Christopher Gornold-Smith (2020, Aug. 4), "Cyprian of Carthage: Finding Purpose in the Plague," International Media Ministries, accessed Sept. 28, 2024 from https://imm.edu/blog/cyprian-of-carthage-finding-purpose-in-the-plague.

4.   Mark Galli (2020), "When a Third of the World Died: During the Catastrophic Black Plague, How Did Christians Respond?" special issue, Plagues & Epidemics (2020): 17-19, *Christian History*, accessed Sept. 29, 2024 from https://christianhistoryinstitute.org/uploaded/ch135s.pdf

5.   Joshua J. Mark (2020, April 16), "Religious Responses to the Black Death," World History Encyclopedia, accessed Sept. 28, 2024 from https://www.worldhistory.org/article/1541/religious-responses-to-the-black-death/

6.   Timothy O'Malley (2021, Nov. 19), "How Did the Church Fare During the Black Death and 400 Years of the Plague?," Church Life Journal, University of Notre Dame, accessed Sept. 28, 2024 from https://churchlifejournal.nd.edu/articles/how-did-the-church-fare-during-the-black-death-and-400-years-of-the-plague/

7.   William Katerberg (2020, March 13), "The Flu Epidemic of 1918-1919 and 'Churchless Sunday'," *Origins Online*, Calvin University > Heritage Hall, accessed Sept. 28, 2020 from https://origins.calvin.edu/2020/03/13/the-flu-epidemic-of-1918-1919-and-churchless-sunday/.

8.   Alan Frow (2020, July 29), "These Precedented Times: Lessons from the Church's response to the Spanish Flu in 1918," Roots & Wings: From the Southland to the Nations [blog], accessed Sept. 28, 2024 from https://alanfrow.

Ironically, although we may have heard of these historical plagues, rarely did any pastors or church leaders during our "unprecedented" times of the COVID-19 pandemic look into whether the Church had previously faced these same challenges in the past to learn if there were any insights or lessons we could learn from them. This is a common oversight I have observed repeatedly in how the Church tends to handle disruptive technology and other challenges: We assume the challenges we are facing are brand new, never experienced before, completely problematic, and the end of life and ministry as we know it (in other words, we catastrophize our experiences). Consequently, we have difficulty seeing the bright side or discerning any redeeming qualities to it.

However, a little historical context can go a long way. As the Spanish-American philosopher George Santayana famously said, "Those who cannot remember the past are condemned to repeat it."[9] When we know we've been down that road before, and we know what mistakes we made previously, we can learn from them and make improvements; these procedural changes we make to adapt can then become the foundation of our early warning system so that we are no longer broadsided by unanticipated challenges, but instead able to respond to them cogently, with hope and confidence. I think it is significant that every insightful futurist I know is also a perceptive historian. It is difficult to navigate an uncertain future when we don't know where we have been. That is why in this book I will explore lessons from church history for each of the disruptive technology innovations we consider (as I have done here with these three major plagues). I will also share important background and context about the technology to hopefully "demystify" it so that you can better understand what we're dealing with and, ideally, how the apparently disruptive technology can also benefit us.

ORIGINS OF LIVESTREAM TECHNOLOGY

Contrary to what many may be tempted to think, livestreaming didn't start with the COVID-19 pandemic. In fact, the technology had been around for over three decades prior to it. Livestreaming actually began in the early 1990s, not long after the development of the Internet. This was before Face-

---

blogspot.com/2020/07/these-precedented-times-lessons-from.html

9. This saying (and various derivatives of it) have been variously attributed to Edmund Burke, Winston Churchill, and a few others. Quote Investigator reviewed the history of the quotations and errant misattributions, determining that it probably originated with George Santayana's 1905 publication of *The Life of Reason, or The Phases of Human Progress*. See https://quoteinvestigator.com/2024/03/04/past-repeat/

book, before YouTube, before X (Twitter) or Twitch…before any social media existed. This was back in the heyday of VHS technology, when Blockbuster Video had hundreds of stores throughout the country and was the dominant player in the video rental market.

Deep in the heart of Silicon Valley, there was a garage band comprised of computer scientists and engineers called Severe Tire Damage[10] who played a 12-song concert, and their friends from Xerox PARC[11] decided to try out a new experimental technology called MBone (multicast backbone) to share it over a niche network on the newly-emerging Internet.[12] Mbone was designed to decrease the amount of bandwidth that was required to transmit video and audio. Even with that, streaming their concert footage consumed about half of the available bandwidth for the entire Internet at the time.[13]

Livestreaming technology solves a very big issue: Most of the time, when you view content on the internet, all of those graphics and images you see have to be physically downloaded to your computer or device so that your browser can easily display them. They exist in a cache, and doing it this way ensures that pages will display quickly, which improves browser performance. If you've ever visited an older website whose graphics were not optimized for the web, you've probably seen those webpages and their images load very slowly, often in chunks; caching files eliminates that, and older browser files are periodically flushed or updated to minimize space usage.

But video files are huge and take forever to download, and if you tried to view a video that had to be downloaded first, you would see the page load and then the video would finally appear several minutes (or possibly even hours) later. Most video players for Internet browsers have a capability built in that allows them to pre-load a certain amount of content so that your video playback isn't delayed, but if the video playback catches up to what has been downloaded so far, you will get a message that says the video is "buffering" (that means it is trying to finish downloading and it can't show you the rest of the video until it finishes downloading more of it).[14]

10.   Tom Meisfjord (2018, April 23), "The Not-So-Ancient History of Live Streaming," Switchboard > Technology, accessed Sept. 28, 2024 from https://switchboard.live/blog/live-streaming-history.

11.   PARC is an acronym for Palo Alto Research Center. Xerox PARC was famous for groundbreaking technology innovations that have been foundational to modern computing – the Graphical User Interface, the mouse, the Ethernet (which enabled Local Area Networks), laser printing, and Object-Oriented Programming.

12.   Restream Team (2021, Feb. 2), "The History of Live Streaming," Restream.io, accessed Sept. 28, 2024 from https://restream.io/blog/history-of-live-streaming.

13.   InterWorking Labs (2012, Dec. 26), "History of the Internet - Severe Tire Damage, The Internet's First Live Band," Vimeo, accessed Sept. 28, 2024 from https://vimeo.com/56349011.

14.   Cloudflare (n.d.), "What Does Buffering Mean? | Buffering in Video Streaming," Cloudflare > Learning Center, accessed Sept. 28, 2024 from https://www.cloudflare.com/learning/video/what-is-buffering/

Livestreaming technology solves that problem by utilizing a Content Delivery Network (CDN) along with a process called transcoding:

- **Transcoding** takes your outgoing content and prepares multiple versions of it with various bitrates (the speed at which your livestreaming setup can transmit data) so that each viewer receives whichever quality of broadcast they can best utilize based on whatever speed their Internet bandwidth and devices can handle: A viewer with a high-speed fiber optic Internet connection can view high-quality versions of your broadcast, but someone with older equipment or in more rural areas without high-speed Internet can still view the broadcast, albeit at a lower quality.[15]

- A **Content Delivery network (CDN)** handles the distribution of the content on your livestream provider's end. It caches each data segment (similar to how graphics from webpages you view are cached) to prevent bottlenecks, and then sends it to all users who are watching the stream. In this way it reduces or eliminates buffering, and also saves streaming bandwidth, too.[16]

When it's done well, livestreaming of services can be a very powerful method of connection, allowing congregation members and potential guests who are unable to be physically present to connect and observe (and ideally even participate) in the worship service. The quality of that experience, however, depends heavily on (1) the quality of the equipment used to record and transmit the livestream – especially the lighting and audio, (2) the placement of the camera, and (3) the intentionality of those leading the service in speaking to and including the online guests – especially in how they say it. I will explore each of these aspects a bit more later in this chapter, but first, let's consider some biblical and theological implications.

INSIGHTS FROM CHURCH HISTORY

Because livestreaming is such a paradigm shift that is counterintuitive for a lot of traditional pastors and parishioners, we can draw insights from the experience of Charles Simeon. When he first came to Christ at age nineteen, he did so alone, as Cambridge was a spiritually destitute place with few believers,

---

15. This was also one of the genius innovations of Zoom videoconferencing: By preparing multiple bitrate versions and auto-detecting which speed your browser and bandwidth could best support, they were able to avoid the choppy playback, latency (delays), and often-dropped calls that plagued so many of their predecessors.

16. Summary based on personal experience, supplemented by verification from Emily Krings (2024, Oct. 16), "What is Live Streaming Technology and How Does it Work?," The Video Experts Blog, DaCast, accessed Dec. 30, 2024: https://www.dacast.com/blog/what-is-live-streaming/

and he knew none of them.[17] For three years his faith grew through personal study, but he struggled to find anyone of like faith to share it with, and he tried visiting multiple churches in vain, finding them shallow and lukewarm and not preaching the truth.[18] Eventually he found and attended St. Edwards' Church in Cambridge, and only a week after his ordination, the priest asked him to fill in while he was on vacation over the summer. The response to Simeon's preaching was astonishing; he filled the church with hearers, "a thing unknown there for near a century" as Henry Venn put it.[19]

A while later, the vicar of Holy Trinity Church in Cambridge died, and the Bishop of Ely appointed Charles Simeon to replace him. The churchwardens and congregation staunchly opposed him; they wanted their curate (Hammond) to serve as vicar, and considered Simeon an interloper. When Simeon preached his first sermon, the churchwardens locked the pews so that nobody could sit in them. So the parishioners gathered in the aisles, and Simeon personally purchased benches for the congregation to sit on (which the churchwardens then threw out).[20] They were not just opposed to him being there; they objected to what he preached and the way he preached:[21] They "disliked the earnestness of his manner and the evangelicalism of his message."[22] He was often held in derision for his biblical preaching and his uncompromising evangelical[23] stance. He was slandered with all kinds of rumors. At the university, people talked about the "fanatical minister" and warned new freshmen to avoid Trinity because of him.[24] Services were often disrupted, and tumults often occurred in the street outside of the church. He was often attacked and had both insults and eggs lobbed at him. Nevertheless, he persisted.

Charles Simeon was firmly convinced that the church did not exist for itself, but for those beyond its walls who were not members yet. To reach them, Simeon started "conversation parties" to make it easier for students to

17. John Piper (1989, April 15), "Brothers, We Must Not Mind a Little Suffering: Meditations on the Life of Charles Simeon," 1989 Bethlehem Conference for Pastors, Desiring God, accessed Jan. 2, 2025 from https://www.desiringgod.org/messages/brothers-we-must-not-mind-a-little-suffering

18. Ian Barter (2001), "Charles Simeon of Cambridge," Banner of Truth, Christian Library, accessed Jan. 1, 2025 https://www.christianstudylibrary.org/article/charles-simeon-cambridge

19. Barter (2001), "Charles Simeon of Cambridge."

20. Julia Cameron, ed. (2013), *Charles Simeon of Cambridge: Silhouettes and Skeletons*, Dictum Press / Evangelical Fellowship in the Anglican Communion, accessed Dec. 31, 2024 from https://efacglobal.com/wp-content/uploads/2024/07/Charles-Simeon-of-Cambridge.pdf

21. Barter (2001), "Charles Simeon of Cambridge."

22. Holy Trinity Church (n.d.), "History of HT," Holy Trinity Church Cambridge, accessed Sept. 29, 2024 from https://www.htcambridge.org.uk/our-story.

23. I use the term "evangelical" here in its historical sense, referring to the movement within the Church of England at the time that emphasized a personal and transformative relationship with Christ, rooted in the authority of Scripture, justification by faith, and the necessity of spiritual rebirth...and which stood in stark contrast to the liberal intellectualism and dominant high-church Anglican ethos of the time that often focused on ritual, tradition, and adherence to established church structures.

24. Piper (1989, April 15), "Meditations on the Life of Charles Simeon."

ask questions about faith and safely inquire (like the seeker-friendly model and the Alpha course today, centuries before there was such a concept). He also started an evening service. In response, the churchwardens actually locked the doors of the church against him. Opposition to his ministry like this continued for twelve years, with Simeon never flinching in his mission.[25]

One of the most controversial, yet successful, innovations he embraced was the purchase of a barrel organ in 1793 which he utilized in worship along with 64 songs. This was a mechanical musical instrument that used a wooden cylinder outfitted with strategically placed pins to depress organ keys in order to produce music (similar to how a player piano works). At the time, barrel organs were used primarily by street performers. They were popular, but considered secular (even "vulgar") and used mostly for entertainment. Furthermore, hymn singing at the time was often done acapella, typically from the psalms, with minimal accompaniment. So, the introduction of an automated mechan-

The barrel organ at Holy Trinity Church in Cambridge, England, emblazoned by Simeon with the verse, "Let everything that hath breath praise the LORD."

ical instrument into worship, especially one associated with street musicians and entertainment venues, was certainly controversial. However, it was a very popular and effective technology in contempo-

The inner workings of a barrel organ. Photo by Petr Brož, used under CC-BY-SA license.

rary culture that everyone was familiar with, especially those who were not regular churchgoers. By doing so, he opened the doors of the church to a wider diversity of people, making clear that everyone was welcome (not just the wealthy and elite), and he made the worship experience enjoyable and even attractive to everyday people.

Charles Simeon's extraordinary influence was significant and longlasting: Holy Trinity Church was the center of a spiritual revival from 1782-1836 and grew to over 1,100 attendance.[26] [27] He led admirably and sacrificially during the corn famine of 1788.Concerned with the nepotism that ensured that ineffective and complacent ministers were entrenched in parishes, he ended

---

25. Holy Trinity Church (n.d.), "History of HT," Holy Trinity Church Cambridge, accessed Sept. 29, 2024 from https://www.htcambridge.org.uk/our-story

26. Julia Cameron, ed. (2013), *Charles Simeon of Cambridge*.

27. In fact, its vitality is still evident to this day more than two centuries later. When I visited Holy Trinity Church in 2013, I was impressed by its great attendance, youthful vigor, enthusiastic worship, and authentic & diverse biblical community. See "More pictures of Holy Trinity Church," by David Swisher, Facebook photo album, June 23, 2013, https://www.facebook.com/media/set/?set=a.10200215252880952&type=3

the practice by establishing the Simeon Trust to ensure that only spiritually mature and biblically faithful ministers led congregations.[28] He was known for his instruction in the art of preaching and biblical exposition, and he oversaw the training of ministers, and established the Church Missionary Society. His students became pastors and missionaries, translated the Bible into multiple languages, and launched Inter-Varsity Fellowship (which today has a global reach). By the end of his life, he was one of the best-known people in Cambridge, and his funeral in King's College Chapel was attended by thousands, with the entire campus and town closed for it.

So, what does all this have to do with livestreaming of church services? Prior to the pandemic, livestreaming was primarily used for larger secular events (graduations, high-profile events, public broadcasts, etc.), and Zoom and similar videoconferencing technologies were predominantly used in business meetings and educational contexts. Charles Simeon took a familiar innovation from the secular world and redeemed it for church and ministry purposes; we can do likewise. Although some churches experimented with these technologies prior, they were few and far between.[29] The social distancing and restrictions on large gatherings of the COVID-19 pandemic forced a lot of churches to explore the use of this technology in ways that would enable the effective ministry of the church, and the result has been surprising growth.

BIBLICAL VALUES & THEOLOGICAL IMPLICATIONS

As we reflect on the potential of livestream technologies as well as the challenges they involve, it is important that we consider the theological implications and identify some relevant Biblical values. Part of why I think this is a challenge for many pastors and ministry leaders to do is that we often presume that since "technology" isn't explicitly mentioned in the Bible, it may not seem relevant or applicable, and because technology can often be used in questionable or inappropriate ways, its utility and appropriateness within the Church might therefore be questioned.

One of the reasons that is difficult to reason through is that today we tend to think of "technology" in digital forms (electronics, powered devices, online

---

28. King's College (Sept. 10, 2021), "King's Treasures: Special Collections of King's College, Cambridge," accessed Sept. 8, 2025 from https://kcctreasures.com/tag/open-cambridge/

29. In fact, when I first developed the "Technology for Ministry" course at Tabor College in 2012, I included an assignment for students to participate in a livestreamed worship service and share reflections on their worship experience. At the time, I could only find 7 congregations in the entire U.S. that were doing it. By 5 years later, the number had grown substantially, but there were still only a couple hundred

platforms, digital tools, smartphone apps, video and multimedia systems etc.). However, technology encompasses far more than that:

- Merriam-Webster's dictionary defines technology as "the practical application of knowledge especially in a particular area" or the manner of accomplishing tasks using technical processes, methods, or knowledge.[30]

- The *American Heritage Science Dictionary* narrows its focus a bit further: "The use of scientific knowledge to solve practical problems, especially in industry and commerce" and "the specific methods, materials, and devices used to solve practical problems."[31]

- My favorite definition of technology comes from Dennis Kuhlman, a now-retired engineer who led the Kansas State Polytechnic campus (K-State's school of technology and engineering) for many years as its Dean: ***"The application of science and engineering principles to solve problems."***

That's really the gist of it, and every definition of technology that I have found involves those aspects...problem solving using the principles of science and engineering. Eliminating the electrical and electronic presumptions of modern civilization help us to better understand the core of what technology is all about. And by this definition, even chairs, doors, the wheel, ladders, levers, and more are all forms of technology...not just cars, cameras, and computers. It also helps us look past the presumptive bias we often bring to things which are new. Fundamentally, technology is a very ancient form of science and engineering (even an art), and ***the Church has been using it for millenia***!

So, when people ask me, "Is technology mentioned in the Bible?," I typically have to qualify what it is that they're really asking:

- Is the *word* "technology" mentioned in the Bible? No, not specifically...not the unique Greek combination of τέχνη (téchnē) = "art, skill, craft" and λογία (logía) = "study of" verbatim (that combination is a modern word anyway).

- But is the *concept* of technology mentioned and addressed in the Bible? Absolutely!

---

30. Merriam-Webster Online Dictionary, s.v. "technology (noun)," accessed February 18, 2012, https://www.merriam-webster.com/dictionary/technology
31. The American Heritage Science Dictionary, s.v. "technology (noun)," accessed February 18, 2012, http://dictionary.reference.com/browse/technology

The first mentions of technology appear in the first few chapters of Genesis, where Tubal-Cain is described as a forger of bronze and iron tools, and where silver money is first mentioned, as well as gold jewelry.[32] Scripture is also filled with mentions of musical instruments: Stringed instruments such as harps, lyres, lutes; wind instruments such as trumpets, horns, flutes, pipes; and percussion instruments such as tambourines, bells, cymbals, & sistrum.[33] These are ALL technological innovations which were used in the worship of God.

Furthermore, we see references to craftsmen (pottery, fabric, carpentry, metal work, and stone) fashioning raw materials into something useful or beautiful for worship or practical needs.[34] There are ample references to technological methods in the design and construction of the tabernacle and the temple, as well as objects of worship – altars, foundations & walls, and other engineering feats.[35] Medicine, too, is frequently mentioned…everything from physicians and embalming to pharmaceutical practices (such as a poultice of figs that was used to heal a boil), as well as prosthetics and physical assistance devices (such as the use of a splint for a broken arm),[36] and many more such examples.[37] And this is just the beginning! I haven't even explored the numerous references to agriculture and biology, military equipment, measurement systems, communication methods, and more. These are all examples of technological innovations through Bible times which were used in nearly all aspects of life, work, ministry, and worship practice.

Although electricity was "discovered" (or rather, harnessed) later, and electronics were later inventions, there is still a solid history of technological innovation throughout all of human history, and the Bible is full of such examples. So, what can we learn about technology from these examples throughout the Bible? Well, although there are certainly ways in which technology can be misused or inappropriately applied, there are also numerous Bible verses and passages that seem to affirm the use of technology (including the relevant technology of the day), as well as the development of new technology and innovation.

---

32. Genesis 4:22, Genesis 20:16, and Genesis 24:22.

33. Numerous references throughout Scripture. See ChatGPT's response to my query for a great sampler list of examples: https://tinyurl.com/MusicalInstrumentsInTheBible.

34. Numerous examples throughout Scripture. See ChatGPT's response to my query for a listing of such examples: https://tinyurl.com/CraftsmenInTheBible

35. Numerous mentions throughout Scripture, including the tabernacle and temple in the Old Testament, the early Church in the New Testament, and even imagery in Revelation. See ChatGPT's response to my query for a great sampler list of examples: https://tinyurl.com/DesignConstructionInBible

36. Gen. 50:2, Gen. 50:26, 2 Kings 20:7, Isa. 38:21, Ezek. 30:21.

37. The examples are rich and diverse throughout Scripture. See ChatGPT's response to my prompted query for a wide-ranging sampler of medical technology in the Bible: https://tinyurl.com/MedicalTechInBible

Here are some primary insights culled from a class I developed on "Technology for Ministry":[38]

- **Technological development can sometimes glorify God.** Noah's ark, the tabernacle and the temple were technological constructs, and God gave instructions for the building of each of them. In fact, in the building of the temple, and other projects completed during the reign of Solomon, there was apparently extensive use of natural resources by craftsmen and artisans. Solomon sent 10,000 workers to Lebanon to cut down cedar trees each month (I Kings 5:14), in addition to the servants of King Hiram who helped them. They may have worked there for as long as seven (I Kings 6:38) or even twenty years (II Chronicles 8:1). All this was at least *allowed* by God, and some of it was specifically *directed* by Him. Furthermore, Jeremiah 22:6 says that God finds the palace of the king of Judah as beautiful as the mountains of Lebanon: "You are like Gilead to me, like the summit of Lebanon" (NIV)! So, if God can find a human construction to be beautiful, one that was created to satisfy human needs, then we surely can, too, at least sometimes. This confirms that technological development is not wrong in and of itself (although it can be done for wrong reasons, or with the wrong attitude).

- **Part of the image of God in humans is the desire to create things.** The fact that we can create and use technology has certainly lead to some unfortunate consequences, such as radioactive nuclear waste and child pornography on the Internet, as well as more commonplace tragedies, like deaths and injuries in highway accidents. However, technology can also lead to our being able to alleviate some of the consequences of our own mistakes of the past, or even to mitigate some of the consequences of the Fall. Our desire to create things has led to the creation of great art, music, and literature, as well as useful articles of clothing, furniture, tools and recipes. These are positive and fortunate consequences of technology, and it is a direct result of the *imago dei* (the image of God) in humans.

- **Technology can be used to make us better stewards and ministers.** We live in a fallen world. Whatever Eden was, and was like, we aren't in it (and we don't deserve to be). Fallen creatures

---

38. David Swisher (2012), "BRS 304 – Technology for Ministry" course, initially developed or Tabor College's Christian Ministries program (School of Adult & Graduate Studies). Many of the insights I share here were first articulated by now-retired professor Martin LaBar of Southern Wesleyan University from some teaching resources he put together in 2005 called "Technology: Some Biblical Basics" (unfortunately, they are no longer available online).

that we are, we have done things with technology that we should not have. However, we also can do good. We can help people be healthier, and obtain food that wouldn't otherwise have been available. We can enable the Good News to be spread widely and rapidly, in ways that grip the viewer, listener, or reader, using technology.

Simply put, technology is morally neutral. It is what you do with the technology that gives it its moral character. By itself, technological innovation is not inherently right nor wrong (although the creative impulse is, of course, from God), but whether it is used for good or evil determines the moral relevance of that application. Also, in many (perhaps most) cases, the same technology can be used for both good or evil.

THE POWERFUL POTENTIAL OF NEW MEDIA TECHNOLOGIES

Innovation through technology doesn't happen in a vacuum, either; it comes on the heels of prior developments and earlier uses of technology and innovation. The rise of livestreaming and other forms of online delivery of church worship experiences is no exception to this. Darrell Bock and Jonathan Armstrong make a solid case for this in their recent book, Virtual Reality Church, where they examine how churches and Christian communities have historically adapted to shifts in media technology. Bock & Armstrong make a compelling case that technological change is both inevitable and also transformative for religious engagement, and I fully agree with this perspective. In Chapter 2 – "The Only Constant Is Change," they outline key developments over the past several decades, illustrating how radio, television, and eventually the internet revolutionized the ways Christians communicate, evangelize, and build community.[39]

The authors rightly highlight how early skepticism often gave way to widespread adoption as churches recognized the potential for outreach and discipleship through emerging media. Their chapter emphasizes that while each new technological wave initially raised concerns – ranging from fears of inauthentic worship to the dilution of doctrinal integrity – many Christian leaders ultimately found ways to integrate these tools effectively. The rise of livestreamed and online recorded services, social media engagement, and now virtual and augmented reality (which I will cover later in this book) all represent a con-

---

39. Chapter 2 – "The Only Constant is Change" (pp. 55-80) in Darrell L. Bock & Jonathan J. Armstrong (2021), *Virtual Reality Church: Pitfalls and Possibilities*, Chicago: Moody.

tinuation of this trajectory. Bock and Armstrong encourage readers to view technological change not as a threat but as an opportunity for innovation, stressing the need for discernment in leveraging new media while remaining anchored in theological convictions.[40]

Long-time church members often underestimate the potential of technology-enhanced distribution modalities. Many years ago (2009), I pastored a small rural church in a tiny little town called Delphos, which sat 40 minutes north of Salina, KS (population then of 46,000) and was surrounded by half a dozen or so scattered small towns ranging in size from 1,000 – 5,000 people. The church itself ran about 25 early in our ministry there. I often found it discouraging to preach to such a small crowd, yet I believed strongly in the potential of new technologies and was convinced that I had a message worth sharing. So, I experimented with podcasting our messages: I found a sermon hosting tool that allowed me to upload edited audio recordings of messages along with a description, relevant Scripture verses, search tags, and notes. Needless to say, our church board wasn't very enthusiastic about this, and felt it was a complete waste of time and effort.

Within about 3 months I was pleasantly encouraged to find that we were regularly seeing anywhere from 150-175 listens, and on our more popular messages and topics, we often had 250-300 or more listens (and anywhere from 75-100 downloads of the sermon notes). Yes, you read that correctly: In a small rural town of under 500 population, with a church attendance of only 25, we were seeing an average of 200+ listens to our messages weekly (4-5 times our attendance), and nearly half of them were downloading the notes, too, so I knew they weren't just casual listeners or curiosity seekers. Soon after that, we started getting emails and messages from shut-ins and missionaries overseas who were connected to the church who had discovered the podcasts and recorded messages and who thanked us for sharing them. They wanted to stay connected and grow, but weren't able to with their current life circumstances. As that congregation grew, so did our digital reach.

That experience confirmed for me the power and potential of new media technologies, and it also cemented the idea in my mind and spirit that far more people are interested in your church than you typically see on Sunday mornings. It is also fairly well documented that in today's culture, church attendance and frequency is declining at an alarming pace, yet interest remains high. Most pastors acknowledge that attending once or twice a month is now consider being a "regular attender," and anything more frequent than once a month at-

---

40. Ibid.

tendance is a positive.[41] Livestream technology helps bridge that gap; it helps connect your members and periodic attenders with your messages, themes, culture, and announcements in between visits and it gives them a sense of connectedness and purpose.

It is also a great first connection. In fact, every church whose livestream ministry I have been a part of (3 now) has reported that the number one way people discover and engage with the church initially is through the livestream. The biblically-faithful megachurch in Wichita whose livestream ministry I was a frequent volunteer in regularly saw over 2,000 people connecting to the livestream on a weekly basis, and over 80% of our first time attenders reported that they first attended online. One of the highlights of my ministry there was when we held a baptism where a dozen people were baptized who had first attended the church online livestream (most of them attended for a good 6-9 months online before checking us out in person). Online & livestreamed services are the modern-day equivalent of a "yellow pages" (phone directory) from a few decades ago.[42]

The church where I currently serve is much smaller (average weekly in-person attendance of 130), and our number of live viewers often seems small (typically 8-10 live viewers during the actual service). But by week's end, we typically have several hundred (250 - 350) views, and with many of our seasonal or popular topics, we've had as many as 700 - 800 views within a week or two. As Elizabeth Rhyno, our Pastor of Relational Ministries, explains, "Almost every first-time guest who comes through the doors on a Sunday morning has already watched one or several of our services online." Simply put, if you want to connect with people in today's culture and be seen as offering any sense of relevance or connectivity, a quality online &/or livestreamed worship service is an absolute necessity. It is NOT some temporary fix to get you through a pandemic and discard once that's over; it's a paradigm shift in how people connect, and it's absolutely vital for establishing your brand and your presence in today's world.

THEOLOGICAL ASPECTS OF LIVESTREAM TECHNOLOGIES

Although the incarnation might seem to imply that it requires physical presence, we would do well to remember that the Church has always adapted to circumstances where physical presence was impossible, such as in times of perse-

41. Carey Nieuwhof (n.d.), "5 Church Attendance Statistics Every Church Leader Needs to Understand in 2025," Church Growth, https://careynieuwhof.com/church-attendance-statistics/

42. A decade or so ago, it was the church's website that functioned in that way, but those are so normative and commonplace now that what establishes legitimacy and provides meaningful connection over time to most people is now the online or livestreamed service.

cution, exile, or illness. After all, the early Church met not just in the Synagogue, but also in homes (Acts 2:46-47), and a significant part of Paul's pastoral and missionary influence was conducted through letters written across great distances (e.g., Paul's epistles). Online worship through livestreaming technology offers a modern extension of this tradition, allowing believers to gather and encourage one another, even when they are physically apart. Online worship provides a means of being spiritually present with one another, allowing us to accomplish the "one another" commands of Scripture as well as to reflect Jesus' call to transcend physical boundaries in bringing the gospel to all nations. God's presence is not limited by geography or proximity.[43]

Furthermore, online and livestreaming technology provides a useful option to connect believers who are physically unable to attend church, such as those who are ill, shut-ins, those whose work schedules make Sunday attendance difficult (truck drivers, frequent travelers, healthcare workers, etc.), and international members who wish to stay connected with their home church. This helps support the Scriptural mandate to encourage and build one another up (1 Thessalonians 5:11). Livestreaming also aligns with the mission to spread the Gospel to all nations (Matthew 28:19-20).[44] It enables churches to reach a broader audience, potentially touching lives across the globe, thus fulfilling the directive to preach the Gospel everywhere.

For example, one of my ministry friends pastors an online congregation that truly transcends borders. The Chapel Online is a global community of faith with over 5,000 participants who meet on Facebook and through WhatsApp. Through recorded messages, livestreamed prayer times, blessing, and spiritual counsel, Pastor Anne Bosarge provides daily discipleship, weekly worship, and a prayer community for people who connect from 50 different countries (many of them from countries where they cannot openly worship).

Despite the advantages and benefits, there are some definite risks and concerns, too:

- **Body, Gathering, & Biblical Community:** Online services challenge the traditional notions of what it means to "gather" as a church body. Also, while digital platforms certainly enable tangible connection, they may lack the embodied, sacramental nature of physical gatherings (e.g., communion or baptism). Also,

---

43. Notice that John 4:23-24 says nothing about a requirement for physical presence or proximity. Instead, with the full context (vv. 19-26), especially in light of the Samaritan woman's location-centric concerns, Jesus appears to be making the opposite case...that where you worship is not nearly as important as the attitude of the heart and spirit.

44. Anne Bosarge, Facebook Messenger communication with author, February 12, 2025. I have personally observed this biblical community in action and benefitted from it.

counting, quantifying, and validating attendance in livestream and recorded contexts is particularly challenging, especially when families and couples often watch a single livestream together, while sometimes people drop in and out, and occasionally others may have more than one device connected.[45]

- **Pastoral Care:** Online participation requires rethinking pastoral care models and how to provide spiritual support to remote attendees.[46] Likewise, online-only participation raises questions about how sacraments like baptism and communion can be meaningfully administered in a digital context.[47] Pastors are called to shepherd their flock, but digital participation makes it harder to discern spiritual health and provide the necessary accountability. Furthermore, a common frustration with online contexts (especially with social media) is that the perceptual barrier created by the screen can lull people into a false sense of comfort or judgement…where they will often say or do things to someone else online that they would never say in person when face-to-face. Pastors who embrace this technology need to remain ever vigilant to encourage and foster supportive and judgement-free environments so that people feel safe opening up about their challenges and truly seek pastoral care and counsel.

- **Discipleship and Spiritual Formation:** Although spiritual formation can – and does – happen online and in livestreamed services, discipleship typically works best through relationships, accountability, and communal practices. These can be much harder to cultivate in digital and online venues. In-person gatherings often foster vulnerability and authenticity through face-to-face interactions, while digital/online platforms can make it easier to remain anonymous, potentially inhibiting deep relationships.

- **Consumerism and Commitment:** Although livestreamed services are an example of meeting people where they are at their point of need, the convenience and flexibility – and anonymity – of online participation can easily encourage spectatorship, minimal engage-

---

45. To mitigate this for official attendance reports, my denomination (The Wesleyan Church) has found that "peak live viewers" is the most accurate approach to quantifying the variables of livestream attendance (and we took our cues for that guidance from the experts at Life Church): Matthew Tietje (2020, March 17), "Finding Peak Live Viewers," Facebook, https://www.facebook.com/legacy/notes/10158040136749605/ . See also Tietje (n.d.), "Live Online Attendance Tracking Guidance for The Wesleyan Church," https://resources.wesleyan.org/live-online-attendance-tracking-guidance

46. Several churches I know who have wrestled with these either utilize livestream hosts or even have dedicated online campus pastors whose specialty and primary role is engaging and nurturing the online participants.

47. For a great exploration of the issues and possibilities, as well as discussion of how various churches and denominations wrestle with this issue, see Chapter 7 – "The New People of God and Visible Signs of Invisible Grace" (pp. 201-234) in Darrell L. Bock & Jonathan J. Armstrong (2021), *Virtual Reality Church: Pitfalls and Possibilities*, Chicago: Moody.

ment, or even allow people to disappear altogether. Likewise, the ability to view recordings of livestreamed services has led to what I like to call the "DVR'ing" of services (watching later instead of live), and although this is likely more a product of consumer culture and current sociological trends, it is all too easy for parishioners to view worship as a product to consume at their convenience rather than a commitment to participate in with others. Watching services on-demand may prioritize convenience over consecrated time for worship. This raises theological questions about how believers sanctify time for God in an increasingly busy, distracted world.

PRACTICAL CONSIDERATIONS & LOGISTICS

Earlier in this chapter, I explained that quality of the livestream experience depends heavily on (1) the quality of the equipment used to record and transmit the livestream – especially the lighting and audio, (2) the placement of the camera, and (3) the intentionality of those leading the service in speaking to and including the online guests – especially in how they say it. This is an extremely important point which cannot be emphasized enough, so let's explore those aspects now.[48]

If the lighting quality is poor, then it will be difficult for online viewers (especially those participating via a smaller screen like a computer, tablet, or smartphone) to visually perceive important details like facial expressions which signal how they should interpret the message. Lighting directly impacts how one perceives shades of color and dimension, so if the lighting is poor, you will have lots of shadows which are difficult to comprehend or interpret. If the audio quality is poor, it becomes irritating and distracting; if it is merely low volume, online participants can simply turn the volume up (to some extent) on their devices, but if the microphone placement isn't intentional, it will overemphasize some elements and minimize others.

Remember, your online guests will only hear what you send through the microphones and they will only see what you include in the camera shots. For example:

- If your worship leader is mic'd well, but other members of the worship band or team are being picked up through overhead mics

---

48. Unfortunately, space and scope limits the extent to which I can address these aspects in a single chapter. If you want to explore these issues in more depth, I highly recommend Jason Moore's (2022) book *Both/And: Maximizing Hybrid Worship Experiences for In-Person and Online Engagement* (Plano, TX: Invite Press).

inside your worship facility, the online audience may only hear the lead without any backup voices. That will sound weird.

- If the mics are near fans or electrical equipment, or have a poor connection, you might not hear it in the main auditorium, but the online audience will hear a very distracting hum or buzz…and it can be bad enough to want to turn it off altogether.

In my experiences managing livestreamed events over the last two decades, I have found it a nearly universal truth that people will tolerate poor lighting for only awhile (presuming it will improve), but if the audio quality is poor – or worse, distracting – they will turn it off rather than continue to listen. This is why it is important to have someone listening to your livestream throughout the service who can make adjustments (or convey issues) whenever they arise. If you are using a soundboard, instead of just relaying a simple audio out, you should have a dedicated mix created for the livestream's audio and someone assigned to monitor and adjust it as needed.

Camera placement matters a lot, too. Your goal in determining where to place the cameras is to position them so that the audience sees whatever someone sitting in a seat would see, and the shot should change whenever the action or voice changes. Nothing is more irritating to an online viewer than hearing a new voice, speaker, or instrument begin and not being able to see it through the one camera view you have provided. That's why it is vitally important that somebody be monitoring and managing those camera views and anticipating what a viewer will want to see. For example:

- If a soloist gets up to sing or perform a specific part, or somebody comes up to a mic to read Scripture or make an announcement, make sure you switch to a good closeup view of that person as soon as it happens so that the online viewers won't feel like they're missing out.

- If you know that you're going to be doing something different in a given service (such as a baptism, a child dedication, a commissioning, testimonies, candlelighting, etc.), make sure that you have one or more cameras positioned ideally to capture that, and also ensure that nobody will stand in front of that camera.

Although it might seem like putting a phone on a mic stand in the back of the room or atop the sound booth zoomed out wide would be a good idea (to get the maximum view and not have to follow anybody or change the shot), the reality is that such camera views are annoying to watch for more than a few seconds.[49] There's a church in my neighborhood that does this, and when I first considered visiting their service, I tuned in to their online livestream to check out what it's like. It was a horrible experience: The camera was positioned from the back of the room on a stand at an awkwardly weird angle, and so it felt very unnatural, and the view looked like I was sitting in the nosebleed section of a stadium watching tiny dots down on the field. I couldn't see any faces or make out any expressions.

Also, the view was so wide that it included one of the side entrances, so every time somebody entered (especially those who were arriving late), the viewer's focus was shifted to the motion on the periphery instead of where the worship was happening. Worse, there were multiple points throughout the service where someone came up to a mic to talk, but they weren't visible on camera, and the camera view never changed, so as a viewer I was hearing a disembodied voice. That was weirdly disconcerting. The whole experience proved to be so unnatural and difficult to watch and listen to that even though I really wanted to learn more about this church and its ministry, I gave up and was never able to watch more than a song or two. Their camera and audio quality ruined the experience and made it worse.

Admittedly, it is helpful every now and then to have what videographers call a "reference" shot (a wider view to see everything), especially if it's unclear where the action is or someone on stage is moving from one place to another, but that should only be for a few seconds. As soon as you know where the action is, the online participant needs to be able to see a closeup view of that. If you only provide a wide shot from the back of the room, the online participant can't see any facial expression, and it gives the feeling that you're a long way away from the action. The perception of distance is not a friend to authenticity or participation in worship; it makes it feel inauthentic and emphasizes the fact that you're not there.

If you don't have enough volunteers to run multiple cameras, that's OK; you can instead invest in a mixing tool or app that allows you to position multiple cameras on mic stands in various places and a single volunteer can easily switch between them. We use Switcher Studio (an iPad-based app), with 3-4 iPhones serving as cameras positioned throughout the experience room, and it allows us

---

49. Jason Moore covers this extensively in Chapter 2 – "Reconceptualizing the Online Experience" (pp. 21 – 50) in *Both/And*. If you're wrestling with any of these challenges – or considering dropping your livestream as people return to worship in buildings – I highly recommend you read it!

to do near-professional quality mixing at a fraction of the cost with only a single volunteer running the technology.[50]

EXPLORING POSSIBILITIES

So, what might this look like in real life? How would it work if a congregation made their livestream connection intentional and used it to strategically engage those who are curious, checking out the church, or unable to attend physically for a variety of reasons? Consider the following fictional vignette that it based on a number of plausible real-world scenarios I'm familiar with.

PASTOR JASON, STEPHANIE, AND THE DIGITAL CONGREGATION

Pastor Jason had been leading his congregation for over a decade, relying on traditional methods of worship and community engagement. However, the COVID-19 pandemic changed everything. Overnight, he found himself needing to pivot to online services to keep his church connected and spiritually nourished.

With the help of Stephanie, a tech-savvy video volunteer, Pastor Jason quickly set up a livestreaming service. Initially, it was a simple setup: A camera, a microphone, and a laptop. Despite the simplicity, the first few services had technical glitches. Audio cut out or was garbled occasionally, the video quality was inconsistent, and sometimes the livestream lagged. Nevertheless, the congregation was patient and appreciative of the effort.

As weeks turned into months, the church's online presence grew more sophisticated. They invested in better equipment and learned how to use streaming software effectively. Stephanie taught Pastor Jason how to engage with the online audience in real-time, reading comments and prayer requests during the service. This interactive element brought a new dimension to worship that he had never experienced before, and participants at home and shut-ins loved it.

Engagement:

One Sunday, after the service, Pastor Jason received an email from Steve, a long-time member of the church who had recently moved to another state. "Pastor Jason, I just wanted to thank you for the livestream services. They've been a lifeline for me. I can't attend in person anymore, but being able to watch the service live and participate in the chat makes me feel like I'm still part of the community."

---

50. See www.switcherstudio.com. Previously we used (& loved) Sling Studio, but that product is no longer in production and their support is marginal. Other such tools include OBS Studio, eCamm Live, Wirecast, & ATEM Mini. For a great listing of multiple such products, including the pros and cons as well as costs, see ChatGPT's response to my query: https://tinyurl.com/CameraMixingTools

A few weeks later, he received a note relayed from Connie, an older member whose health meant she often spent considerable time in the hospital and rehab center. She was grateful that she could watch the service live while in the hospital (or later in the day or week if she was resting or being treated), and it meant that she no longer felt isolated or alone.

Pastor Jason was thrilled to hear this. He realized that the online services were not just a temporary solution but a way to reach people who could not attend in person, including those who had moved away, were homebound, or had health concerns.

However, not all feedback was positive. Some members expressed concerns about the sense of community and the loss they felt. "Pastor, I miss seeing everyone in person," complained Mary during a virtual fellowship meeting. "It's not the same watching from home. I feel disconnected."

Reflection:

Pastor Jason understood Mary's concerns. The digital format, while convenient, lacked the physical presence and spontaneous interactions of in-person gatherings. He began to wrestle with balancing the benefits of online services with the need for genuine community connection.

Additionally, Jason noticed a new trend: many members were DVR'ing the services and watching them later. This raised further questions. Was the immediacy of worship being lost? Were people still engaging with the message as deeply?

Resolution:

To address these concerns, Pastor Jason discussed what he was seeing with his associate pastor Linda, and together they decided to implement several changes. She organized small group meetings on Zoom where members could discuss the sermon and pray together, fostering a sense of community. He also introduced live Q&A sessions after the service to make the experience more interactive.

John also addressed the DVR'ing trend by creating a weekly email newsletter summarizing the sermon's key points and encouraging members to reflect and share their thoughts, regardless of when they watched the service. This approach helped maintain engagement and spiritual growth throughout the week.

Through these adjustments, Pastor Jason found a way to embrace the benefits of online worship while addressing its challenges. His journey highlighted the potential of digital tools to enhance ministry and the importance of adapting to new realities with creativity and care. Pastor Jason's experience became a testament to the church's resilience and ability to innovate in the face of unprecedented challenges, ensuring that their mission continued despite the distance.

NEXT STEPS: LEADING WITH WISDOM

The early days of the pandemic forced most churches into survival mode. For many, livestreaming was just a quick fix – an emergency adaptation to handle an unexpected crisis. But as the dust settled, it has become clear that livestreaming wasn't just a temporary solution, but that instead it is a fundamental shift in how people engage with church in the world we minister in today. The mistake many church leaders make is treating it as a stopgap measure rather than a creative opportunity to not only serve their congregations well but even to sustain long-term ministry growth. So, how can we approach this new paradigm with hope and peace?

1. Resist the Panic (Move From Crisis to Strategy)

This means that now is the time to move from reaction to strategy. Ministry leaders need to assess what has changed and determine how to respond wisely. Rather than longing for a return to how things were before, leaders need to reflect on what they learned during the pandemic: What worked well? What proved ineffective? What lessons emerged from several months (or years) of online services? Our goal should no longer be to just *get through* this time period using online and livestream technologies, but to *leverage* it for more effective ministry.

The first step is to stop viewing online engagement as competition to in-person worship (the tendency to view it that way is pervasive, and my colleagues and I hear it often). However, the reality is that hybrid ministry – where digital and physical expressions of church complement each other – is the new normal. It's time to face the reality that some church members will *never* return to regular in-person attendance, yet they still desire to stay connected. Many more experienced the flexibility and will come when they can and watch online when they can't; they are a vital part of your congregation, too. Others will explore the church through its digital presence before they ever step through the doors.

Online platforms have become the new front porch of the church. Instead of measuring success by how many people are physically present on a Sunday morning, we need to rethink (and likely broaden) our understanding of engagement. Keep in mind, too, that long before the pandemic hit, this was an issue: We have all observed how parishioners might be physically present, but mentally or emotionally checked out...or at least not very engaged. The true measure of impact is not just who is in the pews, but who is being discipled, encouraged, and connected – whether in person or online – and how they are taking next steps for their spiritual and relational growth.

23

2. Embrace the opportunity (Develop a Hybrid Ministry Mindset)

The assumption that physical attendance is the only indicator of spiritual engagement is no longer valid. Livestreaming has changed the way people interact with church, making it possible for participation to happen beyond the walls of a sanctuary. While some may worry that digital church encourages passivity (and it can), the reality is that thoughtful online ministry can foster deep connections and spiritual growth. I have dozens of ministry friends who are doing digital and online ministry very effectively…and they're seeing not just numerical and relational growth, but spiritual growth and life transformation, too. The key is to move beyond simply streaming services for people to "watch" and instead cultivating a genuine hybrid approach to ministry where people "engage" or "participate" in multiple ways and modalities.

That shift begins with intentionality; it doesn't happen by merely adapting to circumstances. Pastors must recognize that those watching online are not just spectators, but can be (should be) active participants who need to be acknowledged, valued, and engaged. This means addressing them directly during services, finding a way to receive their prayer requests and include them, inviting them into conversation, and wherever possible, incorporating them into sacraments. Instead of treating digital attendees as an afterthought, ministry leaders who want to thrive amidst the storms of post-pandemic culture should consider how to actively integrate online and livestream participants into the worship experience.[51]

A hybrid mindset also requires rethinking discipleship. Sunday morning livestreams are just one part of a larger digital strategy. Discipleship can – and *should* – extend beyond the livestream through online small groups, interactive Bible studies, and digital prayer gatherings. While nothing can fully replace the richness and vulnerability of in-person face-to-face relationships, online spaces can be powerful tools for connection, accountability, and spiritual growth. Rather than viewing digital platforms as lesser alternatives, church leaders should explore how they can enhance and support the core mission of the church.[52]

---

51. For example, you could invite a regular online participant to lead prayer or share a Scripture reading. Or mention online guests by name in prayers. Or find a way for hosts to relay their comments or prayer requests to pastoral staff or leaders to be acknowledged publicly.

52. I will discuss this more extensively in the chapter on metaverse and VR, but many of the same principles and examples apply to online and livestream ministry as well. For more on this, see my 2024 journal article "Inconceivable! Field Preaching, Digital Church, & the Metaverse: Embracing John Wesley's Legacy of Innovation to Inform the Virtual Ministry of Tomorrow." *Didache: Faithful Teaching*, 24:1 (Spring 2024). ISSN: 15360156 https://didache.nazarene.org/index.php/volume-24-number-1.

Metrics also need to be reconsidered. In a traditional church setting, attendance is an easy number to track, but in an online context, engagement is far more nuanced. Watching a livestream is different from sitting through a service in person. Some people watch live, others tune in later, and still others engage only with sermon excerpts/highlights or discussions afterward. Churches that succeed in digital ministry are those that recognize these different levels of engagement and learn to track them meaningfully. The question is not just how many people showed up, but *how are people growing, connecting, and living out their faith?*

3. Do it Well (Pursue Excellence in Livestreaming)

Recognizing the importance of livestreaming is one thing; knowing how to improve it is another. Many pastors acknowledge that digital ministry is here to stay, but they feel overwhelmed by the technical side or unsure of what steps to take next. The good news is that excellence in livestreaming doesn't require massive budgets or professional production teams – just thoughtful, incremental improvements. Also, if your church has any teens or twenty-somethings attending, they live and thrive in digital culture and know it well. Find a mature one and ask them (or even invite several to help you develop an online engagement strategy).

The first step would be to evaluate your current livestream experience with fresh eyes. It's easy to focus only on what happens in the room, but ministry leaders need to consider how that in-person experience translates to an online audience. Watching past services from the perspective of a first-time online visitor can be eye-opening: Are the sermons clear and engaging? Is the audio crisp, or does it sound distant and echoey? Is the camera work intentional, or does it feel like an afterthought? Is it easy to see and understand who's speaking and follow all of the action, wherever it happens? Many people will decide whether to stay engaged with a church based on the quality of their first online experience. If they struggle to hear, if the visuals are poor, or if they feel ignored as an online participant, they will likely disengage. A great way to improve in this area is to ask someone (or ideally several people) to participate online and observe and experience everything your online guests do, then share their impressions, findings, and suggestions. These could be ministry colleagues from another church, long-time members who can no longer attend, members who normally attend in person, or even professional mystery shoppers.[53]

---

53. My friend Jason Moore (who wrote *Both/And* and specializes in advising churches on hybrid ministry) is a professional who offers this very service. You can reach him at midnightoilproductions.com

Improving your livestream doesn't have to mean expensive upgrades, but some investments will make a significant impact. Clear, high-quality audio is the most important factor – viewers will tolerate less-than-perfect visuals, but if the sound is muffled or unclear, they will tune out. Upgrading the audio setup so that you can mix and control the sound going out to the livestream independently of the audio for the worship space should be the first priority. Camera placement also plays a crucial role. Place them at eye level so that the online viewer can see faces up close, and use multiple angles to make the experience feel more personal.

Beyond the technical aspects, engagement efforts must be intentional. A livestream should not be a passive one-way broadcast, but an opportunity for real-time connection. Churches that succeed in online ministry typically assign team members to monitor and respond to comments, prayer requests, and questions during the service; some have a dedicated online campus pastor, while others have a livestream host or moderator. Their job is to make guests feel seen, welcomed, and cared for. This simple step (easily accomplished with volunteers) transforms the experience from a one-way passive viewing into an interactive, communal gathering. Additionally, follow-up matters. Churches that do this well send a brief email or social media message to thank first-time online viewers and see if they have any questions or concerns, and when online guests keep returning, they invite them to take the next step – whether that's joining an online small group, coming to an info session to learn more, connecting with a pastor, or even attending an in-person service.

Sustainable success in livestreaming beyond the pandemic requires leadership buy-in and a commitment to ongoing improvement. This means training volunteers to run cameras and sound effectively, designating someone to oversee digital engagement, and making livestreaming a core part of ministry planning rather than an afterthought. Churches that thrive in digital ministry are those that recognize livestreaming as more than a technical necessity; they know it is a front door to discipleship, evangelism, and meaningful community.

MOVING FORWARD WITH CONFIDENCE

Change, especially when it feels forced, can be unsettling. Many pastors still feel a sense of loss, longing for the way church used to be before the pandemic changed everything. Digital engagement can feel foreign and unnatural if it's not your norm. But history shows that every major shift in communication technology has opened new doors for the Church to reach people. The advent of Roman roads made the spread of the gospel in the first century possible. The printing press made Scripture widely available and helped give rise to the Protestant Reformation. The rise of radio and television extended the Gospel's reach into millions of homes and birthed multiple movements at home and abroad. Now, digital platforms allow churches to connect with people in ways that previous generations could never have imagined. Instead of resisting change, wise leaders embrace it with confidence, knowing that God is not bound by any single method or format.

Remember, too, that you are not alone in this journey. Many others are navigating the same challenges, asking the same questions, and experimenting with new ways to engage their congregations. The goal is not perfection, nor is it to keep up with the latest trends; it is to be faithful stewards of the tools available to us today. Technology will continue to evolve, but the mission of the Church remains unchanged. The message of Christ is timeless, even as the methods change.

Just as storm chasers do not try to stop the storm but instead learn how to navigate, predict, and prepare for it, church leaders must recognize that technological disruption is not a threat...it is an opportunity. By understanding the landscape, preparing wisely, and leading with a spirit of confidence, you can ensure that your churches remains a place of hope, connection, and transformation in an increasingly digital world. Online and livestream ministry is not the end of meaningful church engagement; it is merely the beginning of new opportunities. The Church has weathered such storms before, and it will do so again.

Chapter 2

THREATS
OR POTENTIAL

Generative AI and the Church

Although AI itself isn't new, the unprecedented success of ChatGPT in late 2022 and the subsequent emergence of dozens of other generative AIs since then have forced pastors and ministry leaders to offer spiritual guidance on subjects they often know little about. Meanwhile, debates rage about whether AI is good or evil, what the appropriate use of it is, and how to ensure responsible and ethical use...leveraging its potential while (hopefully) avoiding its risks.

The arrival of ChatGPT in late 2022 caught the world by surprise, and its unprecedented success in the years following have been truly mind-boggling. Artificial intelligence isn't new, but suddenly it was on everyone's mind and impossible to ignore. Generative AI has been in the news non-stop ever since, with vendors rushing to add AI to their product line, innovators experimenting with what's possible, and naysayers questioning whether any of this is wise... as well as pundits seizing the opportunity to grandstand about a worst-case scenario future. But believe it or not, generative AI has incredible potential to serve the Church and become a powerful tool for ministry leaders. Many pastors feel stretched thin by administrative tasks, message prep, and communication, and church budgets don't typically allow for extra help. AI can alleviate some of these burdens, allowing pastors to focus on what only humans can do...shepherd, disciple, and lead with spiritual discernment. However, it also comes with some inherent risks and challenges.

My interest in AI goes back almost 30 years to when I was exploring text-to-speech and voice recognition software while in Bible college. Shortly after I graduated, I went to a one-year intensive missions and ministry training school in the Dallas/Fort Worth metroplex, and while I was there, I toured the headquarters of Wycliffe Bible Translators. I was interested in becoming a Bible translator, and there I saw how Wycliffe was using machine learning and early forms of AI to accelerate the process of Bible translation.[1][2] I've been following the development of AI ever since.

Since I work in higher education, once ChatGPT emerged, generative AI has become a major focus of my research and work as well as daily life. I do faculty training, research, conference presentations, and work with faculty and program leaders to incorporate AI into our courses and programs. I've been interviewed on multiple podcasts about AI, served on a couple of AI advisory committees, and I've written a couple of articles and contributed to several books now on AI. Most importantly, though, I practice what I preach: I have researched several dozen generative AIs, subscribe to about a dozen of them, and I regularly use about a half dozen of them (on almost a daily basis).

I was also the co-author and coordinator of a university innovation grant called the AI "Learn & Share" Initiative, which provided funding and train-ing for over three dozen faculty to experiment with various generative AIs and share their experiences in a first-ever "AI Showcase." So, AI doesn't scare me. But I do realize that it can be overwhelming and a bit of a concern for many of my colleagues in ministry. So, in this chapter I hope to demystify it and help you understand its potential for ministry use better.

HISTORICAL FOUNDATIONS

I think it's very important to understand that AI is not new. It didn't start with ChatGPT, and it didn't emerge in 2023. Rather, AI has been around for a VERY long time. In fact, some of its earliest progenitors emerged as early as 1495 through Leonardo DaVinci's *automata*. These were machines he built that could mimic human functions. For example, DaVinci devised a self-pro-pelled cart, as well as a mechanical lion that he designed which could walk for-ward, open a compartment, and present flowers at the end of its performance. This AI-like machine was presented to King Francis I as a diplomatic gesture during a banquet hosted by Florentine merchants and Giuliano de' Medici in Lyon in honor of King Francis I in 515 (the lion is the symbol of Florence and lilies are the fleurs-de-lis of France, so this was a very symbolic automaton). He also developed a mechanical knight which could sit up, wave its arms, move

---

1. For a great short synopsis on this, see Jonathan Robie's Jan. 3, 2024 article "Artificial Intelligence and Bible Translation," *Biblical Archaeology*, available at: https://www.biblicalarchaeology.org/daily/artificial-intelligence-and-bible-translation

2. For a more extensive analysis of the current state of AI in Bible translation, see the papers and synopsis from the "Generating Wisdom: Artificial Intelligence and the Bible" conference I attended which was hosted by Museum of the Bible (July 25-26, 2024): https://www.museumofthebible.org/events/generating-wisdom-ai-and-the-bible-conference

its head, and open and close its anatomically correct jaw. However, seeing this humanoid automaton creeped people out (apparently people weren't ready for that lifelikeness).[3]

Further advancements with computing capabilities have happened over the years, too, starting with Blaise Pascal's invention of a mechanical calculator in 1642. Then, Ada Lovelace and Charles Babbage developing the first programmable machine back in 1837.[4] For AI as we understand it today, the key date is 1956, which is when the term "artificial intelligence" was first coined by a group of computer scientists who gathered at Dartmouth College to create machines that could think like humans.[5] So AI in its earliest forms has been around for centuries, and AI as a distinct field of research has been around for almost 70 years.

So why is generative AI suddenly in the news everywhere? What changed? If AI has been developing for so long without major issues, why is it now suddenly in the news and dominating our focus? What changed is the development of Natural Language Processing in 2017. To explain that, however, I need to explain a few related terms and concepts.

WHAT IS AI?

Artificial intelligence is the "broad field of computer science that's focused on creating machines or software that can perform tasks which normally require human intelligence." Within that field, there are two specialty areas where lots of research has been happening over the last few decades: Machine Learning and Deep Learning.

- **Machine Learning (ML)** is "based on the idea that systems can learn from data, identify patterns, and make decisions with minimal human intervention."[6] Instead of hard coding or programming a computer to do specific functions, it involves teaching a computer system how to use patterns and inference to solve those challenges itself. Some examples applications of that are email

3.   Lisha Pace (July 24, 2023), "The History of Leonardo da Vinci's Automata," History-Computer.com. https://history-computer.com/leonardo-da-vincis-automata/

4.   Daniel Fitzpatrick, Amanda Fox, & Brad Weinstein (2023), *The AI Classroom: The Ultimate Guide to Artificial Intelligence in Education*, The Hitchhiker's Guide for Educators Series (Beech Grove, IN: TeacherGoals Publishing).

5.   Amy Webb (2019). *The Big Nine: How the Tech Titans & Their Thinking Machines Could Warp Humanity* (New York: Public Affairs).

6.   OpenAI. (2023, Aug. 1). ChatGPT 3.5 [Large Language Model]. AI Definitions. Retrieved from: https://chatgpt.com/share/5fc82d02-33ec-4af3-b753-c4b8a8812a19

filtering, detection of network intruders, computer vision, and enabling vehicles to navigate paths.[7]

- **Deep Learning (DL)** is "a subtype of machine learning that attempts to mimic the workings of the human brain in processing data for use in decision making."[8] Deep learning is a key technology behind driverless cars, enabling them to recognize a stop sign or distinguish a pedestrian from a lamppost. One of its most famous examples was in 1997 when when IBM's Alpha Blue beat the world chess champion, Gary Kasparov, under tournament conditions.[9]

In recent years, though, a new emphasis has emerged. **Natural Language Processing (NLP)** is "a subfield of artificial intelligence that focuses on the interaction between computers and humans through natural language." NLP "combines computational linguistics—rule and statistics-based modeling of human language—with machine learning and deep learning models to enable machines to understand how humans speak and write."[10] NLP allows ordinary people with no coding or programming background to converse with an AI just like they would with other humans.

Those require, and need to be trained on **Large Language Models (LLM)**, which are "a type of AI model that has been trained on a vast amount of data." They are "large" because they have a high number of *parameters*, or internal variables, that the model uses to make predictions.[11] A few examples of LLMs are:

- GPT-4 by OpenAI
- Turing-NLG by Microsoft
- BERT by Google
- Claude by Anthropic
- LLaMA by Meta
- Megatron by NVIDIA
- XLNet by Google Brain.[12]

---

7.   Ibid.
8.   Ibid.
9.   Paul McLellan (2018, 3 April). "Deep Blue, AlphaGo, and AlphaZero." Cadence. Community > Breakfast Bytes. https://community.cadence.com/cadence_blogs_8/b/breakfast-bytes/posts/alpha-go-and-alpha-go-zero
10.   OpenAI. (2023, Aug. 1). ChatGPT 3.5 [Large language model]. AI Definitions. Retrieved from: https://chatgpt.com/share/5fc82d02-33ec-4af3-b753-c4b8a8812a19
11.   Ibid.
12.   Ibid. Also updated with: OpenAI. (2024, Aug. 11). ChatGPT4o [Large language model]. Major LLMs Overview. Retrieved from: https://chatgpt.com/share/8079b573-7bce-4319-8853-b7c06b7bd721

So, putting it all together, a Generative AI is the combination of machine learning and deep learning with Natural Language Processing using a Large Language Model:

GenAI = ML/DL + NLP + LLM

Natural Language Processing means that AI research and output is no longer limited to computer science professionals with coding and programming experience, but that now everyday people can communicate with AIs in natural language, and it provides the output in natural language, too…in the same way humans naturally speak to each other. This allows you to chat conversationally with it.

The game-changer that led to the massive growth of generative AI lately is the **transformer model**. Transformer models are a specific type of AI model used predominantly in the field of Natural Language Processing (NLP). They are designed to handle sequential data, such as text, in a way that pays attention to the contextual relevance of each data point, like specific words (or "tokens") and their relationships.[13] They also look at multiple different ways of viewing the words and relationships simultaneously, and they use contextual cues to understand word order.[14]

This makes it possible for them to rapidly learn how humans communicate and provide outputs in very realistic, natural language, imitating our patterns. If you've ever tried to learn a foreign language and been confused by the order of words (is it Subject-Verb-Object, or is it Subject-Object-Verb?) or by the placement of adjectives (before or after the noun) or the use or absence of prepositions, then you understand the quandary: Languages worldwide vary in how these "rules" are applied.[15]

Transformer Models avoid all that complexity by converting the key words of any communication into "tokens" and giving them mathematical values, and this allows the AI to analyze their relationships and proximity to each other. In this way it can see dependencies and relationships that are hidden to us, but make it sound like natural human speech when it's done right. The term "transformer" comes from the model's ability to "transform" input

---

13. OpenAI. (2024, Aug. 14). ChatGPT4o [Large language model]. AI Transformer Models Concepts. Retrieved from: https://chatgpt.com/share/e5956ecc-f351-40e0-85ec-74d144bcc8c6

14. OpenAI. (2024, Aug. 14). ChatGPT4o [Large language model]. AI Transformer Model Overview. Retrieved from: https://chatgpt.com/share/dfce00bb-0294-41a2-a0b5-adfdc09765a8

15. SVO (Subject-Verb-Object) word order is typical of English, Spanish, and Mandarin Chinese: "The cat (S) chased (V) the mouse (O)." SOV (Subject-Object-Verb) word order is typical of languages like Japanese, Korean, and Turkish: "The cat (S) the mouse (O) chased (V)." Other variations include VSO (Verb-Subject-Object), which is found in languages like Classical Arabic and Irish: "Chased (V) the cat (S) the mouse (O)."

data (like a sentence) into an output (like a translation of the sentence) while maintaining the complex dependencies between those data points.[16]

AI IN DAILY USE

We have actually been using AI for decades, quite well, and most of us have been using AI extensively for many years and just aren't aware of it. Here are a few examples: [17]

- When autocorrect on mobile devices suggests alternate words or automatically "fixes" spellings in a word processing document,

- When you're driving in the morning and launch your Maps app and your mobile device recognizes the road you're on and the time of day, so automatically pulls up the route for your school or workplace,

- When your fast food restaurant's or retailer's app detects that you're a quarter mile from their location and automatically puts your order in the oven…or notifies them you're almost there,

- When Amazon recommends products based on your order history (or on what other people who've purchased the same item typically buy),

- When the photocopier you place materials on detects the orientation and placement, so loads up all the available options (or makes cropping recommendations),

- When an online application automatically recognizes that you're doing a typical operation and asks if you want it to complete it for you,

- When app tools like Grammarly suggest alternate wordings or improvements to style, tone, or grammar,

- When your mobile device or computer notices a pattern (such as when you're typically answering work emails) and asks if you'd like to make that your norm (such as your "available hours").

All of these situations are examples of computer algorithms responding to human input to analyze large volumes of data in order to make predictions based on typical responses. That's Artificial Intelligence (AI) at work. These are

---

16. OpenAI. (2023, Aug. 1). ChatGPT 3.5 [Large language model]. AI Definitions. Retrieved from: https://chat-gpt.com/share/5fc82d02-33ec-4af3-b753-c4b8a8812a19

17. David Swisher & Tiffany Snyder (2023, August 24). "Preparing Your Classroom for the World of AI." CAS Faculty Retreat (College of Arts & Sciences), Indiana Wesleyan University; held at Eastview Wesleyan Church, Gas City, IN.

all examples of AI in everyday use that we've been doing for years…for so long that we don't even think about the fact that is an AI algorithm enabling it.[18]

THE TREMENDOUS POTENTIAL OF GENERATIVE AI

When ChatGPT first emerged in late November of 2022, its full potential wasn't even close to being realized; it seemed like more of a novelty (but not for long). That Christmas, I used it in my family's Christmas tradition: After reading the Christmas story from Luke 2 in the Bible, I asked it to tell us the Christmas story from the perspective of Mary. I was blown away by all the nuances and insights that it captured with this innovative twist (of course, soon after that, my kids wanted it to tell them what Christmas means from the perspective of a cat). At first, it was pretty impressive what it could do, but the flaws and weaknesses were quite obvious – errors & inaccuracies, hallucinations (made-up content), obvious bias, etc. But that was multiple versions ago, and both ChatGPT and the other tools like it are now downright impressive.

However, ChatGPT is just the best-known of the generative AIs because it was first to market and consequently amassed massive market share and publicity. There are now hundreds of them, with dozens more being released every month.[19] New generative AIs are proliferating at an almost exponential rate, so by the time you read this, there will most likely be well over a thousand different generative AIs. Today, these generative AI tools offer remarkable possibilities for ministry contexts. As of this writing (in the Spring of 2025), here is a sampling of what generative AI can do to support churches and ministry leaders:

- **Text Generation:** AI tools like ChatGPT, Claude, Jasper, Gemini, Magai, and Perplexity can serve as collaboration partners in ministry, helping you brainstorm fresh perspectives for sermons; ideate series titles, themes, & illustrations; and even recommend Scriptures verses or passages to augment your prayerful sermon preparation. They can also provide feedback on drafts or teaching outlines, suggesting relevant connections, and provide constructive input on how messages or examples/illustrations might resonate with different segments of your congregation (and even

---

18. For a more in-depth review of how you're already using AI on a daily ba7is, see Ch. 1 in Jason Moore (2024), *AI & the Church: A Clear Guide for the Curious and Courageous* (Plano, TX: Invite Press).

19. David Swisher (2024, August 15), "The Current State of AI," AI Advisory Committee Kickoff, The Wesleyan Church (Fishers, IN).

help you see alternate points of view and anticipate objections), all while keeping you firmly in the driver's seat of content creation.

- **Image Generation:** AI tools like DALL-E, Stable Diffusion, Ideogram, Leonardo, and Midjourney can complement existing design resources by creating unique, conceptual imagery that would be impractical or cost-prohibitive to capture through traditional photography, such as biblical scenes, abstract theological concepts, or culturally-contextualized illustrations that aren't available in standard stock libraries. With the more advanced (paid) tools, you can even develop iterations, such as images and sequences to illustrate various scenes of a Scripture passage or stages of your message.

- **Video Generation:** Text-to-video AI tools like Synthesia, Runway ML, Sora, and Kling allow ministry leaders to create professional-quality videos and develop powerful video examples and imagery, all without requiring expensive production equipment, on-scene shoots, or studio time. You simply describe in text form what you want to see in video and it generates an extremely realistic video of what you described. You want to depict Joseph leading Mary on a donkey through the dusty streets of first-century Bethlehem, or show Elijah pouring water on a sacrificial altar to challenge the prophets of Baal? Describe what you want to see in text form, and you can have impressive video renderings of it in minutes!

- **Writing Improvement:** Tools like GrammarlyGO, Microsoft Co-Pilot, and Quillbot help pastors and ministry leaders to refine and enhance their written communications, ensuring that church documents, welcome/visitor communications, pastoral letters, and ministry materials are clear, engaging, appropriate for the audience and community demographics, and error-free, all while maintaining your authentic voice and message.

- **Meeting Assistants:** Tools like Otter, Read.ai, and Microsoft Co-Pilot can transcribe and summarize church meetings, small group discussions, and even client/coaching or counseling sessions (with permission), allowing ministry leaders to focus on personal connection and compassion during the time together, while letting the AI take effective notes, create useful summaries, and identify next steps for action. In combination with workflow tools, you can even use them like a secretary to add follow-up reminders and notes to your calendar, suggest next steps, and draft follow-up communication.[20]

---

20. My friend Rob Laughter (who served as Jason Moore's technical advisor for his *AI & the Church* book) offers a workshop on "Workflow, Automation, & Code" through his **AI Collaborative** where he demonstrates how he does this.

- **Music & Audio Generation:** Tools like Suno and Amper can create custom background music for church videos, youth programs, or special events, or fun on-the-fly soundtracks for youth gatherings, as well as generate unique worship arrangements that fit your congregation's style and needs.

- **Presentation Tools:** AI-powered presentation tools like Tome, Gamma, and Beautiful.ai can transform your sermon notes or Bible study content into visually engaging presentations, automatically suggesting layouts and visual elements that enhance your message. Even if you're not skilled with design and layout or struggle to put together a good presentation, or don't have staff or volunteers who can assist, a few good prompts and a solid set of notes will result in rather impressive presentations that you can easily adapt as you see fit.

- **Audio/Visual Voice Cloning & Translation:** AI tools like Eleven-Labs can help churches create authentic-sounding and culturally diverse voiceovers, or add warmth and personality to videos and multimedia. And tools like HeyGen can can take your existing videos and convert them into different languages while maintaining the pastor's voice, inflection, and facial expressions, making your ministry content more accessible to diverse communities at surprisingly affordable rates (much cheaper than traditional costly and time-consuming translation processes).

And this is just a sampling of the range of tools and scope of abilities that are currently available. Every week I see new examples of pastors and ministry leaders using one or more of these tools to create impressive content that enhances their ability to serve their communities well. And every few days I learn about new tools that are being released. AI is advancing faster than any technology in human history.[21] I consider this development on par with the technology of Roman roads and Gutenberg's printing press, both of which God used to spread the gospel message in strategic ways at just the right time.

So how is all this possible?

HOW GENERATIVE AI "THINKS"

Many of my ministry and education colleagues mistakenly presume that generative AI is simply taking phrases and excerpts from various files and

---

It's part of his "Generative AI Fundamentals" course and can be accessed via a one-time purchase or through a monthly paid membership: https://roblaughter.com/collaborative/

21.   Charles Coxe (Ed.) (2025), *Artificial Intelligence: The Second Wave* [Special issue]. A360 Media.

authors and stitching them all together to form something it claims is new. One even goes so far as to call it a "plagiarism machine." Generative AI is driven entirely by predictive analytics using a large dataset. According to Stephen Wolfram (the computational linguist and programming guru behind Wolfram|Alpha), "…what ChatGPT is always fundamentally trying to do is produce a 'reasonable continuation' of whatever text it's got so far, where by 'reasonable' we mean 'what one might expect someone to write after seeing what people have written on billions of webpages."[22] Believe it or not, it is literally adding just one word at a time![23]

So if we've got the phrase, "The sky is _____," then it's going to be scanning the massive dataset of its Large Language Model to predict the next most likely word in our context. If the data it's using shows high frequency of the word, "blue," then the word it appends here will undoubtedly be "blue."[24] However, it is ALSO scanning the related context of our input window and the LLM's context, and it is adjusting its data through the lens of variable "tokens," so…

- If the context is a weather forecast, it will likely forego the obvious larger number from our GENERAL context and instead look at instances from the LLM when weather forecasting is the context, and in that case, it will likely generate "stormy" or perhaps "hazy" (depending on other tokens in the context window).[25]

- If the context is poetry and art, then it's likely going to forego the obvious larger numbers from the GENERAL and WEATHER context and will look at its LLM for instances where poetry and artistic beauty are the context, and so in that case, it will likely generate "turquoise" or "tranquil."[26]

If you've ever watched the TV game show "Family Feud," you've surely heard the expression, "100 people surveyed, top 5 answers are on the board." Well, that's essentially how generative AI works, except that it's more like "Top 10,000 responses surveyed, top 2,000 words from answers ready to generate."

IS AI JUST STEALING & REPACKAGING OTHERS' CONTENT?

22. Stephen Wolfram (2023). *What Is ChatGPT Doing … and Why Does It Work?* Champaign, IL: Champaign, IL.
23. Ibid.
24. David Swisher (2023, August). "Academic Integrity in an Era of Generative AI." Fall Faculty Professional Development emphasis on "Generative AI and Adult Education" (Faculty Enrichment, National & Global Campus). Indiana Wesleyan University, Marion, IN.
25. Ibid. Screenshots of what I am describing are available in David Swisher & Annie Els (2024). Rethinking Assessment in Light of Generative AI. C2C Digital Magazine, 1 (20), article 3. Colleague2Colleague. https://scalar.usc.edu/works/c2c-digital-magazine-fall-2023--winter-2024/rethinking-assessment-in-light-of-generative-ai
26. Ibid.

One of the most common concerns I hear raised from both faculty and church leaders is the mistaken presumption that generative AI is just plagiarizing other people's content. When we hear about AIs being "trained" on content, or see output that looks similar to other works, it's easy to understand why people might conclude this. After all, the content it generates looks and sounds a lot like how we write, and often the results are very similar to others' published works. However, this assumption is based on an understandable, yet faulty, premise.

My friends and colleagues know that my three longest-running passions and expertise are: (1) Copyright & intellectual property law, (2) Academic integrity & plagiarism, and (3) effective & ethical use of technology. These are what I am known for in professional circles. If you have any doubts about this, look me up on Quora, where I have over two thousand published answers on the site, nearly two-thirds of which are on copyright & intellectual property, and the other third of which are on academic integrity, plagiarism, & originality.[27] And yet, I am a long-time (30-year+) follower of AI's development and an avid AI user. So, how do I reconcile these supposedly divergent perspectives? After all, if I thought that AI was routinely infringing others' copyrights or that it was routinely plagiarizing content, I would be AI's strongest and harshest critic. But the reason I have no qualms with it is that's simply not how AI works.

Training an AI involves showing it thousands of examples of whatever the category or topic is so that it can "learn" how to recognize it (including examples of what doesn't fit the criteria) and then be able to predict it. Large volumes of high-quality data are fed into the tool, and the parameter values are continually adjusted until the AI can reliably predict the next token (word/concept) in the sequence: "It does this through self-learning techniques which teach the model to adjust parameters to maximize the likelihood of the next tokens in the training examples."[28]

What I find most fascinating about this is that this is also how WE learn![29] For example, when I say the word "tree," what do you think of? How do you know what a tree looks like? Well, you've seen thousands of them in your lifetime! From early childhood, when you saw a big tall brown trunk with a green

---

27. Quora (n.d.), "David Swisher: Educator, Multimedia specialist, D.Min, & minister" [Profile], https://www.quora.com/profile/David-Swisher

28. Amazon Web Services (n.d.), "How are large language models trained?" in "What is LLM (Large Language Model)?," https://aws.amazon.com/what-is/large-language-model/

29. David Swisher (2023, August 22), "How We Learn: The Neuroscience of Learning" (6:32 – 11:31) in David Swisher, "Research-Based Best Practices for Developing Effective Presentations," Indiana Wesleyan University (Marion, IN): http://www.kaltura.com/tiny/hk31z

leafy top, a parent or mentor told you that was a tree. Later, you refined that understanding as you saw other types, shapes, and colors of trees and learned that they were also considered trees, and occasionally you may have misidentified a bush or a plant that looks similar but is distinctly different in nature. All of that helped to form your mental representation of a tree. As we "learn" about different kinds of trees and similar-looking vegetation, we've been making mental representations to help us decipher the inputs we're receiving.[30]

And inside our brain, chemicals migrate the synaptic gaps in our neurons to help electrical signals cross, thus reinforcing that connection. And every time we find out we're mistaken or that our old mental representations aren't accurate, our brain either severs those connections or they are broken over time due to pruning.[31] The result is that we learn by reinforcement, over time, with dozens if not hundreds of examples, all by rehearsing and practice to reinforce those neuronal pathways. The result is that if I asked 100 people to draw a tree, we would come up with an awful lot of similarity because, for the most part, we know what a tree looks like. There might be some regional variation, with those in coastal or island regions drawing trees that look more like palm trees and people from the African Savannah drawing trees that look more like umbrella trees. But for the most part, our collective consensus of what a tree looks like will be fairly consistent.

AI training mimics this approach, but in a decidedly mathematical and predictive way. The training process is also not much different than how artisans perfect their craft:

- When an artist wants to paint at a professional level, they "train" on other artists' work: They practice painting in the style of Van Gogh, Picasso, Monet, & others so that they can understand and master the techniques and learn to paint like that.

- When a writer wants to become a professional writer, they "train" on great writing by spending countless hours reading great works of literature, immersing themselves in the writings of Faulkner, Hemingway, Shakespeare, and more, and they practice writing like the greats.

---

30. For a visual illustration of this very process, including how the human brain learns, see my presentation on "How We Learn: The Neuroscience of Learning" (6:32 – 11:31) at: http://www.kaltura.com/tiny/hk31z

31. Harvard University (2011, Sept. 29), "Experiences Build Brain Architecture." Excerpt from Part 1 of "Three Core Concepts in Early Development" Series, Center on the Developing Child, Harvard University, accessed March 18, 2023, https://youtu.be/VNNsN9IJkws

- When a sculptor, engineer, designer, or etc. want to become a professional in their craft, they "train" on great works by working for (under) a mentor in that field.

- Ancient monks did it at Qumran during Jesus' day, and Medieval monks did it, too..."training" on great examples to improve their skills and craftsmanship.

In fact, for more than two millenia, we have used a guild system for people to learn skilled crafts, and nearly all of the skilled trades still follow that model today. Our academic institutions, too, are built upon this premise and its millenia-old model, using experts and mentors to teach newcomers to the field the requisite skills and expertise that can only be acquired through learning from and by imitating the best mentors and examples. Nobody ever questions the skill acquisition or practice efforts of someone learning like this, but everybody gets in an uproar when AI does it. In reality, the only thing that's different about an AI learning is that AI can do that kind of "training" in a matter of hours, days, or weeks, whereas it takes humans years, decades, and even sometimes, a lifetime.

We can fear that efficiency (because it has strong potential to disrupt the way we do things, alter the creative process, and re-shape processes that we're used to), or we can learn to adapt and work with it, utilizing AI to maximize our skill learning and creative efficiency. After all, the best output from AI comes from skilled artisans and professionals who understand the subject matter well, can ideate and communicate effectively, and therefore can craft highly-precise prompts that generate incredible results. It might come as a surprise, but some of the most incredible writers and visual artists I know were some of the earliest adopters of generative AI, and it is absolutely incredible what they can do with it. Rather than see it as a threat or disrupter, they treated it as a new tool to leverage so they could expand their repertoire and design even more incredible works.

On occasion, yes, there are exceptions where sufficient guardrails weren't put in place to prevent overt copying, and I know that there are scrupulous designers out there who don't care about ethics. But those can be handled as exceptions when they arise because laws already prohibit that. And I certainly think AI developers should obtain permission or consent, and preferably compensate for the works they include in their training data. But unclear protocols and vaguely applicable laws do not invalidate the process, they just expose specific issues that need to be addressed.

INSIGHTS FROM CHURCH HISTORY

As we consider the potential and implications of AI for the Church, the example from Church history that I think we can best draw from his Jesus Himself. Ask nearly any Christian about Jesus' upbringing and occupation and they'll tell you that He was a carpenter, and the son of a carpenter. After all, early in the gospels we read about the people's reaction to him teaching in the synagogue and doing miracles: "Is this not the carpenter, the son of Mary and brother of [a]James, Joses, Judas, and Simon? And are His sisters not here with us?" And they took offense at Him."[32] The Greek word ΤΈΚΤШΝ (tekton) used there is often rendered as "carpenter," and the assumption that Jesus was a carpenter is the subject of numerous articles, sermons, Sunday School lessons, as well as the theme of one of the most famous mass-produced books on basic Christianity by a well-respected apologist.[33] The presumption that Jesus was a carpenter is rarely questioned, and so it is practically futile to argue otherwise since it entered mainstream assumptive rhetoric decades ago and is now normative. However, the Western assumptions that are inherent in this very limited rendering create problems in regards to technology and praxis, because that nuance isn't what it meant in Jesus' day.[34]

According to renowned Greek scholar Bill Mounce, the definition of ΤΈΚΤШΝ is an "artisan." That word can refer to a carpenter or woodworker, or even more generally to a construction worker who specializes in stone or metal; that's the semantic range for the term.[35] Strong's Concordance defines it as either "artisan" or "carpenter." So the assumption that Jesus was a carpenter isn't necessarily wrong; it's just an extremely narrow (and VERY Western) presumption because we think we know what a carpenter is: Growing up in America, with our abundance of natural resources and our preference for wood construction and furnishings, it is easy for us to conceive of Jesus as having been a carpenter and to assume that his human work involved wordworking projects.

However, when I went on a pastor's familiarization tour of Israel and later viewed pictures from several friends who operate ministries in the Middle East, one thing stood out to me in stark contrast to my own experience growing up in the Midwestern United States: Trees are sparse. They are not only limited in

---

32. Mark 6:3, NASB.

33. Josh McDowell, *More Than a Carpenter* (Living Books, 1986).

34. Significant portions of this section are adapted from the presidential address I delivered in our inaugural meeting of the Society for the Study of the Integration of Technology with Wesleyan Theology & Praxis (SSITWTP) in concert with the triennial joint session of the Wesleyan Theological Society and the Society for Pentecostal Studies gathering in March 2018): "Not Necessarily a Carpenter: Bridging the Technology Gap by Reconsidering Jesus' Role as ΤΈΚΤШΝ."

35. Bill Mounce, "ΤΈΚΤШΝ," Greek Dictionary, accessed Feb. 24, 2018, https://www.billmounce.com/greek-dictionary/tekton

number, but also small and scrawny…and in Israel, they are certainly not the kind of resource you would want to construct your house with.[36] That's why the cedars of Lebanon had such a reputation and were prized for their durability and were even used in elements of temple construction (both David's and Solomon's).[37]

Because of this, you simply would <u>not</u> want to utilize wood as your primary building material…not in Israel at least. Although we know trees were used, their role was far less common; their main function was to serve as support beams and in the crafting of the furnishings (we see this quite a bit in the descriptions of the tabernacle). Archeological excavations from Nazareth and other first-century villages tells us that the vast majority of construction in the land of the Bible from Jesus' time was done with rough stone foundations and mud-brick walls, not timber.[38] Wood was used primarily for ladders and roofing material. So if Jesus was truly a carpenter in our Western sense…in Israel, in the first century…He would not have had much work (it's certainly hard to believe there would have been enough work to sustain a father/son business).[39]

So, what was he, then? Well, the semantic meaning of the word τέκτων is someone who works with their hands: A craftsman, a handyman, or especially an artisan. In the context of ancient Israel, He was most likely a stonemason. This perspective is also well supported by the proximity of Nazareth to Sepphoris (only a couple of miles away), which underwent a major rebuilding and construction drive under Herod Antipas, who made it his capital.[40] Since the Roman construction project was done primarily in stone and began shortly after the birth of Jesus, hundreds of skilled τέκτων's (artisans) would have been needed for stonemasonry construction work,[41] and it is very likely that news of the planned expansion would have been a major factor in Joseph's decision to settle his family there in Nazareth rather than in Galilee.[42]

Even more fascinating (especially for me in my role) is the connection to technology: A closely-related Greek word τέχνη means "art, skill, craft," and

36. Aviva & Shmuel Bar-Am (2016, 25 January), "Get to the Roots of Israel's Historic Trees," Times of Israel, accessed Feb. 24, 2018, https://www.timesofisrael.com/get-to-the-roots-of-israels-historic-trees/; Rotem Hoffman (2023, Oct. 21), "Trees of the Holy Land," BibleWalks.com, accessed Feb. 24, 2018, https://www.biblewalks.com/trees/.

37. Todd Bolen (n.d.), "Cedar of Lebanon," BiblePlaces.com, accessed Feb. 24, 2018, https://www.bibleplaces.com/cedar-of-lebanon/

38. Elizabeth Fletcher (n.d.), "Nazareth: Jesus' Home Town," *Life of Jesus Christ: Buildings Jesus Knew*, accessed Feb. 24, 2018, http://www.jesus-story.net/buildings_NT.htm

39. David Swisher (2018, March). "Reconsidering Jesus' Role as τέκτων." (SSITWTP).

40. Israel National Parks Authority (n.d.), "Sepphoris," *See the Holy Land*, accessed Feb. 26, 2018, http://www.seetheholyland.net/sepphoris/

41. Ray Van der Laan (n.d.), "The Language of Culture," *That the World May Know*, accessed Feb. 25, 2018, https://www.thattheworldmayknow.com/language-of-culture-article

42. Israel National Parks Authority, "Sepphoris."

this is where we get the word "technology."[43] Etymologically speaking, "technology" combines τέχνη (techne) for "art, skill, craft, or the way, manner, or means by which a thing is gained"and λόγια (logia) for "word, the utterance by which inward thought is expressed, a saying, or an expression."[44] Linguistically, historically, and archaeologically, it is far more plausible (in fact, it's almost certain) that Jesus was a technologist...a craftsman, artisan, or worker with his hands...and He most definitely worked with the latest technology of His day![45] Not only that, but following that famous birth we celebrate every year at Christmas time was his earthly father Joseph's move to Nazareth, and that was driven by technology innovation and development!

So, what does this have to do with AI? Well, whenever I (or any of my similarly-minded colleagues and friends) talk with pastors and ministry leaders about the potential of AI for their church or ministry, inevitably we encounter resistance.[46] Christians, as a whole (and pastors especially), seem to be surprisingly averse to technology, and often we come up with incredibly complex mental gymnastics and develop strong, yet often unfounded (or even absurd), objections to explain why we are hesitant to embrace new technologies and innovations. Often we find "support" for our objections by using inaccurate prooftext examples to substantiate our preconceptions. Sadly, this isn't limited to modern times, either: In Gutenberg's day, Johannes Trithemius was the abbot of Sponheim Abbey, and he was deeply involved in expanding the abbey's library, emphasizing copying of manuscripts during this time of technological transition. He wrote, "Printed books will never be the equivalent of handwritten codices, especially since printing presses produce so many books that they can never be perfect in their execution."[47] Well, we all know how that turned out!

Likewise, when radio first emerged as a new medium in the early 20th century, certain religious leaders expressed apprehension about its potential impact on church attendance and community life. They feared that the convenience of accessing religious content from home would lead to congregants preferring to listen to broadcasts over participating in in-person services. Even-

43. Kenneth H. Funk II (n.d.), "Definitions of Technology," Technology and Christian 'Values,' Oregon State University, accessed Feb. 26, 2018, http://web.engr.oregonstate.edu/~funkk/Technology/technology.html
44. Ibid.
45. David Swisher (2018, March). "Reconsidering Jesus' Role as τέκτων." (SSITWTP).
46. My friend Jason Moore covers this extensively in Ch. 4 "Concerns and Resistance" of his 2024 book *AI & the Church: A Clear Guide for the Curious and Courageous* (Plano, TX: Invite Press). I highly recommend reading that if you want to explore this aspect further (and see his responses).
47. Johannes Trithemius, *In Praise of Scribes*, trans. Roland Behrendt (Lawrence, KS: Coronado Press, 1974), 56, https://archive.org/details/inpraiseofscribe0000trit/page/56/mode/2up

tually, however, the church realized the potential of radio to reach wider audiences, and religious organizations began to adopt the medium to disseminate their messages. One notable example was when Pope Pius XI worked with Italian scientist (and inventor of the radio) Guglielmo Marconi in 1931 to launch Vatican Radio, inaugurating it with a broadcast from the pope.[48] Radio has been a mainstay of religious media for decades ever since, and a huge swatch of the evangelical church exists because of it.

Such reactions to new technologies are so common in church and ministry contexts that initial reactions are nearly always all too predictable: There will be a few early adopters and trailblazers, along with a large number of ardent resisters. And by the time the technology is roughly a decade old (and already mainstream in nearly every context), the Church finally decides it might be worth looking into. I've devoted much of my ministry to changing that paradigm, and I think it's important because if we're going to remain relevant in future decades, we've got to learn how to embrace and fully utilize the new disruptive technologies that are coming (as well as those which are already here).

The simple reality, however, is that change does not come easy, and we often fear what we do not understand (and if we're pastors or ministry leaders, we tend to throw in a few verses to make our objection sound theological). But truth be told, most of the time our resistance is inconsistent with the whole of Scripture and inaccurate in terms of the technology or innovation involved, too. This is definitely the case with AI. After all, some of the very first uses by Christians of machine learning and artificial intelligence was Bible translation!

I believe it was Mustafa Suleyman who first articulated the idea that when new algorithmic technology first comes out, we call it "artificial intelligence," but once we get used to it and incorporate it into our daily life, we just call it software.[49] If you use a smartphone, email, or social media, or ever ship packages, travel by plane, use digital maps or GPS, watch the newsfeeds, or use Google, or Amazon, or Wal-mart, then you've already used AI.[50] How? Algorithmic computations and analysis of past activities and purchases is used to predict current needs and intents or filter what you're shown, and that is artificial intelligence at work. And from what we know of Jesus' life and ministry

---

48. EWTN Vatican (2023, Feb. 12), "Vatican Radio: 92 Years of Broadcasting for the Catholic Church," Fondazione EWTN News (Rome, Italy), accessed Mar. 15, 2025, https://www.ewtnvatican.com/articles/vatican-radio-92-years-of-broadcasting-for-the-catholic-church-505

49. Mustafa Suleyman (2023). *The Coming Wave: Technology, Power, and the 21ᵗ Century's Greatest Dilemma* (New York: "Crown").

50. Jason Moore has an entire chapter where he explores this aspect…about how you're already using AI on a daily basis. See Ch. 1 "AI Already in Your Pocket" in Jason Moore (2024), *AI & the Church: A Clear Guide for the Curious and Courageous* (Plano, TX: Invite Press).

(and especially His occupation), I think it is not the slightest stretch of imagination to contend that since He was using the latest technological innovations of His day on a daily basis for His family's livelihood (and grew up with it), if He were around today, He would be fully embracing and utilizing AI, too.

PATTERN RECOGNITION & PREDICTIVE ANALYSIS

AI excels at pattern recognition and predictive analysis. Although humans do have that ability, and some (like me and a few of my colleagues) enjoy reviewing piles of statistical data to find commonalities and exceptions or anticipate trends, most people really don't enjoy that. It can be very mind-numbing work, and no matter how adept and skillful we are at spotting differences, finding exceptions, and plotting trends and trajectories, we tire quickly from it and often overlook – or can't even see – small details. We require periodic rest, rejuvenation, refreshers and regular motivation to continue analyzing data in order to identify trends, spot outliers, analyze commonalities, etc. But machines don't need that. They can analyze data for days on end without ever tiring, without their eyes glazing over, without needing sleep or motivation, and without missing anything that we can so easily overlook.

A good example of this is when we started reaching our user limit on my institution's Grammarly account (which I had been the admin of for several years). I had noticed a substantial uptick in new user account signups, and the growth rate seemed much faster than usual (plus a lot of it seemed to be coming from a specific program). So we needed to make some adjustments and likely revisit our contract. However, to make any financial or policy decisions, we needed to base that on hard evidence using actual data, so I needed to be able to document the recent increase in new signups on a monthly basis over time. So, first I downloaded the user data from our account and started by using Excel to manually review the data. But with over 14,000 users, that proved nightmarishly challenging.

In the Data Visualization class I teach, we use R Studio, so after getting frustrated by the Excel approach, I ran the data file through that program and attempted to find meaning and plot trajectories from it. The problem? It's a data visualization program, and you need to understand how the data is structured and know what you're looking for to effectively graph those trends. I knew some of the things I wanted to see and analyze visually, but not enough to use that approach efficiently. So then I turned to AI. I used Claude rather than ChatGPT to maintain student privacy, and then, after a bit of prompt engineering where I

45

explained the context and my needs, as well as what format I wanted my results in, I uploaded the data file.

Within minutes, I had a fully interactive graph of new user signups of our Grammarly account on a month-by-month basis for the past 5 years, and it also plotted a trendline with a 3-month moving average. The ebbs & flows of campus semesters were unmistakably clear, and so was the trajectory, which was increasing at a steadily increasing rate. Even better, I could hover over individual data points and see precise details, and it gave me a very helpful written analysis with 5 key takeaways. This was absolutely perfect for documenting the issue and understanding where our growth was headed so that we could make decisions supported by evidence. What took me hours in Excel (with only headaches to show for it) and which proved elusive in my data visualization program only took minutes to create with generative AI.

Imagine doing that in your church with attendance records, enrollments for discipleship or Sunday School classes, or demographics for the neighborhood where your church is located! Imagine being able to analyze shifts in attendance patterns or the demographic makeup of your community, or analyzing small group growth and distribution in light of shifting generational or neighborhood changes. Imagine being able to analyze your last 10 years' worth of messages and evaluate them for tone and theme, generate a list (or chart or table) of Scripture passages and themes you use most, or even runs some correlations between your church's attendance data, engagement patterns, demographic trends, and felt needs of the age groups. These are things we don't usually notice or see because we're living it daily (it's that old "frog in a kettle" issue…you don't recognize the slow incremental changes).

But an AI can analyze all that and spot trends, trajectories, and anomalies quickly, and even make recommendations based on it. That's a sampling of the pattern recognition and predictive analysis capability of AI for ministry contexts. So, what might this look like in a specific church context? Consider the following scenario:

PASTOR ROB AND THE AI-ENHANCED SERMON

Pastor Rob is the lead pastor at a medium-sized suburban church, one that has been around for nearly a century, and it is known for its diverse congregation as well as its creative approach to ministry. Pastor Rob has a very demanding ministry schedule that keeps him extremely busy with pastoral visitation, hospital ministry, coordinating staff, and leading adult discipleship classes, and in the midst of all that, he has to develop timely, relevant, and life-changing sermons to deliver from the pulpit weekly.

Lately, he has been using a generative AI tool to help him develop his weekly sermons. He doesn't have the AI write it *for* him, but he <u>does</u> use it like a colleague or administrative assistant giving him ideas, suggestions, examples, and feedback, as well as helping him with research. After spending time in prayer about the direction he should go with the weekly message, he organizes his thoughts and begins his research. He uses the generative AI tool to help him come up with potential titles that would capture his parishioners' attention, and once he's got an idea of how he wants to organize the message, he asks the AI to help him fine-tune the outline. Often he'll ask the AI for help with alliterating the outline or otherwise making it memorable.

In years past, he made heavy use of commentaries and Bible software that helped him mine the depths of past saints and their perspectives, as well as suggestions of other biblical references or insights he might want to include. Lately, he's been asking the AI to help with that. When he's struggling to illustrate a particular concept, he often asks the AI for examples from Scripture, contemporary illustrations, or ways to explain the concept that might be meaningful to his hearers.

The tool also does an amazing job of analyzing his sermon recordings, providing a text transcript of it, and helping him develop follow-up study materials to use in the Wednesday night adult discipleship class as well as draft a "sermon summary" in the church's newsletter. . All of this saves him valuable time (tasks like those used to take him hours each week), freeing him to focus on doing the work of the ministry that he finds great fulfillment in doing and feels called to do. The AI help also enriches his sermons with insights and perspectives that he likely would have overlooked, and it serves as a great "conversation partner," too, helping him to include ideas and examples he might not have considered.

One Thursday, as Rob was preparing for a particularly challenging sermon on social justice and Christian responsibility, he input his preliminary thoughts into the AI tool and it suggested several powerful contemporary examples of social injustice, along with links to news articles, and quotes from theologians and activists. Intrigued by the depth of the AI's suggestions and their relevance, he used these examples to build a compelling narrative. Later, in a meeting with his leadership team, he mentioned how the AI tool had contributed to that aspect of his sermon. Many on the team were impressed, but some were also concerned.

They raised some concerns, such as: How much of the sermon is truly his if the AI is providing important content, too? Does using AI for sermon preparation dilute the personal touch and spiritual discernment that's traditionally associated with pastoral ministry? How

47

would the congregation feel if they knew that the pastor was using AI regularly in developing his messages? Even if Pastor Rob's uses are perfectly OK, is there a line that others might cross (if they followed his example) that would be inappropriate?

Pastor Rob acknowledges these concerns and appreciates their wise counsel, though he is somewhat surprised at the pushback. In response, he suggests maintaining a balance. He decides to use the AI as a starting point but commits to ensuring that every sermon is filtered through personal prayer and reflection. He also proposes an informational sesion for the congregation to talk about the role of technology in spiritual life, aiming to engage the community in these important discussions.

That week's Sunday message is well-received; it sparks a lively discussion and great follow-up dialogue among congregants about technology, ethics, and spirituality. Pastor Rob reflects on the experience, recognizing the value of AI in enhancing his message, yet also reaffirming the irreplaceable value of human oversight and Holy Spirit involvement in pastoral ministry.

THE RISKS AND CHALLENGES OF AI

Part of the reason why I think pastors and church leaders often fear AI is due to Hollywood depictions. When we think of AI, all too often our minds go to dystopian science fiction movies, so we picture Agent Smith from The Matrix movies, or HAL 9000 from 2001: A Space Odyssey, or Skynet from The Terminator movies. Of course, these are all examples of "worst-case scenarios" when an AI goes rogue.[51] And whenever there's a news report about AI that didn't work exactly right, it's always a really bad outcome that the news media and all reports will focus on. Why? It's simple: Fear sells.

A movie about an AI operating efficiently and intelligently, in a symbiotic co-relationship with humans, making their lives better and helping them creatively ideate and solve problems would have little to no potential at the box office (most people won't pay to see everything going well and there being no issues or challenges). A news report about all the billions of AI-driven interactions that occur daily will never make it on the nightly news, but a scintillating one about an AI that messed up and caused problems will of course get prime coverage.

But AIs behaving badly is usually what happens when humans aren't actively engaged in the process. Sadly, although the misplaced emphasis makes

---

51. For many more examples, see this list and synopses which ChatGPT provided: https://tinyurl.com/Sci-FiRogueAI

perfect sense, it also negatively colors our impressions of AI. Nevertheless, there are some legitimate concerns and risks, along with rampant fear and mis-understanding. In his outstanding book *AI & the Church: A Clear Guide for the Curious and Courageous*, my friend Jason Moore has devoted an entire chapter to those concerns and the resistance which flows from them, and it's a great synopsis of the fears and concerns I have encountered in my own dialogues with pastors and ministry leaders about AI. So, in this section, I will list the specific fear or concern about AI that Jason identified,[52] summarize his words briefly, and then share my response to that concern:

AI is the devil – The perception (or presumption) that any new form of technology must be the devil's work. There are a surprising number of people who espouse this view.

> This concern reflects fear, not theology. Of course, the perception that any new form of technology must be the devil's work has also been said of a multitude of innovations that later proved to be completely benign, including forks, telephones, the Internet, and more. People have always feared new technologies they don't understand. AI is a human-made tool, nothing more or less. And, like all technology – it us morally neutral. It can be used for good or evil. It has tremendously power and potential, but it can also be mis-used. Even with its inherent risks, it can also be used for tremendous good – for the benefits of God's people and mis-sion. What matters is whose hands it is in and how it is wielded.

AI as proxy leader – The concern that we might allow AI to take on roles that should only be assumed by humans, such as delivering sermons, leading worship services, doing pastoral counseling, etc.

> Rather than undermining human uniqueness, AI actually affirms it. AI's capabilities are entirely derivative, meaning that they draw from patterns and data that humans have created. The inability of AI to feel, discern, or spiritually reason serves as a powerful reminder of the uniquely human capacity for creativity, emotion, empathy, and moral judgment. AI can assist, but it cannot shepherd. It can generate ideas, summarize trends, or offer insights, but it cannot lay hands on the sick, weep with those who mourn, or provide the incarnational presence of a faithful pastor. Used right, AI frees pastors to focus more on people, not less.

---

52. Jason Moore (2024), Ch. 4 "Concerns & Resistance" in Jason Moore (2024), *AI & the Church: A Clear Guide for the Curious and Courageous* (Plano, TX: Invite Press), 40-41.

Deepfakes and scams – The risk that AI can be used to generate deepfakes and perpetuate scams, violating trust and generating confusion and deception.

The manipulation of graphics, audio, news, soundbytes, and more (including deepfakes and scams), as well as the confusion and deception they cause, was a concern long before AI ever came on the scene; think chain letter scams, biased news media, Photoshopping of images, deceptively edited videos and audio, etc. Manipulation is a risk inherent in any medium—whether pulpits, printing, television, or social media. The ethical issue lies in the intent and use, not the technology itself. Church leaders must set the standard for transparency, accountability, and Christlike use of powerful tools.

Loss of agency – The concern that overreliance upon AI could cause us to lose our reliance upon the Holy Spirit and/or the irreplaceable value of human connection.

Replacing the value of human connection and/or losing our reliance upon the Holy Spirit is always a risk with any new technology, system, or process; that concern should impact how we approach the technology, not cause us to avoid it altogether. In fact, the ability of new technologies to save time and effort is often the pitch that comes with every new technology: "Imagine how much time and effort you'll save with this new [powered razor, lawnmower, dishwasher, computer, etc.]."

Using AI is cheating – The fairly prevalent concern that the ease of use and access to AI makes it easy to generate quick answers and content, replacing genuine effort and time investment with quick fixes.

The all-too-human-tendency to relegate responsibility for the sake of convenience has existed since the dawn of mankind; it drives our innovation and leads us to experiment further, always seeking better, faster, and more efficient ways of doing things that we find laborious or tedious. But efficiency and capability alone does not inherently make it wrong; humans are wired for this, and we use (& develop) tools for this very purpose. Like any tool, AI can be misused; however, it can also support ministry leaders, inform pastoral insight, and even help deepen spiritual engagement. If AI helps a minister preach more powerfully, lead more effectively, or understand their ministry context and options better, then it can certainly be a ministry tool. If AI can help someone pray more regularly, reflect more deeply, or better understand Scripture, then it can also be a tool for discipleship. The responsibility lies with the user, not the algorithm.

AI will force us to perpetuate biases – Some believe that AI has an agenda or a nefarious plan to perpetuate human biases or force certain views on us. While bias can certainly be more of a problem with AI than with other technologies,[53] bias is inherent in the human heart (it's part of our sin nature) and its influence and the related social/economic disparity has always been a problem when new technologies first emerge.

> Wise users and leaders stay cognizant of the risk and seek to mitigate its impact. Pastors and ministry leaders who understand this can actually be a powerful voice for not only proper use and ethical approaches, but even push for training and fine-tuning of LLMs in ways that recognize and represent ALL people, not just certain groups. In this sense, fear and avoidance only makes the problem worse; active engagement and under-standing actually helps *improve* the ethical use of AI and mitigate against the potential for bias.

AI will turn on humanity – The concern that AI will one day turn on us, enslaving the very humanity that created it and perhaps even eliminating the threat we pose.

> Whether AI will one day turn on us and enslave humanity really depends on how fanciful your imagination is and how many dystopian science fiction movies and "bad AI" news reports you've consumed. However, I would also contend that a fear-based reaction to the development of technology and the emergence of AI is also indicative of a very low view of God's presence and active role in our lives. It's dismissing God's sovereignty, concluding that machines and software created by humans are more powerful and effective than God. Quite frankly, I think the book of Revelation makes overwhelmingly clear that God is far more powerful than anything the enemy (or humanity) can develop.

However, I do want to acknowledge the fear factor and the perceived loss of control we may feel when we think about (or actually start experimenting with) using generative AI to accomplish our work. That apprehension…that fear…is real. In many ways, it would be like hiring an intern or an office assistant to support your ministry efforts: You know that you need help, the administrative tasks and tedium of common things slows you down from doing the real work of the

---

53. This (AI bias) is something that Jason addresses quite a bit in his book (Ch. 6 – Navigating Ethical Concerns) and I address rather frequently in my workshops and teaching about AI.

ministry, you're worried whether they would share the same heart for ministry and commitment to pastoral care and theological accuracy that you have, and you're anxious about what bringing them on might mean for the office. You may even worry about the impressions it gives and perceptions people may have, too (as if they might think less of you or consider you perhaps inadequate to do the job). I've felt every one of these feelings, and every pastor I've known has, too. Sometimes we may even worry if the new hire might even replace us…or wonder (or even fear) what would happen if the congregation likes them more.

These are legitimate feelings that all of us engaged in ministry struggle with, and I don't want to dismiss them altogether. But it's important that we not mix issues. What I'm describing here has far more to do with our own sense of self and ministry calling (fears, loss of control, concerns about spiritual discernment, commitment to accuracy, etc.); they have very little to do with the technology itself. But what I see happen all too often is pastors and ministry leaders conflate the fears and concerns they have about what this kind of change would involve with the technology itself, and then they simply resist the technology. That's a form of escapism (or even imposter syndrome), and it's not only unhealthy, but it's biblically problematic.[54]

Keep in mind, too, that there is a big difference between using AI as a support or conversation partner (ideation, collaboration, etc.) in your ministry and actually having it do the work of ministry. AI can be a wonderful tool to suggest, summarize, and assist, and it can help you organize, think, alliterate, evaluate, and research. But it does not discern, pray, think, or carry the weight of spiritual responsibility. Only human hands guided by the Holy Spirit can do that. My biggest concern in this regard is that when we take this fear-based resistance approach (the proverbial ostrich with its head buried in the sand) rather than critically engage, we end up relinquishing the power of the people (and Spirit) of God to influence the eventual outcome! Do we really want secular leaders, profit-driven businesses, and governments being the sole voices on the future of AI development?

As a positive example of this, one of my favorite AI specialists, T'Neil Walea, is actually a pastor's wife AND an artificial intelligence and quantum computing specialist. She is the Director of Strategic Missions and Technologies at Microsoft, where she oversees product management for intelligence, security, and

---

54. Recent research among pastors and ministry leaders indicates that there is a close correlation with these fears and "imposter syndrome." Simply put, it's easier to resist change and oppose new technology than deal with the deeper issues that may lie behind our resistance. See Steven Grabiner (2024, December), "Silencing the Imposter Monkey," *Ministry: International Journal for Pastors*, accessed Mar. 15, 2025, https://www.ministrymagazine.org/archive/2024/12/Silencing-the-impostor-monkey

other mission-critical aspects of the US Government and serves as a technological advisor to government, Federal contractors, and think tanks. Prior to that she was IBM's Industry Chief Technology Officer for the Federal/Department of Defense space.[55] However, she is active in ministry leadership, as she and her husband Tyler are pastors at First Church of Pearland, TX, a multi-cultural and multi-generational church in the Houston area. Rather than fear the technology or avoid its dangers, she has become a well-recognized expert in artificial intelligence and quantum computing, and uses her expertise to shape policy and develop products that make our country safer and more secure. She also uses her knowledge and expertise to help church leaders better understand and utilize AI tools,[56] as well as to empower young women in STEM fields.

BIBLICAL VALUES & THEOLOGICAL IMPLICATIONS

The integration of generative AI into church and ministry contexts presents both remarkable opportunities and significant theological implications to consider. It is important for ministry leaders to approach this innovation with wisdom, discernment, and a firm grounding in biblical values. While AI has the potential to enhance and expand our capacity for ministry, we must also ensure that its use aligns with our calling to serve Christ and His Church with integrity. In this section, we will explore key theological themes, biblical cautions, and practical ministry applications to help pastors and church leaders navigate the role of AI in the Church. Here are a few specific areas we should consider.

Creativity and the Image of God

The Bible teaches that humans are created in the image of God (Genesis 1:27), and part of that image includes the capacity for creativity and ingenuity. Although generative AI is certainly capable of producing text, music, images, and even video, it does not possess true creativity. Rather, it is simply recombining patterns it observed from vast datasets to produce outputs that mimic human originality. This distinction is critical in ministry. AI can assist in brainstorming sermon series, generating imagery, and automating mundane tasks, but the responsibility of crafting messages, teaching God's Word, and leading with authenticity remains uniquely human. Pastors and ministry leaders need

---

55. T'Neil Walea. "About." LinkedIn, accessed Feb. 14, 2025, https://www.linkedin.com/in/tneilwalea/
56. I've participated with T'Neil in several such workshops, from Jason Moore's AI cohorts to a think tank for the Wesleyan Church's IT group, and I greatly appreciate her perspective as well as her grounding in theology and ethics.

to remember that AI, no matter how advanced, cannot replicate the Spirit-led creativity that God has placed within His people.

Community and Connection

The early Church "devoted themselves to the apostles' teaching and to fellowship, to the breaking of bread and to prayer."[57] The writer of Hebrews exhorts believers, "Let us consider how we may spur one another on toward love and good deeds, not giving up meeting together, as some are in the habit of doing, but encouraging one another."[58] Likewise, there are multiple "one another" admonitions throughout the New Testament that make clear the importance of authentic Biblical community and encourage deep, human relations. AI cannot replace those authentic human relationships. While AI tools can assist with communication, automate administrative tasks, and even help facilitate conversational engagement, the Church must ensure that its use of AI does not diminish the necessity of real human interaction. Pastoral care, discipleship, and evangelism are inherently relational and must remain so. AI can enhance community engagement and provide useful tools to improve it, but they should never become a substitute for face-to-face ministry.

Truth and Integrity

One of the inherent risks of AI is its potential to spread misinformation or unintentionally distort biblical truths. AI models are trained on vast datasets, and thus their predictive potential and ability to analyze is incredible, but they do not possess the ability to discern truth from falsehood. Nevertheless, as pastors and ministry leaders, we have the responsibility to uphold truth: "Therefore each of you must put off falsehood and speak truthfully to your neighbor, for we are all members of one body."[59] Ministry leaders must be vigilant in verifying AI-generated content. Also, just because you can create something with AI doesn't necessarily mean that you *should*. Whether using AI for research, sermon or teaching preparation, administrative efficiency, or outreach and communication, pastors must ensure that the information presented with it accurately reflects Biblical truth and exhibits Christian values. AI can be an asset, but it requires careful oversight to prevent misuse and misinformation.

Stewardship and Responsibility

The Bible also teaches that we are stewards of the resources and opportunities entrusted to us: "Each of you should use whatever gift you have received

---

57. Acts 2:42, NIV.
58. Hebrews 10:24-25, NIV.
59. Ephesians 4:25, NIV.

to serve others, as faithful stewards of God's grace in its various forms."[60] Jesus also teaches in the Parable of the Talents (Matthew 25:14-30) that wise stewardship is an expectation for His followers. This can actually be one of the many justifications for using AI in church and ministry contexts, since it empowers leaders to accomplish far more with limited budgets, staff, and volunteers. However, as AI becomes more integrated into church operations, stewardship also includes ethical considerations such as data privacy, intellectual property rights, and responsible AI deployment. It is important that we exercise caution when using AI to ensure that personal data from congregation members is protected, that our use of AI tools does not infringe on copyright laws, and that the use of AI enhances rather than exploits human dignity. It would be prudent for every church to develop policies to guide responsible AI usage in sermon preparation, outreach, and administrative functions.

The Risk of Idolatry

One of the greatest temptations with any new technology is allowing it to take center stage in our lives, subtly shifting our dependence from God onto our creations and increasing our reliance on human ingenuity. AI is an extraordinary tool, but it is just that (a tool); like all tools, it serves a purpose, and must remain in service to that higher purpose. The people of God are repeatedly cautioned throughout Scripture about the dangers of worshipping created things and/or trusting or relying on our own efforts and ingenuity more than God. AI should be a servant, not a master. The challenge for ministry leaders is to ensure that AI remains a tool that enhances rather than replaces personal engagement, spiritual discernment, and reliance on the Holy Spirit. While AI can help generate ideas for sermons, enhance administrative efficiency, and provide useful insights, it cannot substitute for the prayer, study, and personal reflection nor the intimate connection with God that is required of a faithful shepherd. AI absolutely can support the divine call to shepherd the flock with wisdom and care (just as many technologies can), but it should never supplant it.

Wisdom and Discernment

Lastly, Proverbs repeatedly emphasizes the value of wisdom: "Blessed is a person who finds wisdom, and one who obtains understanding. For her profit is better than the profit of silver, and her produce better than gold."[61] James also encourages us, "If any of you lacks wisdom, you should ask God, who

---

60. 1 Peter 4:10, NIV.
61. Proverbs 3:13-14, NASB.

gives generously to all without finding fault, and it will be given to you."[62] AI certainly presents us with ethical dilemmas – how we use it, when we use it, and what boundaries should be in place. Ministry leaders need to discern the role and extent of use that is appropriate for their context. For example, while AI-generated content can assist with sermon preparation, where does one draw the line? Spell-checking? Of course! Brainstorming ideas, crafting titles, helping with alliteration, refining first drafts? Sure, no worries. Suggesting illustrations, Bible verses/passages, alternate perspectives, etc.? Probably. But would it be ethical for a pastor to use AI to generate sermons without personal input? Same for generating images and videos with AI: Illustrating concepts that are hard to explain, bringing Bible passages to life, & more are great uses. But how do we ensure that any AI-generated images or videos we collaborate in developing are faithful to the Biblical text and accurately convey truth? And where might that cross the line?

Integration

As pastors and ministry leaders navigate the landscape of generative AI, our goal should be to integrate AI in ways that align with biblical values, enhance ministry effectiveness, and uphold the dignity of human creativity and connection. AI is neither inherently good nor evil; it is simply a tool that must be wielded with wisdom, discernment, and ethical responsibility. By keeping technology in its proper place, exercising wisdom and discernment, upholding truth, practicing ethical stewardship, and prioritizing authentic community, ministry leaders can navigate AI's opportunities and challenges in a way that honors God and advances His Kingdom. AI offers incredible potential for enhancing ministry, but it must always remain in service to the higher calling of Christ-centered leadership and gospel proclamation.

NEXT STEPS: LEADING WITH WISDOM

Throughout history, the Church has encountered disruptive technology innovations – from the printing press to the Internet – and has had to decide how best to engage with them. Some have resisted, others have avoided or adapted. However, still others have found ways to redeem and utilize technology creatively to advance the Kingdom. The emergence and proliferation of generative AI is no different. It is no longer a distant storm on the horizon; it is already here, and its winds are already shifting how we communicate, create,

---

62. James 1:5, NIV.

and minister. I will readily admit that some technology innovations are more faddish than others. However, this one is a game-changer, and it's a paradigm shift on par with the computer, Internet, and smartphones. So, the question is not whether AI will affect the church (it already does), but instead how pastors and ministry leaders can best engage with it wisely, faithfully, and strategically. AI is already shaping how your congregation thinks, learns, and engages. However, that is a good thing, because it means that if you're aware and using it and talking with your leadership or congregation about appropriate uses, you will have a voice in how people use it.

Wise leaders do not stand paralyzed in the face of technological change, nor do they rush forward recklessly. Instead, they approach new tools with discernment, seeking to understand their potential along with their theological implications while staying firmly rooted in the Church's mission. Unfortunately, the impact of AI on our world is so pronounced and so far-reaching that those who ardently resist or avoid the technology will simply find themselves increasingly irrelevant in a fast-changing world. Just as a skilled storm chaser tracks an approaching storm cell, these next steps will help pastors and ministry leaders navigate the turbulent shifts of AI with confidence, ensuring that they lead with hope and peace rather than anxiety and uncertainty.

1. Embrace a Learning Posture

By far, the best way to understand artificial intelligence and discern its role in ministry is through hands-on exploration. Pastors and ministry leaders should set aside intentional time to experiment with generative AI tools like ChatGPT or Claude, using them in practical ways that align with their day-to-day work. Experiment, and see what it can do. Whether you use it to craft catchy titles, analyze texts, find relevant Scripture passages, offer feedback on drafts, generate illustrative content, or review attendance and engagement trends, the important thing is to try it out and experiment (after all, I have yet to meet or hear from a critic of AI who has actually used it). Firsthand experience will help you gain a clearer understanding of AI's potential and its limitations. Most concerns surrounding AI arise from unfamiliarity, and actively engaging with these tools can provide the confidence needed to make informed decisions about their use in ministry.

For those interested in diving deeper, I highly recommend Jason Moore's *AI & the Church: A Clear Guide for the Curious and Courageous* as a next step in your AI journey. Also, I developed a white paper called "Pro Tips for Ideating with Generative AI" which you may find insightful.[63] You may also find OpenAI's ChatGPT Prompt Engineering Guide is also a useful resource, offering guidance on crafting meaningful and productive AI interactions.[64] And of course there are lots of great tutorials on YouTube and mini-courses on sites like Udemy: www.udemy.com/courses (tip: search for "AI for beginners" or "AI video for beginners" to narrow the options).

2. Engage with Ministry Leaders About the Role of AI

While personal experimentation with AI is essential, meaningful discussions with other ministry leaders can provide additional wisdom and perspective. Pastors should actively seek out conversations with lay leaders, volunteers, and fellow ministers to explore AI's appropriate role within the church. These discussions can be informal, such as a staff meeting or leadership retreat, or more structured, such as small focus groups dedicated to theological and ethical reflections on the implications of AI for ministry.

In addition to in-person discussions in your own ministry context, I would highly recommend joining an online community where other ministry leaders like you are already wrestling with these questions and experimenting with possibilities and applications. The **AI for Church Leaders & Pastors** Facebook group[65] provides an active space for these discussions; its mission is "to empower pastors and church leaders with knowledge and tools to integrate AI into their ministries effectively," and it currently has over 6,500 members (with hundreds more added every month). Another useful group is the **AI for Churches** group, which is 2,500 strong and designed to "explore the transformative potential of AI in enhancing worship experiences, fostering community connections, and advancing the reach of our collective ministries."[66] All of the ministry-minded AI leaders I know are active participants in one or both of these groups, and we regularly share ideas and new AI tools, ask questions, explore possibilities, discuss use cases, and talk about theological implications as well as practical aspects. If you're already convinced and want to maximize your capabilities with generative AI as a power tool, Rob Laughter's **AI Collaborative** would be a worthwhile investment.[67]

---

63. David Swisher (2023), "Pro Tips for Ideating With Generative AI," https://tinyurl.com/ProTipsGenAI

64. Open AI Platform (n.d.), "Prompt Engineering," accessed Feb. 16, 2025: https://platform.openai.com/docs/guides/prompt-engineering

65. Kenny Jahng (2023, Feb. 17), "AI for Church Leaders & Pastors: ChatGPT, Claude, Gemini Prompts & more" Facebook group, https://www.facebook.com/groups/1230366870910779

66. David Thorne (2024, Nov. 8), "AI for Churches" Facebook group, https://www.facebook.com/groups/aifor-churches

67. Rob is a tech-savvy ministry leader and AI power user who offers workshops, webinars, and classes where he gives a behind-the-scenes look at how he uses generative A.I. in real-world ministry applications: https://roblaughter.com/collaborative/

3. Explore AI's Usefulness for Study & Teaching, Communication, and Outreach

Throughout this chapter, I have identified a dozen or more ways that generative AI can be utilized in ministry contexts to ideate, collaborate, analyze, organize, summarize, and refine whatever the ministry needs and tasks you have before you. If it's something you might delegate to an intern or volunteer (if you had one), or discuss with a staff pastor or colleague, or just plain tiresome or tedious to do manually, it's worth considering whether generative AI can assist you with it. AI can serve as a valuable collaborative partner, freeing your time up from the cumbersome tasks so that you can focus your time on meaningful relationships and ministry connections or on preparation for teaching and preaching. Used appropriately, it can even help you with that (not as a replacement for your own study, research, prayer, and spiritual discernment, but to augment it). But you'll never know what's possible in these areas until you first commit to try and explore, and then talk with other pastors and ministry leaders about how they're using AI effectively in their ministries.

Beyond administrative support and assistance with analysis and content development, AI can also help craft or refine content for newsletters, develop social media posts related to the sermon or teaching series, and even suggest resources, verses, or questions for discipleship and teaching follow-up materials. Space limitations prevent me from diving as deeply into this as I would like, but Jason Moore's *AI & the Church* book has a huge section where he walks you through the tools and gives great advice on how to utilize them well.[68] Additionally, churches with multilingual congregations or communities may find AI-powered video translation tools like **HeyGen** particularly useful in making sermons and ministry resources more accessible.[69] AI tools like **Otter.ai** and **SermonShots** can provide automated sermon transcriptions, while **ElevenLabs** offers AI-powered voice cloning for multilingual outreach, These tools can help you extend your message beyond the walls of your church and into the wider community.

As you explore the usefulness of AI for study and teaching, communication, and outreach, it would be prudent to set limits on what you (and others) in your ministry should and should not do with AI. My pastor, Scott Rhyno, proposed the following list, and I think it is an ideal set of recommendations to serve as a foundational starting point:[70]

---

68. Jason Moore (2024), Part III: Embracing the AI Toolbox, in *AI & the Church: A Clear Guide for the Curious and Courageous* (Plano, TX: Invite Press), 113-215

69. HeyGen is one of my favorite AI tools. See https://tinyurl.com/HeyGenPromote for more info

70. Scott Rhyno, e-mail message to author, March 12, 2025.

- AI should enhance or support, not replace, Spirit-led creativity.
- AI should always be used with full transparency in church communications.
- AI should never compromise biblical truth nor replace deep study and prayer.
- AI-generated content should always be reviewed and refined (and fact-checked) before being used in ministry.
- All churches should consider an AI usage policy.

4. Develop a Thoughtful AI Usage Policy

Once you have explored AI's capabilities and engaged in dialogue with fellow ministry leaders (at both your church and throughout the wider Body of Christ), another important step would be to develop a clear and thoughtful policy for AI use in your church. Establishing guidelines will help ensure that AI remains a useful tool rather than a disruptive force. Key considerations should include defining where AI can provide practical benefits, such as administrative support, communication, and content creation, while also clarifying where its use should be limited (or possibly prohibited) in order to preserve authenticity and human engagement.

This policy should be shaped by both theological reflection and practical discussions with ministry teams. Rather than rush to implement AI without clear boundaries, or caution against its use, you should take the time to listen to other ministry leaders and observe how AI is currently being used in ministry settings, learn from the experiences of others, and seek input from your denomination as well as local church leadership. To assist in developing such resources, I have developed an "Ethical Standards Framework" which is a set of questions to ask and issues to consider when working with generative AI to ensure that your use and handling is ethical.[71] If you prefer to start with an example or template of AI policies for churches, several are available to review and adapt in the Files of the AI for Church Leaders & Pastors Facebook group.[72] Also, some denominations have begun to offer ethical guidelines on AI use, and various faith-based organizations have begun publishing insights on the intersection of AI and ministry. Taking the time to establish thoughtful policies will help ensure that AI en-

Swisher's Ethical Standards Framework

---

71. David Swisher (2024), "Ethical Standards Framework," AI Fusion Conference, https://tinyurl.com/EthicalStandardsFramework
72. Kenny Jahng (2023, Feb. 17), "AI for Church Leaders & Pastors."

hances, rather than undermines, the integrity of church leadership...and can help you avoid embarrassing compromises.

PREPARING FOR FUTURE MINISTRY

As AI continues to shape the landscape of ministry, wise leaders will understandably strike a balance, leveraging its benefits while safeguarding the irreplaceable human elements of pastoral care, discipleship, and spiritual leadership. This requires both wisdom and spiritual discernment as you integrate AI into your ministry work. AI can enhance efficiency, but it must never replace the relational and Spirit-led aspects of ministry that define the Church's calling. This requires an ongoing commitment to ethical stewardship. AI must remain a servant, not a master, and its use must be shaped by theological reflection, community dialogue, and a clear sense of mission. Pastors should remain transparent in how they use AI, actively seek feedback from their congregations, and adjust their approach as needed.

The goal is not merely to adapt to technological change but to engage with it in ways that are faithful, ethical, and beneficial to the Church's mission. Just as early warning systems allow communities to prepare for approaching storms, a thoughtful approach to AI will allow you to lead proactively rather than reactively. The Church does not need to fear this technological shift, but it does need to prepare for a future where AI is commonplace and integrated with wisdom, courage, and a commitment to Christ-centered leadership.

Imagine with me a future less than ten years from now where churches use AI-driven analytics to anticipate congregational and community needs (and are therefore more responsive and perceptive to issues and concerns), craft more effective discipleship pathways (and therefore see greater numbers of people engage and deeper commitments grow), and translate sermons in real-time for multilingual communities...all while pastors focus more on face-to-face ministry. The mind-blowing thing, however, is that *this isn't science fiction*; it is already happening. I hope you and your church will be able to realize this potential, too. AI offers remarkable possibilities, but its greatest potential will be realized when it is guided by human hands working in tandem with a divine calling and sense of purpose.

Chapter 3

AUTHORITY & DECENTRALIZATION

Bitcoin, Blockchain, Cryptocurrency, & DAOs

Cryptocurrency has been fascinating to watch, with meteoric highs and incredible drops, but along with the volatility and consolidation, new models of authentication and trust have emerged such as blockchain and Distributed Autonomous Organizations (DAOs). Unlike traditional currency models whose authority exists by fiat, these newer models have developed unique trust and authentication measures such as the ledger-based and user-validated blockchain, "baking," validation, and even a complete means of managing a distributed organization autonomously without a central governance or hierarchical model of authority.

Although these are on the innovation edge at present, these technologies and divergent models are poised to move into mainstream thinking within the next few years, and they offer some amazing perspectives and opportunities for church structure and management that will challenge the status quo, question traditional hierarchical governance models, and provide alternative methods of trust and validation from within. In its purest form, a DAO appears to be surprisingly similar in concept to the New Testament model of governance, and stands in stark contrast to the consumerist and hierarchical models that are so prevalent in the West today; many churches are already exploring what it might look like to transition to such a model.

In late October of 2008, a computer programmer using the pseudonym Satoshi Nakamoto posted an email to The Cryptography Mailing List announcing that he had developed a new secure peer-to-peer electronic cash system that "would allow online payments to be sent directly from one party to another without the burdens of going through a financial institution."[1] In the email, he copied an abstract of a paper that he had written and posted online.[2] The paper describes how online payments would be sent using digital signatures, utilizing a peer-to-peer network that would record timestamps of

---

1.   Saifedean Ammous (2018), *The Bitcoin Standard: The Decentralized Alternative to Central Banking* (Hoboken, NJ: Wiley), xiv.

2.   Satoshi Nakamoto (2008, Oct. 31), "Bitcoin P2P e-cash Paper," email message to The Cryptography Mailing List, accessed August 30, 2024, https://satoshi.nakamotoinstitute.org/emails/cryptography/1/

all transactions "by hashing them into an ongoing chain of hash-based proof-of-work" (which we now know as a blockchain, which will be described later in this schapter).[3] People would willingly connect to the network, using their computer's processing power to "mine" bitcoins (which amounts to running transactions until a random award was granted), so this meant that those who contributed the most Central Processing Unit (CPU) power to the network would have the greatest likelihood of earning rewards in the form of bitcoin.

This system would require minimal structure, yet would ensure that all transactions could be verifiable from any node on the network because the largest pool of CPU power (which is what would be used to generate the electronic cash rewards) would also create the longest chain on the network.[4] The genius of Nakamoto's design was a set of carrot & stick incentives that "encouraged those who were validating transactions to do so honestly" and by requiring every computer that used the system to conduct a "proof of work" exercise...solving a complex mathematical puzzle that required heavy computational power. Because it used up a ton of processing power, it was expensive to do, which meant that bitcoin "miners" could only gain the rewards if they were heavily invested in the effort.[5]

The network timestamps transactions by recording ("hashing") them into an ongoing chain of hash-based proof-of-work, forming a record (via a public ledger) that cannot be changed without redoing the proof-of-work.[6] This would prove that those who were generating (mining) the cash rewards, who had the most vested interest in its success, would have the longest chain and therefore the most accurate records[7] and serve as a strong deterrent against fraud and abuse (it's too expensive and unrewarding to hack the system). In this way, the design also safeguarded against attackers by demoting the credibility of their efforts. In essence, the system would validate itself through its increasing use as the community using it grew.

Although the principles behind it were radical, few took notice...at first. For many months, there were only a few dozen users joining the network who engaged in mining and would send each other digital coins as if they were collectibles.[8] But about a year later, an Internet exchange sold 5,050 bitcoins at a price of only $1 per 1,000 coins...a whole $5.02 (which was essentially the

3. Satoshi Nakamoto (2008, Oct. 31), "Bitcoin: A Peer-to-Peer Electronic Cash System," Satoshi Nakamoto Institute > Library, accessed August 30, 2024, https://nakamotoinstitute.org/library/bitcoin

4. Ibid.

5. Michael Casey & Paul Vigna (2018), *The Truth Machine: The Blockchain and the Future of Everything* (New York, NY: Picador), 66.

6. Ibid.

7. Antony Lewis (2021), *The Basics of Bitcoins and Blockchains: An Introduction to Cryptocurrencies and the Technology that Powers Them* (Coral Gables, FL: Mango Publishing), 150-153.

8. Saifedean Ammous (2018), *The Bitcoin Standard:* xv.

cost of energy used to produce it).[9] An even more notable moment was when a programmer from Florida used Bitcoin to purchase two pizzas from Papa John's. On May 22, 2010, Laszlo Hanyecz paid 10,000 Bitcoins for the pizzas, which was worth about $41 at the time (today that would be worth around $1.2 billion).[10] This was the first real-world use of Bitcoin for a commercial purchase, and these transactions proved to be turning point in the history of digital assets because "Bitcoin was no longer just a digital game being played within a fringe community of programmers; it had now become a market good with a price."[11]

Over time, the value of Bitcoin has dramatically increased, growing from ten cents to thirty cents in the first couple of years, then reaching $1,000 in 2017. When the COVID-19 global pandemic shuttered so many businesses and made in-person use of cash risky, the cryptocurrency's value skyrocketed, starting the year at $7,161 and increasing in value to $28,993 per Bitcoin by the end of the year.[12] In early 2024, courts forced the SEC to reconsider how it treated Bitcoin-related investment processes, and its value shot up again to a then all-time high of $73,795.[13] With consumer confidence high following Donald Trump's re-election in Nov. 2024, Bitcoin's value surpassed $100,000 multiple times in Dec. 2024 and Jan. 2025, and after dropping for a few months, has stayed above that threshold throughout the summer of 2025 .[14] Today, there are thousands of other cryptocurrencies such as Ethereum and Tether with over $100 billion in daily volume on hundreds of exchanges.[15]

WHY THIS MATTERS

So why have I included a chapter on this in a book for ministry leaders on navigating disruptive technology innovations? Because the technologies that enable cryptocurrencies are poised to dramatically re-shape not just banking and finance, but even how businesses, economies, and even churches are organized!

---

9. Ibid., xv.

10. "Bitcoin History: A Journey Through Memorable Transactions" (2024, June 12), Bitcoin Depot, accessed Mar. 16, 2025, https://bitcoindepot.com/bitcoin-atm-info/a-history-of-memorable-bitcoin-transactions. At its highest valuation to date (July 14, 2025), 10,000 Bitcoins were worth approximately $1.234 billion USD.

11. Saifedean Ammous (2018), *The Bitcoin Standard*: xv.

12. John Edwards (2024, May 26), "Bitcoin's Price History," Investopedia, Cryptocurrency > Bitcoin, accessed August 30, 2024, https://www.investopedia.com/articles/forex/121815/bitcoins-price-history.asp

13. As of the time of this writing (March 2025). Edwards (2024, May 26), "Bitcoin's Price History," *Investopedia.*

14. CoinMarketCap, "Bitcoin," Cryptocurrencies, accessed Mar. 16, 2025, https://coinmarketcap.com/currencies/bitcoin

15. As of the time of this writing (March 2025), there are 12,780 cryptocurrencies, and about two dozen are the most popular. Bitcoin represents about 45% of the current cryptocurrency market. CoinMarketCap, "Today's Cryptocurrency Prices by Market Cap," Cryptocurrencies, accessed Mar. 16, 2025, https://coinmarketcap.com

But before we go there, I need to clear up some misconceptions. Many conservative Christians have mistakenly equated cryptocurrency with digital cash, and then presumed that what we saw during the COVID-19 global pandemic with many businesses avoiding the acceptance of cash (and a temporary coin shortage) meant that we were rapidly moving to a cashless society. Those circumstances have very little relevance to cryptocurrency and digital assets. As Christian financial consultant Dave Ramsey adeptly explains, "The vast majority of transactions (90-something % of them, probably north of 95%) in the U.S. are already digital. But is the U.S. going to do away with the greenback? Not in my lifetime or yours."[16]

Unfortunately, we tend to fear what we do not understand, and since there aren't many Christian financial planners (and far fewer pastors and ministry leaders who were trained in business finance and economics), we tend to embrace the worst-case scenarios that are peddled by those who are trying to sell us something.

HISTORICAL FOUNDATIONS

Although the technologies behind cryptocurrencies, blockchains, and Distributed Autonomous Organizations (DAOs) are new, the principles and concepts undergirding them are not. In fact, many of these principles have been around for centuries.

- During the period of the Crusades (in the 12th and 13th centuries), Christian pilgrimages to the Holy Land were frequently undertaken, but travelers to the Holy Land were at great risk of being attacked and robbed while en route. To address these challenges, a Medieval order of militaristic monks who became known as the Knights Templar arose during this period to serve as protectors of travelers.[17] [18] One of their inventions was an early form of a letter of credit, whereby pilgrims could deposit funds in one Templar commandery (a sort of regional headquarters) and withdraw them at another. This system was one of the earliest forms of what we

16. Dave Ramsey (2023, Sept. 22), "Get Ready for a Digital Currency? The Ramsey Show Highlights, YouTube video, 1:44, accessed August 30, 2024, https://youtu.be/mUywzuPY7xY. For more explanation on this perspective, see Ramsey Solutions (2024, April 5), "Are We Really Headed for a Cashless Society?" Budgeting > Spending, accessed August 30, 2024, https://www.ramseysolutions.com/budgeting/cashless-society

17. Al Bustani, Hareth (n.d.), "Templar Banking: How to Go From Donated Rags to Vast Riches," Medievalists. net, accessed Sept. 1, 2024, from: https://www.medievalists.net/2021/08/templar-banking

18. For more on the historical context and the birth of the Knights Templar, see Dan Jones (2017), *The Templars: The Rise and Spectacular Fall of God's Holy Warriors* (New York, NY: Viking), pp. 28-35 and Kelly Pete (2017, Oct. 25), "Hughes de Payens & the Birth of the Knights Templar" HistoryTime UK, YouTube video, accessed Sept. 1, 2024, https://youtu.be/0DAUN6V4brA

would consider modern banking: The letters of credit served as a form of traveler's checks, their deposit and withdrawal system paralleled many of the functions of modern banks, and their safeguarding of assets (especially valuable documents and treasures) laid the groundwork for vaults and safety deposit boxes which are features of modern banking today. [19]

- Hawala is an ancient and informal method of transferring money that originated in India and is primarily used in Islamic cultures such as in the Middle East, Africa, and on the Indian subcontinent. It is derived from an Arabic term for transfer or trust.[20] Rather than go through traditional banking systems, hawala makes use of a network of dealers called *hawaladars* who keep coded journals/ledgers of all deposits, along with any passwords or stipulations regarding who can retrieve the funds and under what conditions.

It is fascinating to me to see all the parallels between these legacy methods and modern digital assets: Both the conceptual underpinnings of the system the Knights Templar established and the encoded journal/ledger system of hawaladars are very comparable to the approach utilized with blockchain, and these are often referred to as permissionless or "trust-based" approaches because they don't require the approval of third parties (government or financial/regulatory agencies) but instead rely on the system itself to validate the accuracy of transactions.

For those whose only experience with money has been Western systems of cash in various forms (including checks, deposits, loans, banks, & more), the idea of digital assets can be confusing and often unsettling because it seems like a radical departure from the familiar. However, there is a reason we call it "currency": That term comes from the Latin "currens" which means "running" or "circulating" (and it's the same word from which we get "current," as in a river or stream or events or happenings).[21] And throughout time, various civilizations and cultures have used all kinds of instruments as currency.

Many millenia ago, livestock (particularly cattle) and grain were used as commodities for monetary exchange, and in 1200 BCE, cowry shells (from sea snails) were used as currency in China and parts of Africa.[22] In fact, the zoological name for a particular species of shells used in Africa is *Monetaria*

---

19. OpenAI (2024, Sept. 1), ChatGPT 4o [Large language model], "Hawala System & Templar Banking," accessed Sept. 1, 2024, https://chatgpt.com/share/b5d08600-6745-40a6-bda8-37557caa2f76

20. CFI Team (n.d.), "Hawala," Corporate Finance Institute, accessed August 26, 2024, https://corporatefinance-institute.com/resources/wealth-management/hawala

21. "Currens," Wiktionary, accessed Sept. 1, 2024, https://en.wiktionary.org/wiki/currens

22. Antony Lewis (2021), *The Basics of Bitcoins and Blockchains*, 44-48.

Moneta (literally, "money money").[23] It is a medium of exchange that is still in use in Polynesian cultures today where seashells often serve as money: Why do you think we talk about "shelling out" funds? In Roman times, when refrigeration was unavailable, salt was particularly valuable because it functioned as a vital preservative, and Roman soldiers were paid with it (this is literally where we get our modern word "salary," from the Latin *salarium*, which refers to "salt money").[24] In today's prison systems, often cigarettes function as currency because they are difficult to come by, so they have value and therefore function as a medium of exchange.

The origins of coinage for many cultures dates back to the days when valuable metals (gold, silver, copper, etc.) were actually used as the medium of exchange. The Roman emperor Constantine issued gold coins called *solidus* in the early 300s CE, but also issued debased silver and copper coins for lower-value transactions.[25] In fact, the design of modern coins (with the round shape and ridges) is often a direct result of measures taken to reduce the likelihood of devaluing the currency through clipping or trimming them to harvest the precious metals;[26] it's a reflection of the days when coins were made of precious metals.

PRECURSORS TO DIGITAL ASSETS

In earlier days, coins were often cut to yield smaller denominations: For example, If you sell me something that costs one and a fourth of the value of a silver coin, I'm not going to round up and give you two (nor would you want me to reduce your profit by rounding down), so often they would clip off a fourth of the coin and you would give that to me and keep the remaining three-fourths. Of course, this was before smaller denominations of coins (such as nickels and pennies) were minted to facilitate incremental transactions.

Much has often been said (especially in conservative Christian circles) about the "gold standard," with the idea being that behind every dollar spent, there is gold backing that transaction (often in "Fort Knox"). The logic behind this is: Have you ever carried gold bars into a store to conduct business? Of course not! Very few people have ever held gold bars, and they're far too valuable for smaller transactions, so instead of carrying a briefcase full of gold bars, precious metal

---

23. Ibid., 47.
24. Wim Hordijk (2014, Nov. 8), "From Salt To Salary: Linguists Take A Page From Science," NPR > Cosmos & Culture, accessed Sept. 1, 2024, https://www.npr.org/sections/13.7/2014/11/08/362478685/from-salt-to-salary-linguists-take-a-page-from-science
25. Antony Lewis (2021), *The Basics of Bitcoins and Blockchains*, 54.
26. American Bullion, Inc. (2023, April 28), "Why Do Modern Coins Have Ridges?," *American Bullion*, retrieved from https://www.americanbullion.com/why-do-modern-coins-have-ridges/

coins, or other "real money," you will instead pay for the transaction with paper money (which isn't actually money at all, but merely a "promise to pay"). If you take a close look at any US paper money, you will see a large heading that reads "Federal Reserve Note" along with fine print that reads, "This note is legal tender for all debts public and private." In other words, it is not *actually* money; it merely <u>represents</u> money. It's called a "bearer instrument," which means whomever is bearing that instrument can present it in exchange for its actual value in precious metals.

But the reality is that this "gold standard" is more myth than reality. After all, its definition and value has changed at least a dozen times throughout U.S. history.[27] There are at least three different types of gold standard, and what people often think of is actually a *gold bullion standard* where a note represents a defined amount of gold and can be redeemed for it.[28] What happens in this case is that an issuer of currency (typically a central bank), "pegs their currency to a fixed weight in pure or fine gold and tells the world that they will exchange one unit of currency for a certain amount of gold stored in their vaults."[29] But that's actually a currency peg, and it only works if you actually have the gold in your vaults and actually let people redeem it.[30]

That's typically what people presume to be the case, but it hasn't been how the U.S. has operated for decades. As the Congressional report "Brief History of the Gold Standard in the United States" makes clear, the classic gold standard ended in 1933, and "what followed was only a partial—and not full— gold standard."[31] Furthermore, as the links to gold became impossible to maintain, the U.S. stopped redeeming dollars with gold for international transactions in the early 1970s.[32] What we have now is *fiat money*, which is value determined by decree (it has value because a government entity has declared it to have value.)[33]

THE VALUE OF MONEY

One of the most common concerns (or complaints) I hear about cryptocurrency is that it has no *intrinsic value*. The perception is that its value is

---

27. Lewis (2021) has an excellent synopsis of the evolving gold standard in *The Basics of Bitcoins and Blockchains*, 63-68. A fuller analysis can be found at Craig K. Elwell (2011, June 23), "Brief History of the Gold Standard in the United States," Congressional Research Service, retrieved from https://crsreports.congress.gov/product/pdf/R/R41887/2

28. Antony Lewis (2021), *The Basics of Bitcoins and Blockchains*, 54.

29. Ibid., 63.

30. Ibid., 64.

31. Elwell, Craig K. (2011, June 23), "Brief History of the Gold Standard in the United States," 13-14.

32. Ibid.

33. Fiat is Latin for "decree, order, or authorization." Saifedean Ammous (2018), *The Bitcoin Standard*, 41.

volatile, so how can you trust it? But that's why it's important to understand what fiat money is and how that shapes our use of currency: *U.S. dollars have no intrinsic value, either.* They are just promissory notes on paper, which is worthless. Our currency only has value because the U.S. government says it has value.

This isn't an alarmist or skeptic's perspective, either; even the European Central Bank says so in a very helpful explanation:

> Fiat money is declared legal tender and issued by a central bank. It can't be directly converted into, for example, gold. The paper used for banknotes isn't worth much, yet is accepted because it is widely usable and central banks work to keep the value of money stable.[34]

After explaining how money has evolved over time and then stating the above about fiat money, they go on to explain how money can take many forms, not only banknotes and coins, but "can also exist in a bank account as a computer entry or be stored in a savings account," and also functions in digital form to complement cash.[35] And the perceived volatility we see with cryptocurrencies is how much they're *trading* at, which is not necessarily a direct correlation to what that particular token is actually *worth.*

My boys and I experienced this issue firsthand while sightseeing in Peru a couple of years ago. In most Latin American countries, American dollars are well regarded as having enduring value (often while the local currency is highly volatile and the exchange rate changes daily). But because of this, there is also a problem with counterfeiting, and local shop owners aren't as familiar with the features and security measures of a U.S. dollar bill, so they are very leery of any U.S. currency that is worn, torn, nicked, or damaged in any way, and they usually won't accept it. Now, if you're from the U.S., you know that it doesn't matter how beat up that dollar is or even if pieces are missing or it's torn; as long as more than 50% of it is there, it's worth the full face value of the dollar amount printed on it...and you also know that we tend to be suspicious of fresh, crisp bills (that can sometimes be a sign of counterfeit bills). But not so when we were shopping in Peru! It didn't matter how much value was printed on it, or how much exchange (or goods or services) I would get for it in the U.S., or how much I insisted it was worth; to local Peruvian shop owners wary of counterfeiting, it was absolutely *worthless*; they wouldn't be able to deliver it to their supplier in

---

34. European Central Bank (2024, June 19). "What is Money?," Explainers, retrieved from https://www.ecb.europa.eu/ecb-and-you/explainers/tell-me-more/html/what_is_money.en.html

35. Ibid.

exchange for goods, and their bank wouldn't take it, either. If I didn't hand over fresh, crisp brand-new bills (straight from the ATM), I wasn't going to be able to purchase anything with it.

And that's really the core of the issue: Currency has value because the people involved in the transaction agree upon that value; there's some kind of a central standard somewhere that we all agree is immutable. It makes no difference whether it's shells, stones, round metal coins, cigarettes, plastic buttons, paper bills, digital assets, Non-Fungible Tokens (NFTs), or cryptocurrencies (digital tokens), it's worth whatever the community says its worth. If you walk into a collector's shop with an old baseball card or bring a Pokémon card or *Magic: The Gathering* card to GenCon (the largest tabletop gaming convention in North America), it has value because the community involved agrees it has value. But if you walk into a grocery store and try to pay for groceries with such a card there, they're going to look at you funny and wonder what kind of a fast one you're trying to pull. It's worthless in that context, just as our well-worn and slightly-damaged U.S. bills were worthless to Peruvian shop owners.

So it's not about intrinsic value; after all, no physical form of currency (except actual precious metals, arguably) has any intrinsic value. It's about *utility*. If you can use it for what you want to spend it on, then it has utility. So in terms of fiat money, that's the significance of government declaration that a particular kind of currency is *legal tender*. As Anthony Lewis (FinTech influencer and cryptocurrency author) explains: "When a currency is declared legal tender, it means that by statute (law), people must accept it as a settlement mechanism to meet a financial obligation."[36] However, that just means that it *can* be used as payment, not that a private business must accept that form of payment.[37]

CRYPTOCURRENCIES & DIGITAL ASSETS

In traditional financial exchanges, a trusted third party is usually required (typically the bank, sometimes a broker) who can verify that you have sufficient funds in your account and make the monetary transfer[38] (and they charge fees or interest for these services). Cryptocurrencies "remove that middleman from the exchange, instead validating transactions with every computer on the

---

36. Antony Lewis (2021), *The Basics of Bitcoins and Blockchains*, 71.

37. Board of Governors of the Federal Reserve System (2020, July 21), "Is it legal for a business in the United States to refuse cash as a form of payment?" FAQs, accessed Mar. 16, 2025, https://www.federalreserve.gov/faqs/currency_12772.htm.

38. Peter H. Diamandis & Steven Kotler (2020), *The Future is Faster Than You Think: How Converging Technologies are Transforming Business, Industries, and Our Lives* (New York, NY: Simon & Schuster), 57

network,"[39] and they are entirely digital (the assets are tracked by computer using software; there isn't any physical coinage, paper, or other form of currency. Once that transaction is determined to be valid, it is recorded along with other transactions on a "block" (of code or data), and bundled with the record of all prior blocks (the "chain").[40] This public ledger makes it distributed and mutable, because everyone on the network has a copy of it, and when anyone enters new information in the ledger, all ledgers automatically get updated.[41]

Until recent years, cryptocurrencies and digital assets have been viewed with suspicion. Most people have heard of Bitcoin, but people have mixed perceptions of it. But did you know that you can make Xbox purchases on Microsoft with it, pay your AT&T bill with it, purchase movie tickets at any AMC theater in the U.S. with it, order Quiznos subs with it at specific branches, and use it to purchase ExpressVPN services?[42] Many technology vendors (such as NewEgg, Pirate Bay, Namecheap, & more) also accept payment through Bitcoin; after all, the tech community tends to value and support technology-based digital innovations.[43]

Cryptocurrency and digital assets not only represent a paradigm shift in banking and finances, but they are undoubtedly going to be a gamechanger in future years because they are already demonstrating explosive growth and poised for exponential growth. This will disrupt multiple industries, and most certainly impact the church. Clearly, Bitcoin's popularity and acceptance is growing: In 2020, Hartford Steam Boiler (HSB), a specialty insurer and provider of inspection, risk management, and Internet of Things (IoT) technology services, conducted a nationwide survey and found that 36% (more than a third) of small to medium-sized businesses accept cryptocurrency, and 59% of those companies purchased digital currency for their own use as well.[44] Current estimates are that we'll be looking at closer to 80% acceptance within the next few years.

When Diamandis & Kotler were writing their book on converging technologies (2018), blockchain and cryptocurrency technology was "exploding": Firms like J.P. Morgan, Goldman Sachs, and Bank of America were rolling out crypto-strategies at scale, and Initial Coin Offerings (ICOs) had a market

---

39. Ibid.
40. Ibid.
41. Ibid.
42. Alexander Reed (2024, Aug. 7), "Who Accepts Bitcoin as Payment?," 99Bitcoins, retrieved from https://99bitcoins.com/bitcoin/who-accepts/
43. Ibid.
44. Dennis Milewski (2020, Jan. 15), "HSB Survey Finds One-Third of Small Businesses Accept Cryptocurrency," *Business Wire*, retrieved from https://www.businesswire.com/news/home/20200115005482/en/HSB-Survey-Finds-One-Third-Small-Businesses-Accept

value of $10 billion.[45] Obviously the more lucrative the market is, the more major business and investors will venture into the space. In 2019, Gartner, Inc. forecast that the value of blockchain would grow to more than $176 billion by 2025, then surge to exceed $3.1 trillion by 2030.[46] However, by 2022 (only 3 years later), the same firm reported the cryptocurrency market was then worth around $2 trillion, which is more than the amount of U.S. dollars in circulation,[47] and represents a 1036.% increase. With exponential gains like this, I can only imagine how much higher the valuation and how much faster the acceptance rate will be within just a few years of this book's release (especially after courts forced the SEC to re-evaluate their handling of Bitcoin, which cleared the way for much wider adoption).

Ethereum is another very popular cryptocurrency. Introduced in 2015 by Vitalik Buterin, it has since become one of the most significant and widely-used cryptocurrencies, second only to Bitcoin in terms of market capitalization. Although Bitcoin is primarily used as a digital currency, Ethereum is a decentralized platform that enables developers to build and deploy decentralized applications (dApps) using smart contracts. These smart contracts automatically execute transactions when predefined conditions are met, providing the foundation for a wide range of decentralized financial services (DeFi), games, and other blockchain-based applications. Businesses that currently accept Ethereum for payments include Overstock, Gucci, Emirates, Amazon (through Bitpay), NewEgg, Chipotle, and Shopify.[48] [49]

Other popular cryptocurrencies include:

- Tezos
- Litecoin
- Tether
- Basic Attention Token
- Compound
- Stellar Lumens
- EOS
- Dai
- Chainlink

---

45. Diamandis & Kotler (2020), *The Future is Faster Than You Think*, 58-59.

46. Katie Costello (2019, June 3), "Gartner Predicts 90% of Current Enterprise Blockchain Platform Implementations Will Require Replacement by 2021," Gartner, Inc., Newsroom > Press Releases, accessed Sept. 4, 2024: https://www.gartner.com/en/newsroom/press-releases/2019-07-03-gartner-predicts-90--of-current-enterprise-blockchain

47. Jordan Turner (2022, March 22), "A CFO's Quick Guide to Cryptocurrency," Gartner, Inc., Insights > Finance, accessed Sept. 4, 2024: https://www.gartner.com/en/articles/a-cfo-s-quick-guide-to-cryptocurrency

48. Georgia Straight Team (2024, June 15), "Detailed Guide: Companies That Accept Ethereum in 2024," https://www.straight.com/guides/finance/crypto/companies-that-accept-ethereum/

49. Mr. Creatonics (2022, Dec. 16), "A List Of Merchants Accepting Ethereum In 2024," CoinSutra, retrieved from https://coinsutra.com/who-accepts-ethereum/

- XRP
- Dogecoin
- Maker
- the Graph
- and more.

Like I said earlier, there are *thousands*; these are just the ones that appear fairly high up on the "top assets" list on the CoinBase platform. A closely-related concept that has been rising in popularity are NFTs (non-fungible tokens), which are physical (and sometimes digital) assets like a piece of art, digital content, or video that have been tokenized via a blockchain.[50] They are non-fungible, meaning that they are one-of-a-kind and unique, and therefore cannot easily be swapped out for another without a change in value, because each one's value has distinct properties.[51] They are "minted" in a process where the asset's information is encrypted and recorded on a blockchain, and they can be traded and exchanged for money, cryptocurrencies, or other NFTs.[52]

If the statistics and trends are even remotely accurate and your church is comprised of typical people, at least 10-15% of your congregation is already using cryptocurrency, and that number is likely to double within the next 3-5 years. They just haven't told you about it because it's not a typical "church" conversation...yet. Have you had any parishioners ask if they can contribute funds via cryptocurrency? Tithe using Bitcoin or Ethereum? Or minted an NFT to fund a mission or building project? Perhaps not, but get ready! These will be very natural and likely questions in most churches within the next few years, and pastors and ministry leaders need to understand what it all means and how rapidly this is all changing to be prepared for the realities that are already underway.

So what would this look like if we were using cryptocurrencies and digital assets in a ministry context? Here's a plausible scenario:

PASTOR JUAN CARLOS AND THE INTERNATIONAL CRYPTO LAUNCH

Pastor **Juan Carlos**, who pastors a vibrant multilingual church called Comunidad de Fe, has been, looking for ways to connect with their dispersed global community. Many members of Comunidad de Fe have family members back home or who have emigrated to other

---

50. Rakesh Sharma (2024, June 12), "Non-Fungible Token (NFT): What It Means and How It Works," Investopedia, accessed Sept. 4, 2024: https://www.investopedia.com/non-fungible-tokens-nft-5115211

51. OpenAI (2024, Sept. 4), ChatGPT 4o [Large language model], "NFTs Explained - Basics," accessed Sept. 4, 2024, https://chatgpt.com/share/ea3262dc-c585-40ee-ac66-c91721ee5b82

52. Rakesh Sharma (2024, June 12), "Non-Fungible Token (NFT): What It Means and How It Works."

countries throughout Latin America. These family members remain deeply connected to their home community and church, often sending financial support to help fund church initiatives or community outreach programs.

However, the international exchange rates, wire transfer fees, and other banking charges often take a big bite out of their contributions and make it a bit of a challenge to contribute regularly.

When **Juan Carlos** learned about cryptocurrency, he immediately saw it as a potential tool to facilitate international donations, particularly from members who had moved abroad but still wanted to support the church. So, he introduced a cryptocurrency-based offering option, partnering with a cryptocurrency exchange to ensure security and ease of use. He educated the congregation on how to use it, emphasizing its benefits for international donors.

During a service that was livestreamed, Pastor **Juan Carlos** explained, "This new offering method allows our brothers and sisters in Christ around the world to contribute easily, without worrying about currency exchange rates or wire transfer fees. It's a great way to stay connected and support our ministry from anywhere." Members who didn't have convenient access to a bank, those who lived in countries where their currency was being devalued or had poor exchange rates, as well as those who didn't have bank accounts or the kinds of IDs that banks required, could all contribute without prejudice. It was a great equalizer.

The initiative was a success. Former members from various countries started contributing, and members who had not been able to give previously were finally able to contribute. The church saw an increase in international donations. These funds supported local projects, mission trips, and eventually their online ministry efforts...which helped bring the messages of the church and opportunities for inclusion to those who were geographically dispersed.

The cryptocurrency offering also sparked interest among younger members, who were excited about using modern technology to support their faith community. Pastor **Juan Carlos's** innovation effectively bridged both generational and geographical gaps, showcasing the potential of cryptocurrency in fostering a global church community.

THE POTENTIAL OF BLOCKCHAIN

As I mentioned earlier in this chapter, Nakamoto's design for Blockchain incentivizes accurate and honest validation of transactions through "proof of work" exercises and time-stamped network transactions that use "hashing" to make it very difficult to falsify records. Later cryptocurrencies have developed even more complex and distributed blockchain methods to decentralize and validate transactions and reinforce security. In the typical cryptocurrency exchange, transactions are bundled into blocks which function like pages on a ledger.[53] However, these blocks are passed around the network due to its distributed nature, which can mean that they sometimes get distributed more slowly than the individual transactions they are recording.[54]

With a book, the pages are numbered, so even if they were removed from the book or fall out, they can easily be reassembled in the correct order. Although blocks *could* be similarly numbered, the challenge is that we wouldn't want people knowing a later block number, and therefore being able to mine it, until the current one's processing is completed (this would result in varying types of gamesmanship to try to jump ahead of the process in order to prematurely gain rewards).[55] So the blockchain is an optimal solution: Instead of a "block number," the technology uses a *hash* to refer to how the previous block was processed.[56]

Antony Lewis' description from his book *The Basics of Bitcoins and Blockchains* is very helpful:

> To mine block 1,002, minsters need to know the hash of block 1,001. Until 1,001 has been mined, 1,002 can't be mined. This forces miners to focus on block 1,001, which in turn includes the hash of block 1,000, and no miner can skip ahead. Thus a chain of blocks is created, held together not by block numbers (which can be predicted) but by block hashes (which can't). Each block refers to a previous block by the previous block's hash, rather than by a number that goes up sequentially. This is the chain of blocks, or blockchain.[57]

The networks created for handling cryptocurrency mining and transactions are beautifully self-balancing: When more hashing power is added (newer arrivals), blocks get created faster for a period of time until the next difficulty change, which then slows down block creation by making it harder to find valid blocks.[58]

---

53. Antony Lewis (2021), *The Basics of Bitcoins and Blockchains*, p. 176.
54. Ibid.
55. Ibid. For an excellent laymen's terms explanation of blockchain and the underlying technologies like this which empower it, I would highly recommend the section on "How Does Bitcoin Work" in Part 4 of Antony Lewis (2021), *The Basics of Bitcoins and Blockchains*, pp. 153-201.
56. In cryptography, a file hash is a unique sequence of alphanumeric characters that function as a sort of digital fingerprint. It is a text representation of data, and it is nearly impossible to replicate without having the original data… and every file (even if it's a copy of a previous one) will have its own unique hash. waymonho (2023, Dec. 5), "What is a File Hash?," KC7 Foundation, https://kc7cyber.com/blog/what-is-a-file-hash
57. Antony Lewis (2021), *The Basics of Bitcoins and Blockchains*, 177-178.
58. Ibid, 175.

Because it provides secure, transparent, and immutable records of transactions and data, blockchain technology is particularly beneficial for:

- Finance and banking (as described already)
- Supply chain management (ensuring traceability and transparency)
- Healthcare (validating medical records and tracking drug manufacturing)
- Real estate (land registration and recording property transactions)
- Voting systems (ensuring their integrity)
- Intellectual property (rights management and tracking of royalties)
- Energy (trading and grid management)
- Government and public sector (public records and tax collection)
- Retail and e-commerce (loyalty programs and product sourcing)
- Insurance (claims processing and policy management)
- Education (credential verification, student records, & transcripts)
- Entertainment and media (content distribution and ticketing).

The potential applications for other industries are undoubtedly going to increase in coming years. Hopefully by now you can see the tremendous potential and wide range of applications behinds this newer technology.

What has really impressed me is how resistant the technology is to hacking and exploitation. Early in my experimentation with cryptocurrency (Jan. 2019), I remember hearing about an attempted hack on Ethereum Classic (ETC), which was one of the digital assets I had nominally invested in at the time. Hackers temporarily gained control of more than 50% of the network's hash rate, which briefly allowed them to double-spend transaction, effectively falsifying records in order to (hopefully) siphon off funds.[59] However, due to the decentralized nature of the platform and active monitoring by the community, the intrusion attempt was detected within minutes by cryptocurrency exchanges, and the community rallied to thwart the effort, and within about 20 minutes, they had locked out the intruders, and within a few hours the community had restored everything back to what it had been prior (by identifying and restoring the uncorrupted blockchain that had been in effect just prior to the intrusion attempt).

---

59. OpenAI (2024, Sept. 2), ChatGPT 4o [Large language model], "Blockchain Security Examples," accessed Sept. 2, 2024, https://chatgpt.com/share/8babed47-7d35-46e8-849b-cd73c2ed996d

This wasn't the first cyberattack on digital assets, and it wasn't the last, either. Over the last decade or so, there have been dozens of attempted attacks, some of which have been successful. But significant losses from such attacks are fairly uncommon; often the perpetrator is identified fairly quickly and it results in negotiation to minimize or even restore the losses. Every time a new vulnerability is discovered, the crypto community rallies quickly to find solutions to remedy it; consequently, it is nearly impossible to successfully repeat an attack.[60] Compared with traditional banking methods, cryptocurrency has been significantly more secure. In fact, the number of threat incidents have increased, but their effectiveness has rapidly diminished in recent years.[61]

INSIGHTS FROM CHURCH HISTORY

Although the technology underlying Bitcoin, blockchain, cryptocurrency, & DAOs[62] is fairly new, the principles and issues involved have been around for millenia, and this certainly isn't the first time in church history where Christian leaders have wrestle with this challenges. For this topic, we need to look no further than the apostle Paul! He routinely wrestled with issues of trust, authentication, validation, accurate record-keeping, dispersal of funds, governance, hierarchies, and accountability. Let's explore how the apostle Paul navigated these challenges in his ministry to learn how his strategies can provide insights for dealing with similar issues today.

1. Trust and Authentication of Ministry

One of Paul's primary challenges was establishing and maintaining trust and credibility within the early Christian communities, especially since he was not one of the original twelve disciples[63] and also had a notorious past as a well-known persecutor of Christians before his transformative Damascus Road experience. If you will recall, many of the early disciples (including Ananias) struggled with whether to embrace him. [64] Paul frequently referred to his dra-

---

60. Imagine trying to get a typical corporation to address a known software vulnerability…or even admit that they were successfully targeted through a cyberattack! All too often, it is days or even weeks before company leaders learn of such security breaches, and it can often be months before it is disclosed to their consumers and shareholders.

61. ChainAnalysis Team (2024, Jan. 24), "Funds Stolen from Crypto Platforms Fall More Than 50% in 2023, but Hacking Remains a Significant Threat as Number of Incidents Rises," ChainAnalysis > Crime, accessed Sept. 2, 2024, https://www.chainalysis.com/blog/crypto-hacking-stolen-funds-2024/

62. DAOs are Decentralized Autonomous Organizations, a blockchain-based governance system developed to distribute decision-making, management, and entity ownership.

63. Paul specifically mentions this fact in 1 Corinthians 15 by referring to himself as "one abnormally born" (NIV) or "one untimely born" (NASB); verses 3-8 (especially v. 8).

64. Acts 9:11-15. Interestingly, Ananias' struggle parallels Peter's own hesitation at doing ministry to the Gentiles (Acts 10:1 - 11:30), a fact which Paul specifically mentions in Galatians 2:6-10.

matic conversion experience on the road to Damascus as a key proof of his divine calling (Acts 9:1-19, Galatians 1:11-24). This testimony was a foundational element in building trust and authenticity. Paul sought the endorsement of other apostles, notably Peter and James, to validate his ministry (Galatians 2:1-10). This endorsement helped authenticate his authority among the early churches. Paul also called attention to the miracles and spiritual gifts that were evident in his ministry as a further validation of his apostolic authority (2 Corinthians 12:12).

Just as Paul needed to establish trust and authenticate his ministry, modern technologies like blockchain can be used to create secure, transparent records of identity and authority. For example, digital credentials stored on a blockchain could authenticate a minister's qualifications or a church's legitimacy, preventing fraud or unauthorized leadership. Additional uses within the church would be marriage certificates, baptismal and confirmation records, voting documents, and so much more. Similar to Paul's approach of gaining endorsement from multiple apostles, a decentralized network could use consensus mechanisms to validate decisions or authenticate leadership within a church or organization, ensuring trust is distributed rather than centralized.

2. Validation and Establishing Authority

Paul had to consistently validate his authority and the message he preached, especially in the face of false teachers and divisions within the churches he founded. Paul often referenced letters of recommendation, which were a common way to validate a person's authority and credentials in the ancient world (2 Corinthians 3:1-3). These letters served as formal endorsements of his ministry. Paul emphasized the consistency of his teachings with the message of Jesus and the teachings of the other apostles. He stressed the importance of holding to the gospel he had received directly from Christ (Galatians 1:8-9). Paul's letters to the churches were a means of reinforcing his authority, addressing doctrinal issues, and providing guidance. These letters were circulated among the churches, becoming foundational documents of Christian doctrine.

Just as Paul used letters and consistent doctrine to validate his authority, modern technologies like smart contracts in DAOs can enforce agreed-upon rules and principles, ensuring that decisions and actions are consistent with a community's established values. Blockchain's ability to create immutable records can mirror Paul's use of letters to establish a permanent and unalterable record of teachings or agreements within a church or ministry, preserving the integrity of doctrine over time.

3. Accurate Record-Keeping and Transparency

Paul needed to ensure that the funds collected for the Jerusalem church were handled transparently and distributed fairly. Accurate record-keeping was essential to maintain trust and accountability, especially since these collections involved multiple churches across different regions. Paul appointed trustworthy individuals from various churches to handle the collection and transportation of funds (2 Corinthians 8:16-21). This collective approach ensured transparency and accountability, reducing the risk of accusations of mishandling. Paul was transparent about the process and purpose of the collections, making it clear to the congregations how the funds would be used and ensuring they were informed about the outcomes (1 Corinthians 16:1-4).

Paul's method of appointing delegates and publicly reporting on fund distribution is comparable to the use of blockchain for financial transparency in contemporary organizations (and some churches). Blockchain allows for the transparent tracking of donations and expenditures, ensuring that funds are used as intended and that all transactions are visible to the community. The use of multiple delegates to manage the funds reflects a decentralized approach to financial management, where authority is distributed among several trusted individuals or entities. This is a fairly common approach with shared assets like retirement funds, investment portfolios, and strategic decision-making, but it can especially be enhanced today with DAO structures that allow for collective decision-making in financial matters.

4. Dispersal of Funds Internationally

Paul was responsible for organizing the collection of funds from various Gentile churches to support the believers in Jerusalem, navigating the complexities of long-distance fund transfers in an era without modern banking systems. Paul carefully planned the logistics of fund collection and distribution, coordinating with local church leaders to ensure the safe and effective transfer of resources (Romans 15:23-33). Paul emphasized the unity of the body of Christ, encouraging wealthier Gentile churches to support the impoverished believers in Jerusalem as a way of fostering solidarity and mutual care (2 Corinthians 9:6-15).

Paul's method of collecting and transferring funds across regions can be compared to the use of cryptocurrency for international financial transactions in modern churches. Cryptocurrency allows for quick, low-cost, and secure transfers across borders, bypassing traditional banking systems and reducing the risks associated with long-distance fund transfers. Just as Paul coordinated the conditions under which funds would be collected and distributed, smart contracts can be used to automate the release of funds once certain conditions are met, ensuring that resources are only used for their intended purpose.

5. Governance, Hierarchies, and Accountability

Paul had to navigate the complexities of governance within the early Christian communities, addressing issues of authority, leadership, and accountability, often in the context of disputes or differing interpretations of doctrine. Paul advocated for a plurality of leaders in the churches, including elders and deacons, to ensure accountability and shared responsibility (1 Timothy 3:1-13). This distributed leadership model helped maintain balance and prevent the concentration of power in a single individual. Paul frequently wrote letters to correct false teachings, address moral failures, and provide guidance on governance. He held leaders and congregations accountable to the teachings of Christ and the apostles (1 Corinthians 5, Galatians 2:11-14).

One of several ways that Paul's emphasis on shared leadership and accountability can be applied today is by using DAOs to create decentralized governance structures within churches and ministries. DAOs allow for collective decision-making, reducing the risk of power imbalances and ensuring that all members have a voice in governance. Just as Paul provided transparent correction and guidance through his letters, modern technologies can facilitate transparent communication and accountability in church leadership, using platforms that allow for open discussions and records of decisions.

6. Building and Maintaining Relationships Across Distance

Paul was responsible for maintaining relationships and ensuring doctrinal unity among widely dispersed Christian communities. Communication and coordination were key to maintaining the integrity of the early church. Paul maintained close contact with the churches he founded through frequent letters, personal visits, and sending trusted associates like Timothy and Titus to represent him (Philippians 2:19-24, Titus 1:4-5). Paul helped to establish a network of interconnected churches that supported and communicated with each other, fostering a sense of unity and shared mission across geographic distances (Colossians 4:16, 2 Corinthians 8:18-19).

Paul's use of letters and personal representatives mirrors the way modern decentralized communication networks can be used to maintain relationships and ensure unity across dispersed communities. Platforms like decentralized messaging apps or blockchain-based communication systems can provide secure and transparent communication channels. The interconnectedness of

Paul's network of churches can be likened to the use of interoperable systems in modern technology, where different platforms and communities can work together seamlessly, sharing resources and information to achieve common goals.

Conclusion

The Apostle Paul's ministry, with its focus on trust, authentication, validation, transparent governance, and the effective management of resources across a decentralized network of churches, offers profound insights into the challenges and opportunities presented by modern technologies like blockchain, cryptocurrency, and DAOs. By examining Paul's strategies and responses, church leaders today can draw parallels and apply these ancient principles to navigate the complexities of a rapidly-changing technological landscape.

DAOS & THEIR POTENTIAL APPLICATIONS

There's more, though! These blockchain and cryptocurrency technologies, along with many of the principles we see embodied through the apostle Paul's ministry, have given birth to a new type of administrative and organizational structure called a Decentralized Autonomous Organization (DAO). A DAO is an autonomous organization run by the community, with smart contracts establishing the underlying laws and predetermined behaviors that carry out chosen courses of action. And it is entirely transparent, meaning that at all times, the proposals, votes, and even the code itself are available for review by the public.[65] [66]

This is in stark contrast to the traditional model of governance which is typically used by corporations and finance companies…one that is deeply hierarchical, and where power is concentrated at the top (by CEOs, senior management, and officials who answers to boards and/or stakeholders). Decisionmaking in contexts like this nearly always reflect what's best for the company's bottom line or maximizing the revenue for the top leaders. Incremental changes come slowly, and threats are often responded to very slowly.

Picture a large software corporation learning of a vulnerability in their flagship product that was recently exposed through a cyberattack: The first thing that's going to happen is the company goes into damage control mode,

---

65.   Jerome Aquino (2022), *DAO Explained: Comprehensive Guide on Decentralized Autonomous Organizations (DAO)*, Independently published, 25 & 35.

66.   A good synopsis with links to actual vote measures and updates that were under discussion for the Lido DAO can be viewed in "How do DAOs govern?" in the article: ChainAnalysis Team (2023, April 7), "Introduction to Decentralized Autonomous Organizations (DAOs)," Crypto Basics, accessed Sept. 2, 2024, https://www.chainalysis.com/blog/introduction-to-decentralized-autonomous-organizations-daos/

Chapter 3

activating their public relations team to carefully craft the messaging about what happened and monitoring social media to mitigate against any perceptions that might be unflattering to the company's reputation. They will carefully control the messaging to customers, stakeholders, employees, and government watchdog groups. Then corporate executives will be looking at the actual and potential losses to determine how significant the breach is and how costly it will be to fix. Layers and layers of institutional bureaucracy will slow progress on this, and a software patch could take days (and most likely weeks, sometimes months) to develop. Meanwhile customers are still buying and using the product, unaware of the dangers they are not privy to, with customer service still in the dark about what happened and unable to advise or assist customers who begin to experience issues because they don't want the public to be aware of what happened. Sadly, this is an all-too-common scenario.[67]

With a DAO, however, there are no hierarchies and no concentrated clusters of power. When the DAO is first established, there are a set of rules created and a set of basic requirements that all members agree to abide by.[68] Tokens are developed and sold to raise funding for the DAO, and holders of tokens receive voting rights.[69] Everything about the company is clearly documented and transparently available for review by anyone.[70] Blockchain technology undergirds the back-end,[71] and smart contracts written by developers execute code following pre-written rules that everyone in the DAO agreed to.[72]

The idea and function of a DAO is very simple: It is a contract that takes the form of a computer program capable of automatically executing the terms of its contract. Put differently, a DAO is a computer program that mimics the functions of a board of directors or an executive management team. And instead of using company resources to achieve its goals, it uses capital contributed by stakeholders in the form of cryptocurrency.[73]

Some leading DAOs in the cryptocurrency space are:

---

67. I don't have a specific company in mind for this scenario; rather, it is an amalgamation of multiple situations and scenarios I have read about and learned of in the software and computing industry over the years. I am deliberately trying to keep it vague and general so that it is both easily recognizable and broadly applicable.

68. Alex Anderson (2021), *DAO - Decentralized Autonomous Organizations for Beginners: The Ultimate Beginner's Guide*, Independently published.

69. Jerome Aquino (2022), *DAO Explained*, 10.

70. Alex Anderson (2021), *DAO - Decentralized Autonomous Organizations for Beginners*, 6 & 8; ChainAnalysis Team (2023, April 7), "Introduction to Decentralized Autonomous Organizations (DAOs)," Crypto Basics.

71. Ibid., 6.

72. Aquino (2022), *DAO Explained*, 25-26.

73. Anderson (2021), *DAO - Decentralized Autonomous Organizations for Beginners*, 22-23.

- MakerDAO (fintech, Dai token)
- DAOstack (developers)
- Digis (precious metals, DGX – Digis Gold Tokens)
- IMMO (global network of cryptocurrencies)
- Aragon (network for launching DAOs)
- GnosisDAO (platform for developing DeFi applications)
- MetaFactory (funding retail product manufacturing).[74]

Others (all of which have over a billion dollars in market capitalization) include:

- Uniswap Foundation (DEX)
- Lido DAO (a liquid staking protocol)
- Ape Foundation (NFTs, metaverse, and entertainment in Web 3)
- BitDAO (Web 3 project funding).[75]

If issues arise or changes in how the DAO operates become necessary, the entire community is informed and decisions regarding those revisions are achieved by consensus through voting.[76] And we know that community members will vote in ways that best benefit the DAO itself because the value of its tokens is impacted accordingly, and they will want the network to flourish because they have a vested interest in its success.[77]

Decentralized autonomous organizations are most commonly used in the cryptocurrency field and are often completely integrated into blockchain initiatives. They are also used in the decentralized finance (DeFi) field to ensure that applications can operate in a completely decentralized way.[78] However, the unique character, capabilities, and agility of DAOs make this organizational structure especially attractive to businesses in a wide variety of industries.[79] DAOs have formed to run a variety of types of organizations, including businesses, nonprofits investment schemes, and more.[80]

---

74. Ibid., 41-49.
75. ChainAnalysis Team (2023, April 7), "Introduction to Decentralized Autonomous Organizations (DAOs)," Crypto Basics.
76. Aquino (2022), *DAO Explained*, 35-36. Anderson (2021), *DAO - Decentralized Autonomous Organizations for Beginners*, 35.
77. Aquino (2022), *DAO Explained*, 28.
78. Ibid., 32-33.
79. Anderson (2021), *DAO - Decentralized Autonomous Organizations for Beginners*, 8.
80. ChainAnalysis Team (2023, April 7), "Introduction to Decentralized Autonomous Organizations (DAOs)," Crypto Basics.

BIBLICAL VALUES & THEOLOGICAL IMPLICATIONS

In addition to all the principles and issues we explored in the apostle Paul's ministry related to trust, authentication, validation, transparent governance, and resource management, there are significant theological implications for church structure, too. At a Metaverse Church Learning Community gathering in Tampa, I participated in meaningful conversations with a church planter and a metaverse pastor about the feasibility of starting a church using the DAO framework, and it was a VERY intriguing idea that has tremendous potential for success.[81]

After all, there are SO many Scripture passages which describe and seem to advocate for this kind of non-hierarchical, altruistic model of gathering... one that emphasizes shared participation and contributions, as well as shared governance:

- Acts 2:42-47 (the Early Church's worship)

- Acts 15:1-21 (The Council at Jerusalem)

- 1 Corinthians 12:12-27 (Paul's admonitions on the unity of the Body of Christ)

- Galatians 3:28 (on equality regardless of status)

- Matthew 20:25-28 (Jesus' teaching about altruistic servant leadership)

- Ephesians 4:11-16 (Paul's teaching about gifts and roles)

- Romans 12:4-8 (more of Paul's teachings about roles in the body and varying gifts)

- 1 Corinthians 14:26 (Paul's teaching about the value of shared contributions and participation in worship).

As you can see, it's practically the New Testament model of church gatherings and governance.

And yet, the history of the organized church through the ages has been a far cry from this kind of model; from Roman Catholic organizational structure to denominational governance, the primary expressions of church governance have nearly always been hierarchical with a heavy concentration of power and authority at the top, all of which seems contrary to Biblical teaching. The Believer's Church tradition (a loosely-affiliated approach that arose out of the

---

81. Jason Dukes (church planter), Stuart McPherson (metaverse pastor), and Joey Santos (church planter), in discussion with the author, Nov. 15, 2022 at the Metaverse Church Learning Community gathering held at Tampa Underground Network's Hub, Tampa, FL.

Radical Reformation in the 16th century) is one of the few church governance models that seems to resist hierarchical models of control in favor of a more decentralized authority structure. While exploring this issue further exceeds the scope of this book, I do think this is something that pastors should consider and explore further (and if we don't, organizational structures arising from technological change like DAOs may force us to).

NEXT STEPS: LEADING WITH WISDOM

So, how can you lead your church or ministry confidently in these uncertain times, offering hope and peace when all too often confusion and misunderstanding reigns? First, resist fear-based appeals and conspiracy theories. We tend to fear what we don't understand, and unfortunately, several hyperconservative quasi-Christian groups (and especially those who market to them) have become skillful at exploiting those fears; most of the time, they're trying to try to sell us something. If it sounds too good to be true, it usually is. If it sounds sensational or alarmist, it's probably overexaggerated and, at best, only partially true. Remember, in the conclusion of his Sermon on the Mount, Jesus told us to watch out for false prophets who would outward manifest in sheep's clothing, but inwardly are ravenous wolves.[82] Peter taught us to be sober and alert because our enemy, the devil, prowls around like a roaring lion looking for someone to devour.[83]

To sift fact from fiction, it often helps to take a close look at the messenger and evaluate what they gain from convincing you to act. For example, some groups and commentators argue that cryptocurrencies are too volatile and speculative to provide real security during a financial crisis. This fear-based narrative often is accompanied by advertisements to purchase gold or other tangible assets as protection against a predicted economic downturn. However, if they're warning you about a coming economic catastrophe, but selling gold, there's your clue: They're exploiting your fear of the unknown and the risk of a shaky future to sell you something they personally gain from.

Another common fear-based argument targets the concept of a cashless society. Critics claim that transitioning to a fully digital economy, including the use of Central Bank Digital Currencies (CBDCs), will lead to an unprecedented level of government surveillance and control. They warn that such systems could allow governments to "turn off" an individual's access to their

82. Matthew 7:15-20.
83. 1 Peter 5:8-9 (NIV).

funds, effectively "canceling" you if you dissent or fail to conform to certain societal norms. Ironically, these concerns are often used to promote cryptocurrencies as a more private and secure alternative, free from government interference. But all that does is transfer the risk to yet another group, and in this case it is one that has already proven itself to be dishonest, manipulative, and untruthful.

Besides, these are very tired arguments: They said the same thing about credit cards, mobile banking, and even online bill payment (and pretty much any new technology that has emerged for centuries, if not millenia). The simple reality is that no matter how much we utilize digital assets or embrace cryptocurrency and other newer blockchain-based tools, we are not moving to a cashless society anytime soon. That would be nearly impossible. Although I invest in cryptocurrency, have used digital tools and mobile apps to make purchase, use online bill payment and banking regularly, have created an NFT, and have traded digital assets, I still carry cash and pay for many things with it, and I still write checks on occasion. And, as we learned from Dave Ramsey earlier, most transactions today are already digital,[84] and yet we are not any closer to this mythical cashless society. In fact, I don't know a single ministry, education, or technology leader who works with cryptocurrency or trades digital assets who has gone completely cashless. That serves no purpose or function (it's mostly only talked about in niche circles to instill fear in people to manipulate them).

Second, educate yourself about these technologies and learn all you can so that you can better understand what your parishioners are hearing about, experiencing, or even involved with. Chances are VERY good that a healthy percentage of your congregation have used or considered one or more of these technologies. If they work in education, finance, healthcare, technology, retail, supply chain, economics, or more, it's nearly certain that they have already become acquainted with these technologies and are using them on the job in some form.

Two of the best user-friendly platforms for learning about cryptocurrency, blockchain, and DAOs are CoinBase and Robinhood:

- Coinbase is a cryptocurrency platform that facilitates buying, selling, storing, and trading cryptocurrency.[85] They are also the largest cryptocurrency exchange,[86] and they offer digital wallets.

84. Dave Ramsey (2023, Sept. 22), "Get Ready for a Digital Currency?, https://youtu.be/mUywzuPY7xY; Ramsey Solutions (2024, April 5), "Are We Really Headed for a Cashless Society?"

85. Gloria Chinemerem Chimelu (2024, July 18), "Coinbase Review," Buying & Selling > Crypto Exchanges, accessed Sept. 2, 2024, https://www.investopedia.com/tech/coinbase-what-it-and-how-do-you-use-it/

86. Ibid.

The platform is intuitive and has a very user-friendly interface, and they make it easy to understand and follow various crypto-currencies…whether you just want to see what's trending and what's performing well (or not), or if you want to dive in deeper and analyze real-time trading data like an investment broker or financial analyst would.[87]

- Robinhood is an online broker that offers an easy-to-use platform that offers both desktop access and an easy-to-navigate trading app for buying, selling, storing, and trading stocks, ETFs, and cryptocurrency.[88] One of its primary draws is being able to trade fractional shares of stocks and ETFs, allowing novices and those who aren't wealthy the opportunity to engage in the stock market.

I have been using the Coinbase platform for 8 years now, and am very pleased with it. One of my favorite features of the site is Coinbase Learning Rewards, where they offer helpful videos and tools to introduce and explain new tokens, assets, and cryptocurrencies, and then reward you for learning with a few dollars' worth of that particular token or cryptocurrency. Much of what I know about cryptocurrency, digital assets, and other tokens as well as blockchain has come through educational videos and arti-cles I viewed on the site, and most of my earliest crypto investment (when I was still a bit skeptical and unsure) came from rewards the platform provided. If you're interested in giving Coinbase a try, here is my referral ink: https://bit.ly/CoinbaseTry (or you can scan the QR code).[89]

I have been using the Robinhood app for 4 years now, and find it extremely easy to use and understand. I first became interested in the stock market back in 8th grade when our class participated in a mock trading exercise over several weeks (and I did exceedingly well). Unfortunately, traditional investing requires a stockbroker, regular attention to the status and performance of your stocks, and quite a bit of wealth, none of which I had. But what Robinhood does is pool the purchasing power of millions of small-time investors who purchase fractional shares and then they collectively trade whole shares at

---

87. For the advanced functions, you would need to use their "Advanced Trade" feature (which used to be called Coinbase Pro).

88. Emily Guy Birken (2024, June 25), "Robinhood Review 2024," Advisor > Investing, accessed Sept. 2, 2024, https://www.forbes.com/advisor/investing/robinhood-review/#how_does_robinhood_work_section

89. This is an affiliate link that benefits both of us: If you follow my referral link and then (1) create a Coinbase account, (2) verify your account, and (3) make a qualifying purchase of $100 (or 100€) or more within 90 days of verifying, we will each receive a bonus of $10 worth of Bitcoin. See "Coinbase Referral Program" at https://help.coinbase.com/en/coinbase/getting-started/getting-started-with-coinbase/new-customer-incentive

volume. This allows the platform to eliminate (or drastically reduce) brokerage fees, and also allows average people like me to hold and transact partial shares of major stocks like Apple, Tesla, Amazon, and Nvidia. Robinhood also sells and enables you to trade cryptocurrency in the same way. If you're interested in giving Robinhood a try, here is my referral ink: https://bit.ly/ RobinhoodTry (or you can scan the QR code).[90]

Finally, I would highly recommend reading Antony Lewis (2021) book *The Basics of Bitcoins and Blockchains: An Introduction to Cryptocurrencies and the Technology that Powers Them* (Coral Gables, FL: Mango Publishing), which is quite affordable on Amazon at: https://amzn.to/4gcv22U. I have found it to be extremely helpful for providing valuable context and a laymen's understanding of all the interconnected topics without requiring a finance or economics background nor presuming any technological expertise.

---

90. This is an affiliate link that benefits both of us: If you follow my referral link and then (1) create a Robinhood account, (2) verify your account, and (3) link your bank account, we will each receive a small portion of a share of stock (typically $5 value). See "Invite Friends" at https://robinhood.com/rewards

Chapter 4

VIRTUAL PRESENCE

Church in the Metaverse

Virtual reality has been around for decades, as has the metaverse, but for the first time, immersive head-mounted display units have become affordable and readily available…and nearly ubiquitous. When Facebook rebranded as "Meta" to focus on this new platform, business leaders took note! There are now hundreds of businesses (including the majority of the Fortune top 20 who are doing employee training in VR, major sports franchises (including the NFL) which are doing training and performance improvement in VR, hundreds of educational institutions which are offering courses in VR and metaverse spaces, and a few dozen churches which now meet in virtual reality and on metaverse platforms.

What was once the domain of geeks and gamers, and a mere curiosity factor for innovators, is now a rapidly-emerging delivery modality and vital platform for conducting business, school, and church. Mission trips into the metaverse are already underway, and within the next few years, most churches with a heart for outreach and a desire to engage with their community will need to explore whether to plant churches in VR, partner with existing ones, or offer virtual campuses. The cost savings and opportunities to reach unchurched denizens is undeniable, but these new models bring paradigm-changing theological questions regarding identity, as well as practical challenges.

The summer of 2020 was a difficult time for many of us; for me, it was an eye-opener that paved the way for a slew of new technological possibilities. The COVID-19 pandemic was in full swing by then, with lockdowns and mask mandates in place, and my daughter's tenth birthday was approaching. One thing you need to know about me may surprise you given my technological aptitude and geeky side: Cake decorating is a side hobby, and I have been doing my daughter's birthday cakes for years. Understand, however, that these are not your ordinary grocery-store bought or typical home-made cakes, either; these are full-blown creative expressions that would be right at home as a centerpiece in a holiday showcase at the mall. I learned how to decorate cakes from my mother, Jeannie Swisher, and she was the 4-H project leader in our county who taught dozens of us how to decorate. I was, of course, her best student, and I had received numerous recognitions and honors for my cake decorating work.

My cakes are smaller-scale versions of what you would see on Cake Boss, employing many of the same techniques and skills. In fact, one of my decorated wedding cakes made it all the way to the State Fair: It was a three-tiered wedding cake with multiple layers of intricate three-dimensional stringwork and cornelli lace, topped with a hexagonal birdcage made of royal icing that featured a realistic bird made of marzipan, perched on a working swing. That cake was not only a Grand Champion at the fair that year, but an oft-discussed showstopper. Over the years, I've created photo-realistic edible storybooks, ice castles, extravagant princesses, and even her favorite animated character in the midst of rune-covered standing stones, nestled among actual working fog. So, for my daughter, birthday cakes are a BIG deal!

But that year I was faced with the dilemma of how to make this day special for my daughter, cater to her extroversion (after all, birthdays for pre-teen girls are ALL about having friends over, right?), and still be safe and compliant in terms of masks and social distancing, too. It was clear that we couldn't have a group of her friends over (and she certainly didn't want to choose just 2-3 of them to join her for the big day), nor could we have a big gathering, so I did what I knew best...I turned to technology. I had already noticed that as her classes shifted to virtual and lockdowns forced us to stay home, she enjoyed hanging out with her friends for multiple hours a day on her iPad, playing Roblox together. I even signed up for an account, created a virtual avatar, and joined them on several adventures. That gave me a perfect idea.

We decided to have her birthday party in her favorite park in town, but only she and I would be physically present. All of her guests would connect remotely via Zoom on their devices, and the highlight of the party would be a series of games we picked out that they would all play together in the virtual world of Roblox. For the party treats, all of her friends wanted to see the cake I had made, and of course share in it, too. So, I still went all out on her cake which we displayed on the table in the park for us to eat (and we also took plenty

Figure 1 – In the park, Susannah connects with her friends in the metaverse through the Roblox app on her iPad while I manage and monitor the Zoom call.

of pics and video of it to share), but I also made a smaller cake, decorated similarly. The day before the party, I took kits around to all her friends: Each one had a themed plate & napkin, slice of cake, plastic silverware, candle, and a ziplock bag full of themed party favors. This way when it was time to sing "Happy Birthday" and cut the cake, her friends could actively participate with us – lighting their own candle, singing along with each other, and eating their very own cake along with her.

It went incredibly well, and her friends loved being a part of it. She had so much fun connecting with her friends, showing off her cake, and playing games with them, even though they couldn't physically be together. The most amazing thing about this was that *none* of them thought this was weird, out of character, "virtual" (or less real), or anything of the sort. For this tight-knit group of preteens, they considered this a *perfectly normal* way to interact with friends.[1] This was when I first began to realize the potential of the metaverse for ministry.

METAVERSE POSSIBILITIES AND POTENTIAL

So, what is Roblox? Roblox is an online platform and game creation system featuring immersive 3D experiences and multiplayer collaboration as well as in-game chat and friend lists. You can see when your friends are online and join them. Furthermore, it provides a sandbox environment where players can create and monetize their own games and virtual items, allowing friends to spend time together in virtual worlds created by their peers. As of the fourth quarter of 2024, the platform had 380 million *monthly* active users, and reported approximately 79.5 million *daily* active users.[2] There are also over 4.6 *billion* registered users on the platform (a 53% increase over the 3 billion total users they had just 3 years prior).[3] Even more astounding is that well over half (58%) of those users are under the age of 16, and 42% are under age 13![4]

Seriously…how many children that age are coming to your church's gatherings? The potential is incredible. There are over 40 million user-created

1.   Significant portions of this section are adapted and expanded from a presentation I first gave at the Wesleyan Theological Society in March 2023 titled, "Inconceivable! Field Preaching, Digital Church, & the Metaverse: Embracing John Wesley's Legacy of Innovation to Inform the Virtual Ministry of Tomorrow," which were later published in *Didache: Faithful Teaching*, 24:1 (Spring 2024). ISSN: 15360156 https://didache.nazarene.org/index.php/volume-24-number-1

2.   Backlinko Team (2025, Feb. 25), "Roblox User and Growth Stats You Need to Know," accessed Mar. 3, 2025, https://backlinko.com/roblox-users

3.   Angela Kulevska (2024, February 9), "How Many People Play Roblox?," CyberCrew, accessed Mar. 3, 2025, https://cybercrew.uk/blog/how-many-people-play-roblox

4.   Backlinko Team (2025, Feb. 25), "Roblox User and Growth Stats You Need to Know."

games and activities ("experiences") on Roblox,[5] with the most active ones featuring anywhere from 80,000 to 120,000 kids playing them at any one time worldwide.[6] If you could reach even 1% of the young people who are online playing Roblox at any given time, it would exponentially multiply your church's reach. Roblox is also a global phenomenon, with 21.5% of the users in the U.S. and Canada, 25.9% in Europe, 25.4% in the Asia-Pacific region, and 27.2% in the rest of the world.[7] Roblox even has its own in-game currency. Cumulatively, users have spent over 17.4 billion hours engaging on the platform every quarter.[8]

Roblox is a "metaverse" application because it is a persistent, shared, virtual space where users can interact, create, and engage in various activities. While in many ways, it might look like a video game, there isn't a singular storyline or objective, but instead it is an open-ended network of multiple interconnected virtual spaces (that's why it's called a metaverse). Players customize their avatars with thousands of accessories, skins, and animations to reflect their digital identity on the platform. As a result, players can appear as people of various types, shapes, ethnicities, and personalities, as well as foxes, cats, robots, or even dragons...and any kind of adaptation or conglomeration thereof. There is really no limit for the creative expression that's possible in virtual worlds like this (although Roblox does have appropriate age restrictions due to its primary demographic); for all practical purposes, if you can imagine it, you can create it.

My second indicator of the potential of the metaverse for ministry was when my oldest son was a freshman at college and his brother (a year younger) was still at home. To ease the transition, these introverted teen boys of mine set up a server in Minecraft and hung out there, crafting and chatting for hours on end. Keep in mind, too, that these are teenagers for whom the traditional church simply doesn't connect or resonate...intellectually-minded teens who aren't impressed with the pat answers that are so often espoused by church leaders. And they are NOT very social and do not enjoy crowds. But give them a Minecraft server, and they come alive, talking about the issues, frustrations, and challenges of life. As I watched my boys engage so readily in this space (it was as natural to them as their little sister's presence with friends was in Rob-

---

5. Nena Shubham (2023, December 27), "How Many Games Are in Roblox? (2023)," GamerTweak, accessed Mar. 3, 2025, https://gamertweak.com/how-many-games-roblox/#how-many-roblox-games-are-there-in-total-2023

6. Personal observation derived from dozens of visits, including active participation in two of the Top 10 games (MeepCity and AdoptMe!). See also Nikita Hariname (2023, Feb. 21), "Most Popular Roblox Games (February 2023)," GamerTweak, accessed Mar. 4, 2025, https://gamertweak.com/most-popular-game-roblox

7. Backlinko Team (2025, Feb. 25), "Roblox User and Growth Stats You Need to Know."

8. Ibid.

lox), I couldn't help but think how this would be an awesome place to plant a church…a church that speaks to teens and young adults, on their turf, in the spaces they frequent, where life is "real"!

Minecraft is also a "metaverse" application because it is a persistent, shared, virtual space where users can interact, create, and engage in various activities. Rather than having a singular storyline or objective, it is a wide open creative canvas, with infinite automatically-generated worlds to explore. You can play solo games, or set up servers to play with other friends; they also have multiplayer options where you can play with thousands of other players, as well as several huge server hubs (the most popular of which are The Hive and Hypixel) where users can play user-created games. So Minecraft is also an open-ended network of multiple interconnected virtual spaces, and players customize their avatars with thousands of accessories, skins, and animations to reflect their digital identity on the platform.

How big is Minecraft's server world? According to their Live Player Count & Statistics,[9] as I write this paragraph in early 2025, in the middle of the afternoon (5 pm in the Eastern U.S.), there are just under a million people playing Minecraft (959,314 to be exact); there are 218,755,945 active Minecraft players who logged in within the last 30 days. In 2024, an average of 45 million people played Minecraft on any given day, and in the first two months of 2025, that number rose to almost 60 million.

But these are just a few of the metaverse platforms. Fortnite is another, one which is primarily game-based, but also open-ended and multiplayer. Back in 2006, I remember helping my oldest daughter Lydia get connected with Club Penguin, an online multiplayer game that featured a virtual world where players could create and customize penguin avatars, explore snowy environments, play mini-games, and interact with other players in a highly moderated and safe online space. That platform was known for its tight parental controls and strict chat filters, ensuring a safe environment for younger users. It also had seasonal events, parties, and in-game activities, making it a popular choice for kids. It was eventually acquired by Disney, but shuttered in 2017.

I have spent considerable time in multiple metaverse platforms while engaged in ministry and education. My first foray involved Second Life, and later I explored Roblox, Minecraft, and Pokémon GO, and I also observed Fortnite. In recent years, through my university research, I have developed characters and explored Horizon Worlds, Engage, AltSpace VR, Campfire, and Virbela,

---

9.   ActivePlayer.io (n.d.), "Minecraft Live Player Count & Statistics," Minecraft, accessed Mar. 4, 2025, https:// activeplayer.io/minecraft

and I have attended metaverse church gatherings in AltSpace VR, Big Screen, and VRchat. However, by far my favorite metaverse experience was in my doctoral program at Portland Seminary (George Fox University), where we met weekly in Second Life, and then later transitioned to a now-defunct platform called SpotOn3D.[10]

What you see here is a place in that platform called "SpiritLife Cathedral," and it was designed to be eclectic and theoretical, employing concepts that couldn't happen that way in real life (thus ideal for a virtual world):[11] The waterfall is gorgeous, and the water actually flows, the trees rustle in the wind, there's realistic stained glass in the background, and a library of great books from our faculty mentor and re-

lated subjects in the rear. That's our instructor (Leonard Sweet) on the carpet in the center, and up against the rock in the center, that's me (in virtual worlds, my avatar always dresses like Indiana Jones with a fedora and has wings so I can fly). Some of us were hovering, some swimming, and some seated in deep thought. But what you can't really see in that screenshot is that the James Bond theme song "SkyFall" from Adele was playing in the background and snow was gently falling...inside the cathedral. This was for a class session on imagination, creativity, & metaphor, so it was the ideal learning environment for that topic!

When I last checked, there were at least three dozen current metaverse platforms that are fairly well known and heavily populated. They range in size and influence from smaller niche networks of a few thousand users to larger ones in the tens of millions. The very first one was Habitat, which launched in 1986, and another early but still active (though niche) platform is Active Worlds, launched in 1995. The longest-running still-active (and best-known) platform is Second Life, which today has somewhere between 600,000 to a million users. Some metaverse platforms tend to cater to specific needs, such as developers (OpenSimulator), gamers and creatives (The Sandbox), or business collaboration (Viverse, Spatial, and Virbela), and some (like Decentraland

---

10. Second Life is an open world, and our class was crashed a couple of times by a group of unsavory characters in inappropriately-attired *"avatars"* who were clearly drunk and intentionally disruptive. So, our program's leadership rebuilt in SpotOn3D, which was a closed world that we could enjoy and explore without such issues.

11. David Swisher & Jase Teoh (2023, January), "Bakhtin, Vygosky, & the Metaverse: Why Learning Flourishes in Virtual Reality," Colleague2Colleague Professional Development Workshop, Overland Park, KS, https://tinyurl.com/BakhtinVygotskyMV-C2C

and Upland) are geared toward cryptocurrency enthusiasts and are hosted on a blockchain. But by far, the biggest and most active user communities are Horizon Worlds (tens of thousands), Roblox, Minecraft, and Fortnite (tens of millions). There are also loosely moderated platforms like IMVU (over 7 million), VR Chat (tens of thousands), and Rec Room (hundreds of thousands).

Consider the possibilities in this fictional, but entirely plausible, scenario. Because the shift to metaverse ministry is both emerging and complex, I've chosen to follow Pastor Jeff's story in three parts, corresponding to key moments of discovery, resistance, and transformation. You'll encounter these scenes throughout the chapter as we explore the practical and theological implications of metaverse engagement with the scenario woven throughout:

PASTOR JEFF AND THE METAVERSE EXPERIMENT
Scene 1: The Leadership Roundtable

Pastor Jeff adjusted his reading glasses and sighed as he scanned the agenda for the monthly leadership meeting. He had been in ministry now for over three decades, and in that time he had weathered countless trends – everything from the seeker-sensitive movement to the rise of megachurches, as well as CCM, and lately livestreaming. But this? This was something else.

"Virtual reality church?" he said, shaking his head. "I just don't see how that's real ministry."

Across the table, Jordan, the church's tech-savvy youth pastor, leaned forward excitedly. "It's already happening, Pastor. VR churches are planting and growing faster than many traditional ones. I've been spending time in the metaverse using my VR headset, and I've already met several kids who wouldn't set foot in a church but they engage in deep conversations in VR small groups."

Elder Mark folded his arms. "You can't disciple an avatar," he harumphed.

Sarah, a church planter, cleared her throat. "Actually, you can. I've been part of a VR church plant for six months now. I've seen people come to Christ who never would have walked into a physical church building. One woman in our group is disabled and homebound; she can't go anywhere, so VR is her only option for corporate worship. And she's a regular."

The room fell silent as that sank in.

"Well, that would be a big stretch for us," Jeff retorted. "Why can't we just let the cool church across town do it?"

"They already do," said Jordan. "But they're reaching entirely different people than we could. When I'm hanging out in VR, the kids I see

95

aren't likely to go there. But they know me, and they'd probably come if I started up a VR service."

"So, what does that mean for us?" Jeff asked.

Jordan grinned, delighted at the opportunity. "I have an idea. I know you're not yet convinced, and that's OK. But I've also seen what's possible. I can't guarantee it's going to work for us, here but we don't have to jump in blind, either – we can learn and experiment first. So, why don't we test it? Let's do three experiments: A VR small group, a VR outreach event, and a partnership with an existing VR church. That would mean less work on our part for now, and a chance to adjust as we learn. And we can pursue (and adjust) whatever seems to work best."

"Alright," Pastor Jeff exhaled. "But if I end up looking like a floating cartoon character, I'm blaming you."

DEMYSTIFYING VIRTUAL REALITY AND THE METAVERSE

So, what exactly is virtual reality, and how does that involve the metaverse? Unfortunately, although there are at least three dozen movies from the last couple of decades where virtual reality featured heavily into the narrative, those movie depictions are not particularly accurate. What they depict is typically a highly-romanticized and fictionalized version so the filmmakers can tell a compelling story. **Virtual Reality (VR)** is a three-dimensional computer-simulated environment that can be experienced using special equipment. It utilizes a cycle of tracking, rendering and display which takes place continuously in real time, and this involves sensors that detect a user's movements and translate them into data that can be used to update the VR content."[12] VR experiences can be self-contained (typically one person using an app), social (offering a network of users who appear as avatars and build or experience VR scenes together), or industrial (such as businesses or educational institutions offering "digital twins" of their office, building, campus, etc., or even products and factory workfloors to explore possibilities and flow).[13] That's what virtual reality involves.

However, there are multiple variations and options for different kinds of media in virtual contexts. In an article my IWU colleagues and I co-authored,[14]

---

12. See Chapter 4: "Virtual Reality and its Opportunities and Risks" (pp. 119-139) by Jeremy Bailenson and Molly Lesher in OECD (2024), *OECD Digital Economy Outlook 2024* (Volume 1): Embracing the Technology Frontier, OECD Publishing, Paris, https://doi.org/10.1787/a1689dc5-en, 120.

13. Ibid., 121.

14. Significant portions of this section are adapted and expanded from a presentation my IWU colleagues and I

mixed media expert Mike Jones explains the various terms and how they overlap. One of the simplest forms is **Augmented Reality (AR)**, where you are looking at the actual physical world through a built-in camera, but electronic equipment (usually either a smartphone or a headset) overlays that physical world with text or three-dimensional assets.[15] One example was an app that Kansas State University built years ago where you could aim your phone's camera at a building, and it would recognize it and overlay that building with its name, listing what offices and classes were in there, and even a map if you wanted. Google Glass is another example of this kind of VR technology.

For one case study, my friend and colleague Mike Jones created a virtual patient who could appear in the center of a room in a variety of environments, and through the student's mobile device which was running the app, nursing students could interact with it. There was no actual physical patient simulator, but a stethescope would appear on screen, and the student would move their phone until the stethescope image came in contact with the correct placement for listening to the patient's heartbeat. The phone would then play the sound of the heartbeat through the speakers of the mobile device, and also cause the device to vibrate at the same rate as the randomized heartbeat.[16] In this way, it was fairly experiential, and great practice for learners.

Another type of experience involves **360-degree video**. These are non-immersive technologies that can usually be viewed through an Internet browser. You may have seen some Facebook or other online images where if you're viewing it on a smartphone or tablet, you can turn your device various ways to see different angles and views.[17] That's 360-degree video, done with a photo. There are also many websites which offer this as a video (for example, museums and visitor sites where you can explore various angles of a displayed object, or realtor's sites where you can click through a home and pan the camera around to see what it looks like from the camera's point of view within the home). That, too, is 360-degree video. This can be achieved with a special camera or smartphone app that takes multiple still images in all directions, then digitally stitches them together to give the illusion of a fully-immersive environment. These can be viewed using a head-mounted display, but more commonly using a simple smartphone inserted in an inexpensive Google Cardboard viewer,

---

gave at a Fall convocation for our National & Global campus, which was later published in Annie Els, Mike Jones, and David Swisher (2023), "Modalities & Experiences: Unlocking the Gamified Metaversity," C2C Digital Magazine, 1 (18), 22, article 2, Colleague2Colleague. https://scalar.usc.edu/works/c2c-digital-magazine-fall-2022---winter-2023/gamified-metaversity

15. Els, Jones, & Swisher (2023), "Modalities & Experiences: Unlocking the Gamified Metaversity."
16. Ibid.
17. Ibid.

though they can also be viewed two-dimensionally using computer or tablet screens or smartphones.

Yet another type of immersive virtual viewing experience is **Mixed Reality (MR).** With this technology, three-dimensional objects or sets of instructions are mapped to real-world objects, and these 3D objects are tracked in real time by the mixed reality hardware. This way, the views and perspectives of the digital asset overlays will change based on the current state of the physical object in the real world. One example Mike likes to demonstrate is a childbirth simulator that looks at a pregnant woman in a lab gown and the mixed reality software superimposes a visual representation of how the child is positioned within the womb. Students can examine the orientation and actions of the baby from their specific vantage point in the room, and the instructor can modify the views and simulated situations as needed. As the state of the physical simulator in the room changes, the mixed reality overlay changes accordingly.[18]

Collectively, this range of technologies is referred to officially as **"Extended Reality" (XR)**, and that term encompasses Virtual Reality (VR), Augmented Reality (AR), and Mixed Reality (MR), as well as 360-degree video. However, in casual conversation, most of the time people just call all of this immersive technology-enabled experience simply "VR." The experiences range considerably from low-end experiences using merely a smartphone or a simple viewer, to augmented reality, to full-blown virtual reality like what people often think of as VR. These types of VR systems usually "display the virtual environment to users in real time, allowing them to experience the environment as if they were physically present." That is typically achieved "through a VR headset, which provides a stereoscopic view of the virtual environment and spatialised sound via multiple speakers synchronised with the user's movements."[19] This way, everything you see happens within the unit (sights, sounds, etc.), and you typically hold handheld devices that communicate with the base unit.

In many ways, this is simply a step up from the old Nintendo Wii that used **infrared (IR) light** to help the Wii Remote (Wiimote) determine its position and movement relative to the television screen. The technology behind this was called **optical sensor tracking**, and it used a sensor bar to relay the position of your props (steering wheels, bats, golf clubs, etc.) so that the character on screen would do whatever you do. Microsoft's Kinect was similar, also using **infrared (IR) light** to determine the user's location; however, it used **infrared depth-sensing**, which projected IR dots and read them back to map

---

18. Ibid.
19. Jeremy Bailenson and Molly Lesher (2024) in *OECD Digital Economy Outlook 2024* (Volume 1), 121.

depth and movement (which enabled facial recognition and gestures). However, the major difference – and improvement – with virtual reality is that you are completely immersed in the scene…you're not watching a character on a screen that is imitating your movements, but are instead *inside* the experience visually, seeing what that character sees.

You may have noticed that I am using the terms "virtual reality" and "metaverse" somewhat interchangeably. I wish I could be more precise, but unfortunately the terms, technologies, and experiences do often overlap (it would take a very complex VIN diagram to accurately depict it all, and even then, some concepts and terms are evolving as technology improves). Generally speaking, though, the **social** forms of VR are the ones that occur within the "metaverse." Those involve two-dimensional augmented reality games that are open-ended and played with thousands of other players simultaneously (like Pokémon GO and Fortnite) as well as virtual worlds that are more visually immersive and usually experienced using head-mounted display units (like Meta's Horizon Worlds, Engage, the former AltSpace VR, Big Screen, and VRchat).

But some of the **industrial** forms of VR also have their own more localized metaverse. For example, college campuses and businesses with digital twins can design their space to allow hundreds of users to simultaneously wander and interact. Similarly, "The Pickup Tower," one of the most frequently used corporate training modules (and on which Walmart has trained over a million of its associates)[20] and the NFL training model developed by Strivr do involve interaction with other users, but it is not an open-ended network. These applications (like Viverse, Spatial, Engage, and Virbela), can also utilize head-mounted display units and involve interaction with dozens, hundreds, or thousands of others. Because it is a very inexpensive and "safe" way to role play scenarios, training through devices and systems like this is rapidly increasing in business and corporate contexts, and likely to transform the way most training is conducted in the future.[21] An entity can also use a platform like Engage to create a limited-access, localized space that is still fully-immersive and accessed using head-mounted display units, but limited to only designated or authorized participants. It is questionable whether that would count as a "metaverse."

---

20. Jeremy Bailenson and Molly Lesher (2024) in *OECD Digital Economy Outlook 2024* (Volume 1), 125.

21. Annie Els, Michael Jones, & David Swisher (2022, December), "Q&A About Extended Realities and Gamification: The Future of Work, Training, and Education," live virtual panel discussion, Alumni Association, Indiana Wesleyan University, Marion, IN, http://www.kaltura.com/tiny/2t9u3

That is why I think the best way to define the "metaverse" is an open-ended network of multiple interconnected virtual spaces, where players customize their avatars which reflect their digital identity on the platform. Bailenson & Lesher acknowledge that the term "metaverse" is broad, not well-defined, and overused. In their definition, they explain that the term metaverse (which is sometimes called Web 3.0) "is the overall architecture that includes XR, block-chain technology and virtual worlds that offer real estate, currency and plat-forms for events and activities."[22] While that is entirely true, I think it overly complicates the issues and isn't helpful as a definition because it muddies the terms with overlapping concepts. What *does* matter about VR, however, is the potential of those fully immersive experiences, and what matters about the metaverse is the interactive social engagement that can happen within these virtual spaces, regardless of which technology people use to access it.

THE POTENTIAL OF FULLY IMMERSIVE VR EXPERIENCES

Jeremy Bailenson was an early adopter and scholarly thought leader on virtual experience and the science and evidence behind its experiential and learning power. He runs the Virtual Human Interface Lab at Stanford University where a significant amount of VR testing and research is being generated, and he's ALSO the co-founder of Strivr (a corporate training VR solutions pioneer). In his book *Experience on Demand* (2018), he explains:

> When VR is done right, all the cumbersome equipment – the goggles, the controller, the cables – vanishes. The user becomes engulfed in a virtual environment that simultaneously engages multiple senses, in ways similar to how we are accustomed to experience things in our daily "real" lives. This is distinctly different from other media experiences, which only capture fragmented aspects of what our senses can detect. For instance, the sounds you hear in good VR don't come from a speaker rooted in one place, but instead, they are spatialized, and they get louder or softer depending on the direction you are facing (or if you are in a tracked environment, how close you move to the source of the sounds. When you look at something in VR, it is not framed by the dimensions of a monitor, or television set, or movie screen. Instead, you see the virtual world as you see the real one. When you look to the left or right, the virtual world is still there.

The introduction to Bailensen's *Experience on Demand* book describes Mark Zuckerberg's visit to the Virtual Human Interaction Lab at Stanford

---

22. Ibid., 120.

where he introduces first-time VR inquirers to "the plank." He says it is "one of the most effective ways to evoke the powerful sensation of presence that good VR produces."[23] When a team of us from Indiana Wesleyan University visited a VR Escape Room as part of our metaverse potential explorations, I decided to try this one out for myself. It was mind-blowing! You step into a virtual elevator, push a button, and then watch (through the crack in the doors) as the elevator takes you "up" 80 stories. When you arrive, you're presented with a 6-foot long wooden plank that extends out from the elevator over the cityscape, and you can look "down" and see the ground 80 stories below. That experience is captured in this must-watch video: https://tinyurl.com/Richies-Plank.

Now, you know *for a fact* that you're standing on a hard, level floor in a room a safe distance away from other obstacles, and you've seen others try it (and probably laughed as they reacted because it's so obviously "fake" from the observer's vantage point). But once you strapped on those VR goggles, the Head-Mounted Display unit, and your eyes see only the virtual world and your ears are covered with headphones that only hear the sounds of the in-game experience, all of your dominant senses are telling you otherwise. You "feel" like you're really there. Often people gasp, clutch their heart, or bend their knees to lower their center of gravity. Some even crawl. Pulses quicken, and fear often sets in. And yet, it's literally "all in your mind." There is no plank or elevator, and you're standing on solid ground. But tell that to your dominant senses! In the words of another famous VR-themed movie, "There is no spoon...you'll see that it is not the spoon that bends, it is only yourself."[24] This is why there is such incredible power and potential for immersive learning and experiential ministry with VR-empowered experiences.

The "plank" was simply using basic VR equipment, such as an Oculus or HTC Vibe head-mounted display unit. But imagine if you could add technology that captures your *movements* within the virtual world. Well, you can! This is the kind of immersive, interactive gameplay that my wife and I experienced in Indianapolis with our friends recently at a place called Sandbox VR...a place my friend Mike Jones connected us with. Six of us at a time were fitted with motion-capture equipment, and stood in an empty room that was lined with various capture cameras, fans, and mist sprayers (to help us experience wind, motion, and water sprays). We donned virtual reality headsets (similar to an HTC Vibe, which is a bit more advanced than Meta's Oculus) to wear and

23. Bailenson, *Experience On Demand*, 2.
24. *The Matrix* (1999), directed by Lana Wachowski and Lilly Wachowski, produced by Joel Silver (Warner Brothers Pictures, 1999), DVD (Warner Home Video, 1999).

view the experience through, and we were provisioned with "weapons" that were roughly-shaped objects made of dense foam that also had motion-capture sensors on them so that they would appear on-screen as swords, phasers, or battle axes. Then we commenced gameplay. In one experience, we fought through a horde of skeletons and a protective fire-breathing dragon to rescue a valuable shard, and in another we fought off spiders and aliens as we ascended a futuristic space elevator to defend a shipping port and deploy a crucial item.[25] It was incredibly immersive and felt amazingly realistic.

But it isn't all fun and games, either. A great use for this kind of technology within the church would be for illustrative teaching and interactive sermons: The pastor could take parishioners on a tour of Peter's house or the synagogue in Capernaum, or walk through the tabernacle or Solomon's temple in Jerusalem, and any parishioner who is wearing a head-mounted display unit or using a smartphone with the app enabled (or someone who displays their view on screen for others) could provide a fully-immersive, up-close-and-personal view as it happens, making the viewer feel like they are actually there, witnessing it in person. Or in a workshop or denominational conference, imagine taking a group of youth workers or counselors through a series of role-play scenarios using virtual environments to discuss how best to handle specific situations. It is often said that you don't really know how you'll react to a situation until you experience it firsthand; well, with VR, you can do just that, yet still review and analyze it later with no consequences.

Personally, I dream of the day I can take people to the hillside on the Sea of Galilee where Jesus delivered his Sermon on the Mount and let people experience it virtually. It won't be many years before I will be able to create a virtual world that simulates what that setting would have looked like, complete with realistic and immersive scenery as well as characters such as disciples, Pharisees, and curious onlookers. Using motion capture technology (like we experienced with Sandbox VR, and which Hollywood movies with realistic CGI characters typically use), I could re-enact scenes and scripted interactions, so that future virtual users could walk through the crowd, listen to Jesus teaching, stop and ask questions, and even observe the reactions of various onlookers up close and personal.

Realistically, this isn't that big of a stretch: All of the individual technologies that it would take to accomplish a project like this currently exist in 2025, but at the present time, it requires a very extensive (and cost-prohibitive) mo-

---

25. Words are so inadequate to convey what we experienced, so I recommend checking out some of the pics and video from our experience: https://tinyurl.com/SandboxVR-SwisherMay.

tion-capture set to both create it and a similarly-sized and costly platform in which to experience it.[26] Not only did we get to experience that at Sandbox VR, but our team from IWU got to experience two fully-immersive educational applications in an impressive experiential VR lab called "Dreamscape Learn" on a field trip to Arizona State University.[27] Given the exponentially accelerating pace of research and development in this area, and the increasing public embrace of immersive VR (and profitability), I am fairly confident that within the next 5-10 years, the equipment will be far more practical and mobile, the technology will be much more adaptable and user-friendly, and the costs will come down substantially. So, by 2030-2035 (and likely sooner), it should be entirely possible for a well-equipped larger church with the right equipment to create immersive virtual experiences like I am envisioning, and I can only imagine the possibilities for immersive church, ministry, and teaching experiences like this!

As we explore the possibilities and potential of ministry in the metaverse, let's revisit our fictional yet entirely plausible scenario to see what transpires:

PASTOR JEFF AND THE METAVERSE EXPERIMENT
Scene 2: Experiencing the Virtual Service

The team gathered in Pastor Jeff's office, adjusting their VR headsets. As the system loaded, the church conference room faded away and in its place, each participant saw a stunning virtual sanctuary. The space was surreal…towering stained glass windows glowed with shifting colors, a pulpit stood before them in front of a beautiful wooden cross, and sunlight streamed through the wide open roof that revealed a gorgeous sunny blue sky interspersed with clouds.

"Welcome to the service," a friendly avatar greeted them. "Feel free to explore before we begin, and if you have any questions, let us know."

As they wandered around the virtual space, they noticed avatars of various shapes and sizes. Some appeared as realistic human figures, while others took on fantastical forms – one even resembled a glowing sphere. Jeff raised an eyebrow at that. Another avatar flickered in and out, apparently struggling with their Internet connection.

Pastor Jeff muttered under his breath, "This is ridiculous."

Jordan, overhearing, grinned. "Keep in mind, this service isn't for you; it wasn't designed with you in mind. You've grown up in church, and

---

26. See "The Holodeck is Here" in Peter H. Diamandis & Steven Kotler (2020), *The Future is Faster Than You Think: How Converging Technologies are Transforming Business, Industries, and Our Lives* (New York, NY: Simon & Schuster), 133-135.

27. See https://dreamscapelearn.asu.edu/ for more information. For a video highlights reel, see ASU Online (2022, May 2), "Take a Virtual Field Trip to the Alien Zoo with Dreamscape Learn," Arizona State University, YouTube video, accessed March 4, 2025, https://www.youtube.com/watch?v=m-T1z8Lx6r4

church to you is pews, pulpits, and stained glass in a physical building. But the folks who attend here grew up as digital natives, and they do VR all the time. For them, THIS is normal, and what's weird – or even ridiculous – to them is pews, pulpits, and stained glass."

Then the worship began. Unlike a pre-recorded livestream, this was surprisingly interactive: Many congregants lifted their hands, or clapped, and some gyrated or bowed. Others used in-world reactions like floating hearts and thumbs-up emojis to indicate their responses and reactions. When the sermon started, a familiar avatar whom they had met earlier (evidently the pastor) appeared in front, standing behind the pulpit and walking around naturally, while gesturing towards a floating Scripture passage.

Jeff was taken aback by the level of engagement. People responded, posted reflections in the chat, and even formed discussion groups immediately after.

Then came the testimony time.

A woman's voice spoke: "I'm Maria. I've been coming here the last few months, and I am grateful for this church community. I have an autoimmune disease that keeps me home most days, and this is my only church. I know some people question why we do church this way. But I love how you all pray with me, study Scripture with me, answer my questions, and even hold me accountable. I need that. And if that's not real, I don't know what is."

As the service continued, Jeff observed a moment of deep worship: An avatar in a wheelchair lifted their hands in praise, then slowly rose out of their chair, twirled around several times, then relaxed and hovered several feet above. Sarah smiled, and explained, "That's Frank. He's been paralyzed since his teenage years from a diving accident. But here in VR, he's not bound by physical limitations."

Another typed in the chat, "I needed this so much. Thank you for creating a space where I belong."

Jeff frowned. He hadn't expected this level of sincerity or interaction. In fact, it seemed they were even more expressive and engaged than his own congregation was.

The worship experience in VR was unlike anything they had imagined. As the team observed, they saw a real-time prayer circle forming near the back of the virtual church. People gathered around, laying virtual hands on a man's avatar. The chat filled with words of encouragement and sincere prayers

Jordan motioned toward the prayer group. "That guy? He's a soldier stationed overseas. This is his only way to join a church in real time because he's always on patrol when the chapel at the base meets."

Pastor Jeff raised his eyebrows again. "I didn't think about military personnel. We've never been able to minister to people like that before."

Sarah nodded. "Or people in hospitals. Or those with social anxiety. Or people in restrictive countries where attending church at a physical building simply isn't an option."

For the first time, Elder Mark looked intrigued rather than skeptical. He wasn't quite sure what to make of it, but the sincerity and depth of engagement was surprisingly…real.

As the service concluded, several of the avatars who were obviously regulars invited them to join a discussion group on a hillside afterwards. So the team made their way out the virtual doors, across a bridge over a gurgling creek, and followed a winding path toward a grove of trees which appeared to be swaying in the wind. There a set of rocks, stumps, and floating lily pads beckoned, grouped amidst a group of signs with Scripture verses. The team sat, wandered, and floated, taking it all in.

The discussion was incredibly insightful. People opened up freely, asking good questions, even hard questions. And avatars of all types responded, offering affirmations, challenges to consider, encouragements, and prayer.

As they left, the team was quiet, pondering the experience they had just observed. Jordan quietly said, "I look forward to debriefing with you back in the office."

OUTREACH MINISTRY OPPORTUNITIES IN THE METAVERSE

So, let's revisit the idea of the "metaverse." Thinking of the wider, open-ended social versions…who hangs out in these virtual spaces? Real people from all walks of life, but especially hurting people. People who are frustrated, lonely, strung out, burned out, tired, curious, or dissatisfied with life as they know it. Admittedly, different metaverse platforms tend to cater to different audiences, and because they have different protocols, expectations, and filters, they inevitably tend to attract different types of people or varying demographics. However, one very common theme I see reported consistently from digital missionaries and metaverse pastors is that a significantly high percentage of the people who populate metaverse spaces are atheists, agnostics, unchurched, de-churched, or spiritually seeking or dissatisfied people.[28]

Why is that? Well, some turn to the metaverse out of curiosity or boredom, while others are seeking entertainment, an escape, or a way to disconnect from the challenges and stresses of real life or to get away from the judgementalism of peers and critics and go somewhere they can be anonymous and yet

---

28. Jeff Reed (2022), *VR & the Metaverse Church: How God is Moving in This Virtual, Yet Quite Real, Reality* (Dallas, TX: Leadership Network).

known or appreciated without anyone caring what they actually look like.[29] Some actively seek dialogue and want to meet people, while others simply want to get away from people. The Cheers theme song seems especially fitting here: "Sometimes you want to go Where everybody knows your name, And they're always glad you came; You want to be where you can see, Our troubles are all the same; You want to be where everybody knows your name."[30] That describes the draw of the metaverse quite well. The same things that draw people to a bar also attract people to the metaverse (and I think it's no coincidence that they are the same desires that attract people to caring and considerate churches). We call it Biblical community; it's what everyone is craving, yet often simply doesn't know how to find.

In 2023, thanks to an invitation from my denomination's church multiplication department and a mini-grant through my university,[31] I was blessed to be able to participate in the Metaverse Church Learning Community, a ministry of Leadership Network. It was coordinated by digital church pioneer Jeff Reed in partnership with TheChurch.Digital and DigitalChurch.Network. Through that opportunity, I spent considerable time getting to know many metaverse pastors and VR ministry leaders, and through them I was introduced to the earliest pioneers: Daniel Herron, who started the Robloxian Christians church network in 2011 (when he was 11),[32] and DJ Soto, who started the very first church in the metaverse in 2016, called Virtual Reality Church.[33] Their sense of missionary calling to the unique culture of the metaverse is undeniable.

My friend Jason Poling (also a metaverse pastor, based out of Yuba City, California) elucidates this connection in a great whitepaper he wrote on the "Theology of the Metaverse."[34] Drawing clear purpose and example from both David Livingstone's ministry in Africa in the 1800s and the apostle Paul's ministry to the unchurched, Poling observes:

> Throughout the history of the Church, Paul's model of cultural adaptation has been followed by countless missionaries, and at times, not without a little con-

29. Personal conversations with multiple VR and metaverse pastors, especially Stewart Freeman, Jason Poling, Stuart McPherson, Joey Santos, and DJ Soto. See Jeff Reed's (2022) *VR & the Metaverse Church* for multiple very insightful personal reflections and descriptions from most of these digital missionaries.

30. Gary Portnoy (1982), "Where Everybody Knows Your Name," The Cheers Theme: Music, accessed Mar. 3, 2025, https://www.garyportnoy.com/cds-cheers-theme.

31. I was serving as "Digital Church Architect" as part of an exploratory research and development project for The Wesleyan Church and also evaluating the potential of "digital church" opportunities for Indiana Wesleyan University.

32. Daniel Herron (2018, Dec. 11), "Daniel Herron: Lessons from The Robloxian Christians Online Church," *Faith & Leadership*, accessed Mar. 3, 2025, https://faithandleadership.com/daniel-herron-lessons-the-robloxian-christians-online-churc.

33. VR Church (n.d.), "VR Church in the Metaverse," accessed Mar. 3, 2025, https://www.vrchurch.org.

34. Jason Poling (2022), "A Theology of the Metaverse" [White paper], Cornerstone Church of Yuba City, accessed Mar. 4, 2025, https://bit.ly/TheologyOfTheMetaverse

troversy within the established, sending churches. These churches simply could not understand the culture the missionaries were seeking to reach. Today is no different. God in His sovereignty has ordained the emergence of the Metaverse. This unique culture requires some degree of adaptation on the part of missionaries seeking to reach these largely unchurched and young digital natives from around the globe.[35]

The reason I think this is so essential for pastors and ministry leaders to understand and encourage is that, although signs of Christianity seem to be everywhere and most towns in America have dozens (and in many cases, hundreds) of churches, there are still huge pockets of cultural expression – and even resistance – in the U.S. where the work of Christ is barely known. These are places where people live their entire lives without any redeeming presence of Christ-followers, places where a church is just a relic of a bygone era or a place where you go for weddings or funerals. These communities can be found in abundance in the metaverse, but these same denizens of the metaverse will never darken the doors of your church or mine.[36]

INSIDE THE METAVERSE: HOW WORSHIPING IS GOING VIRTUAL

Indeed, DJ Soto, the pastor who established the very first VR expression of Church observes, "There are people who come to our church, VR Church and MMO Church, that would never step foot in a church, and I think that's really important to consider."[37] To better understand the unique opportunity and the driving passions of those who minister there, I highly recommend that all pastors and ministry leaders (and anyone intrigued with the missional potential of this type of ministry) watch this 5-minute interview from the NBC

35. Ibid.
36. David Swisher (2024, April 22). "Inconceivable! Field Preaching, Digital Church, & the Metaverse."
37. Jason Daye (July 28, 2021), "DJ Soto: Why Virtual Reality Church Is Just as Legitimate As Gathering in Person," *Church Leaders*, accessed Mar. 4, 2025, https://churchleaders.com/podcast/402303-dj-soto-virtual-reality-church-legitimate.html

Today Show featuring my friend, metaverse pastor Jason Poling:[38] https://bit.ly/MetaverseChurch-NBC

INSIGHTS FROM CHURCH HISTORY

Although virtual reality and metaverse platforms may seem to be extremely modern technological challenges, this certainly isn't the first time in church history when ministry leaders have had to wrestle with the appropriateness of specific modalities, the missional aspects of some places, or question whether God could work there. In fact, John Wesley struggled with a very similar dilemma when he first learned about field preaching and was challenged to try it. His introduction to field preaching came about due to the amazing success that his Oxford friend George Whitefield was having.[39]

Even the secular media of the day noted that Whitefield was regularly drawing crowds of 5,000-6,000 at Hannam Mount (a hilltop outcropping near Bristol which served as an ideal elevated point from which to preach), and on some occasions, multitudes as large as 20,000.[40] Whitefield was familiar with Wesley's preaching power and organizational prowess,[41] and asked for his help. But up to this point, John Wesley had only preached in regular church services in England.[42] Uncertain about whether he should help with the open-air meetings in Bristol, he submitted the decision to the Fetter Lane Society. After casting lots, it was decided he should go.[43] Yes, you read that right… Wesley couldn't decide if he should venture into it, and resorted to casting lots to make the decision for him. But at least he did it in a spirit of accountability with his close friends and colleagues.

That decision led to one of the most fascinating entries in John Wesley's *Journal*:

> "In the evening I reached Bristol and met Mr. Whitefield there. I could scarcely reconcile myself at first to this strange way of preaching in the fields, of which he [Whitefield] set me an example on Sunday; I had been all my life (till very lately) so

---

38. NBC Today Show, S2022, E183, "How the Metaverse is Changing the Way People Attend Church," produced by Erin Farley, directed by Lee Miller, featuring Jason Poling and Cornerstone Church of Yuba City, aired Aug. 3, 2022 on NBC, 2022, accessed Mar. 2, 2025, https://www.today.com/video/how-the-metaverse-is-changing-the-way-people-attend-church-145390661832

39. Significant portions of this section are adapted and expanded from a presentation I first gave at the Wesleyan Theological Society in March 2023 titled, "Inconceivable! Field Preaching, Digital Church, & the Metaverse: Embracing John Wesley's Legacy of Innovation to Inform the Virtual Ministry of Tomorrow," which were later published in *Didache: Faithful Teaching*, 24:1 (Spring 2024). ISSN: 15360156 https://didache.nazarene.org/index.php/volume-24-number-1

40. Howard Snyder (2014), *The Radical Wesley: The Patterns and Practices of a Movement Maker* (Franklin, TN: Seedbed), 38-39.

41. Ibid., 39.

42. Ibid.

43. Ibid.

tenacious of every point relating to decency and order that I should have thought the saving of souls almost a sin if it had not been done in a church."[44]

That was on a Saturday (March 31st). The next day, he spoke to a little society on Nicholas Street about the Sermon on the Mount, reflecting in his *Journal* that this (Jesus' own example of delivering his famous teaching) was "one pretty remarkable precedent of field preaching."[45]

While we don't know the extent or substance of Wesley's dialogues with Whitefield on the matter, Kenneth Collins reasonably speculates, "Whitefield probably convinced Wesley that he could save more souls outside a church than within it, especially since Wesley was now being excluded from so many churches."[46] Whatever it was that Whitefield shared, it worked: On the following day (Monday), Wesley explains, "At four in the afternoon, I submitted to be more vile and proclaimed in the highways the glad tidings of salvation, speaking from a little eminence in a ground adjoining to the city, to about three thousand people."[47] In fact, that week he preached outdoors *multiple* times...to a crowd of about a thousand in Bristol, then 1,500 atop Hannam Mount, then about 5,000 at Rose Green (on the other side of Kingswood).[48] As Howard Snyder notes, "The Wesleyan Revival had begun," and characteristically, Wesley began organizing.[49]

Furthermore, "within a few months of beginning field preaching in 1739, Wesley had set up the basic structure that was to mark Methodism for more than a century."[50] Fairly often at these open-air gatherings, there were outbursts and disturbances (understandably), and his older brother Charles – also raised an Anglican and accustomed to the "decency and order" of church services – raised concerns about the appropriateness of preaching in such places and dealing with so many improprieties like that. In his response, John not only justified what he referred to as his "new measures," but chastened his brother. John replied to his brother Charles, "How is it that you can't praise God for saving so many souls from death, and covering such a multitude of sins, unless he will begin this work within 'consecrated walls'? .... But I rejoice to find that God is everywhere. I love the rites and ceremonies of the Church. But I see, well-pleased, that our great Lord can work without them."[51]

---

44. John Wesley, *Journal of John Wesley*, 29 March 1739, Ed. By Percy Livingstone Parker, Christian Classics Ethereal Library, https://www.ccel.org/ccel/wesley/journal.vi.iii.i.html

45. Snyder, *The Radical Wesley*, 39. Wesley, *Journal*, 1 April 1739.

46. Kenneth J. Collins (1999), *A Real Christian: The Life of John Wesley*, (Nashville, TN: Abingdon), 72.

47. Wesley, *Journal*, 2 April 1739.

48. Wesley, *Journal*, 8 April 1739.

49. Snyder, *The Radical Wesley*, 40.

50. Ibid.

51. Kenneth J. Collins (1999), *A Real Christian: The Life of John Wesley*, (Nashville, TN: Abingdon), 72; Frank

The same can most certainly be said about virtual reality and the metaverse. For the uninitiated, the virtual (often cartoonish) context can seem weird, unfamiliar, perhaps even questionable or disturbing, and quite often humanity will be on full display in all its rawness (people who haven't grown up in church and don't know church "expectations" will certainly express themselves naturally).[52] But as Ken Collins observes, "For the sake of giving the gospel as wide a hearing as possible, Wesley not only, at times, put aside the 'rites and ceremonies of the church,' not only preached outside consecrated walls, but he also violated the parish boundaries of the Anglican Church to the annoyance and frustration of many of its clergy."[53] Why? Because it worked!

As innovative and entrepreneurial as John Wesley was, he was even more pragmatic.[54] And if it was working and God was using it, who was he to deny it? In fact, Wesley justified his "new measures" by appealing to their effectiveness: "My ordinary call is my ordination by the bishop: 'Take thou authority to preach the Word of God.' My extraordinary call is witnessed by the works God doth by my ministry, which prove that he is with me of a truth in the exercise of my office."[55] As we wrap up our exploration of the possibilities and potential of ministry in the metaverse, let's revisit once again our fictional but entirely plausible scenario to see what they ended up deciding:

> **PASTOR JEFF AND THE METAVERSE EXPERIMENT**
> **Scene 3: Debriefing and Next Steps**
>
> Back in the real world, the team removed their headsets and returned to the office so they could debrief together.
>
> "Well," Pastor Jeff said, rubbing his temple. "That was...something."
>
> Elder Mark shook his head. "I'll admit, I didn't expect to feel anything. But hearing Maria's testimony hit me. I never thought about people who physically can't come to church."
>
> Jordan nodded. "And did you notice how engaged everyone was? Although there were certainly some distractions, I have never seen a church service so active, enthusiastic, and completely supportive and engaged."

Baker, ed. (1980), *The Works of John Wesley*, Bicentennial ed., vol. 25, Letters (Nashville, TN: Abingdon), 694-695.

52. Especially in metaverse platforms like Rec Room which have few filters and rules for interactions. Moderated environments generally tend to be safer spaces for first-time missionary pastors and church leaders. See Jeff Reed's (2022) VR & the Metaverse Church for more on this, including Stewart Freeman's firsthand testimony.

53. Collins (1999), *A Real Christian*, 72.

54. For more on this, see my article in *Didache*, where I primarily explore John Wesley's legacy of technological innovation.

55. Reginald W. Ward & Richard P. Heitzenrater, eds., The Works of John Wesley, Bicentennial ed., vol. 18, *Journals and Diaries* (Nashville: Abingdon Press, 1988), 223. As cited by Collins (1999), *A Real Christian*, 72.

Pastor Jeff leaned back in his chair. "I can see why people like it, but I still have questions. Like, how would we handle communion? Or baptism? Or ensure accountability?"

Jordan shrugged. "Those are great questions. But I'm not claiming to have all the answers. Why don't we talk to those VR church leaders and ask them how they handle these kinds of questions? Surely they've wrestled with these same issues and know how to do it." That response seemed to resonate well with the others.

Sarah leaned forward. "So, what's next? Do we take this seriously?"

Elder marked crossed his arms. "I'm not convinced. But I also can't ignore or deny what I saw. The prayer groups, the testimonies, the engagement, and the follow-up discussion. That was genuine."

Jeff sighed, then smiled. "I think we owe it to ourselves – and to people like Maria, Frank, and the soldier – to explore this further. I certainly don't want to move to this entirely, but I'm open to adding an option to reach those who are far more comfortable in metaverse spaces. Sarah or Jordan, is that something you would be open to leading if we do that?"

Both nodded agreeably. "Well, then I think we move forward with the three experiments and see where God leads."

If these concepts are new for you, my friend Jeff Reed's book *VR & The Metaverse Church* provides an outstanding introduction.[56] In it, he introduces the concepts, defines the terms, identifies the most widely-used platforms, explores the issues and applications, and introduces readers to about a dozen metaverse ministries and leaders. He also includes some great testimonies from metaverse pastors and from those whose lives have been changed through such ministries. It is no longer a question of "whether" or "if" God could work in this space; instead, Reed provides numerous tangible examples and first-hand testimonies of how God is actually moving already, where He is actively working, and how people are finding Jesus today in these virtual reality and metaverse spaces.

BIBLICAL VALUES & THEOLOGICAL IMPLICATIONS

Virtual Reality and metaverse contexts certainly raise a host of theological questions and issues, but you may be surprised to learn just how much Biblical wisdom and guidance pertains to it. Also, one of the most intriguing aspects of these conversations is that, in many cases, the objections that some raise based

---

56. Jeff Reed (2022). *VR & the Metaverse Church: How God is Moving in this Virtual, Yet Quite Real, Reality* (Dallas, TX: Leadership Network).

(presumably) on Scripture can also be justified, or even advocated for, based on those same verses, all depending on how you approach the subject and what presumptions and denominational or theological perspective you're coming from. This will become more apparent as we venture into it.

1. The Nature of Presence: Physical vs Virtual

One of the most controversial aspects of the metaverse is the challenge it poses for our understanding of presence, embodiment, and identity. Although digital spaces offer incredible opportunities for connection, evangelism, and innovation in ministry, they also force us to re-examine long-held assumptions about what it means to gather as the church, how we participate in worship services, and how we represent ourselves in digital spaces. For example what does it mean to "gather" as a church? After all, the Biblical word for church is ἐκκλησία (ecclesia), which refers to an assembly or gathering, and whose root words literally mean the "called out ones." Can that exist virtually?

As I mentioned in the online & livestream chapter, one verse often cited in criticism of technology-enabled worship is, "Let us not neglect meeting together, as some have the habit of doing. Rather, let us encourage each other, and all the more as you see the Day approaching."[57] However, advocates of virtual reality and metaverse ministry would readily explain that this is one of the important reasons WHY they meet virtually...and that by gathering in such spaces, they ARE meeting together, even when illness, physical impairments, geography, or life circumstances prevent them from meeting in person. Furthermore, Jesus reminds us that whenever two or three are gathered together in His name, He is there in their midst."[58] Again, depending on your assumptions and theological background, this verse could be read presumptively, as insisting on the importance of physically meeting together, or it can be seen as a validation that when two or more followers gather in virtual spaces, God is already there in their midst...in the metaverse.

The practices of the early church in Acts 2:42-47 are also relevant here. The psalmist observes that God's presence is everywhere...that there is nowhere where you can flee from God's presence, whether heaven, the depths, on the wings of the dawn, or even the far side of the sea.[59] Could that passage be affirming that God's presence is in cyberspace, virtual reality, and the metaverse, too? I think so. Solomon even reminds us that God does not dwell in temples made by humans, and they certainly cannot contain Him.[60] Furthermore, when Jesus

---

57. Hebrews 10:25 (EHV).
58. Matthew 18:20.
59. Psalm 139:7-10.
60. 2 Chronicles 6:18.

went out of His way to meet with the Samaritan woman (ostracized and rejected by Jews and her own community), she raised the same criticism that is often raised about metaverse worship gatherings today…about where it was acceptable to worship: "Our fathers worshiped on this mountain, and yet you Jews say that in Jerusalem is the place where one must worship."[61] Jesus promptly redirected her thinking, explaining that the "where" of worship isn't the issue at all: "A time is coming, and even now has arrived, when the true worshipers will worship the Father in spirit and truth; for such people the Father seeks to be His worshipers. God is spirit, and those who worship Him must worship in spirit and truth."[62]

Another question that begs to be asked is whether true fellowship can exist without physical embodiment. Both 1 John 1:3 and Romans 12:3-8 seem to emphasize the importance of such fellowship. However, the apostle Paul shares a lengthy reflection with the Philippians, emphasizing how he is "with" them, and underscoring his affection for them, while he is imprisoned and awaiting trial. In that passage, he even rejoices in their suffering while apart and celebrates how Christ will be exalted through it.[63] In fact, the majority of the New Testament (at least the parts Paul wrote) we have today because he was physically apart from them, unable to meet or converse in person. But, does virtual presence "count" as real presence? Elsewhere, Paul certainly makes that case: He speaks of being "present in spirit" with the church at Corinth and being with the church at Colossae "in spirit."[64] In fact, most of Paul's ministry involved showing up in person when he could and delivering greetings and letters whenever he couldn't be physically present. If anybody in Scripture understood the importance of fellowship and connection while apart (i.e., virtual presence), it was the apostle Paul.

2. Identity and Representation: Theological Concerns

One of the most common concerns and theological tensions involving the metaverse involves the role of avatars, those digital representations that users create and through which they navigate virtual spaces. These avatars can take nearly any form, from lifelike recreations to fantastical creatures. But this raises an important question: Does our representation in a digital space change who we are? In fact, one of the harshest objections and criticism I have ever encountered online when explaining metaverse and VR ministry is the claim that "you can't save (or disciple) an avatar," so how can this be "real" ministry? I always chuckle when I see that contention, because inevitably (1) the person making that claim is using a virtual representation of themselves (a screen-

---

61. John 4:1-45 (NASB), espec. v. 20.
62. John 4:1-45 (NASB), espec. vv. 23-24.
63. Philippians 1, espec. vv. 7-8, 13, 18, & 20.
64. 1 Corinthians 5:3-4; Colossians 2:5.

name or other digital identity) to represent themselves while debating me, and (2) they would have to deny the nature and primary ministry of Jesus to successfully make that claim. And (3) the fact that they get upset or bent out of shape while debating it only further confirms that avatars, screennames, and digital identities DO matter because they represent real people with real feelings, hearts, and emotions!

I think this is such a pivotal issue because it centers around the very incarnation of Christ: Paul declares that Jesus is "the image of the invisible God"[65] – i.e., the divine made visible and interactive within human history. The Greek word εἰκών (eikón) used there means "image, likeness, or representation," and it is derived from a root word that means "to be like" or "resemble."[66] That word carries the idea of an exact representation, much like how an avatar represents the presence of its user in a digital world. The author of Hebrews reinforces this, stating that Jesus is "the exact representation of His [God's] nature," and the word used for representation is the Greek χαρακτήρ (charaktēr), a term and concept for impressions that closely parallels the way identity is managed in digital and virtual spaces."[67]

So, in this sense, Jesus functions as the "avatar" of God in the sense that He became tangible and knowable to humanity in a way we could understand and relate to, representing God as a direct impression or "exact representation." The word "avatar" itself comes from Sanskrit (अवतार, avatāra), meaning "descent" or "manifestation" (and this was typically used in reference to Hindu deities taking on a physical form), so it is not a linguistic equivalent, but conceptually it follows the same idea. Jesus was fully God, yet He took on a form that allowed Him to walk among us, teach us, and ultimately redeem us; that's what an avatar does. He navigated our world in a representative and knowable form that we could relate to. Also, this comparison does not suggest that all avatars are inherently Christlike, but it does provide a theological precedent for representation in an alternate form without any loss of identity.

Another related question that we need to consider is whether we have a responsibility to reflect our real selves, or if digital self-expression is essential neutral or flexible? Scripture does call believers to integrity and truthfulness.[68] So, if avatars serve merely as masks for deception (as some critics perceive them), that would create a space for dishonesty and disconnection rather than genuine community. Those who think that argue that our avatars and screen-

---

65. Colossians 1:15.
66. "1504. eikón," *BibleHub Interlinear*, accessed Mar. 5, 2025, https://biblehub.com/greek/1504.htm
67. "5481. charaktér," *BibleHub Interlinear*, accessed Mar. 5, 2025, https://biblehub.com/greek/5481.htm
68. Ephesians 4:25, Colossians 3:9-10.

names online should always be faithful representations of our real selves. I would tend to disagree, however, because that is simply not how online and virtual spaces operate; anyone who shows up in a metaverse or virtual space with an actual name or avatar that precisely matches their real world persona would be immediately considered a noob and not be taken very seriously…they're just exploring, and obviously not a "real" player.

Plus, there is ample precedent for such creative expression. Even the apostle Paul, who was formerly called Saul, *changed his name* after his conversion to reflect his new-found identity in Christ. And in 2nd Corinthians, Paul even exhorts us, "Therefore if anyone is in Christ, this person is a new creation; the old things passed away; behold, new things have come."[69] Plus, identity can be truthfully represented even without exact matches. I mentioned earlier that my character in virtual worlds always dresses like Indiana Jones and has wings; this is an intentional choice of mine *to reflect my identity* (love of adventure and archaeology, professor, avid fan of linguistics and cultural artifacts, and yet brave and bold, even capable of flight). So although it may not "look" like me, it certainly IS me. And my screenname has deep meaning, too.

What also intrigues me about such criticisms of digital identity in online worlds is that those who make such complaints seldom acknowledge nor criticize the rampant forms of deception, manipulation, and hiding that routinely occur in physical church gatherings. My metaverse pastor friend Jason Poling articulates this well: "Many Christians attend physical church and yet they continue to hide. Just because someone sees your literal face and knows your given birth name, does not mean they truly *know* you. In fact, we have found that in many cases, we often learn more about the real lives of those in the Metaverse than we do of those in the physical Church."[70] I have experienced this as well. In fact, there is an immersive iPad-based game (Evony: The King's Return)[71] that I enjoy playing when I have free time. Although we are all global (I know players in Germany, China, the U.K., Lebanon, and the U.S.) and all of us have screennames, I know most of the regular players in my alliance fairly well; I even know where they live, what they do for a living, a bit about their family dynamics, what struggles they face relationally, and more. We've grieved together and prayed together over job losses, relationship struggles, natural

69. 2 Corinthians 5:17 (NASB). Note also how the verse immediately preceding reaffirms this representational avatar idea.
70. Jason Poling (2002), "A Theology of the Metaverse" [White paper], Cornerstone Church of Yuba City, accessed Mar. 4, 2025, https://bit.ly/TheologyOfTheMetaverse, 12.
71. See https://pc.evony.com

disasters, and more. So, while it might "seem" that we're all hiding behind our avatars, in a community like that, you get to know each other especially well.

3. Evangelism and Mission in the Metaverse

The metaverse certainly creates new opportunities for outreach that the Church should embrace. The sheer volume of people engaged in virtual spaces is staggering, and SO much larger than any communities where our churches are currently located. But they are also filled with need. After all, what tends to draw people to the metaverse also provides ample opportunities for redemptive change: People who spend time in virtual worlds are often lonely, hurting, struggling, questioning, or seeking. Sometimes they are looking for an escape, sometimes for a balm for the boredom, occasionally they are active looking for answers, and often they are looking for community. Virtual spaces are filled with people who don't fit in, have been cast out, are suspicious or distrusting of organized religion, embrace alternative lifestyles, don't feel like they belong, or are generally dissatisfied and searching for something. In short, people who inhabit the metaverse and virtual spaces need Jesus, just like those of us we encounter in physical places (there just tend to be a lot more in need in the virtual).

So, this makes it all the more important for pastors and ministry leaders who "get" it to do evangelism and mission work in the metaverse, as well as to establish a church presence. After all, our Great Commission tells us to "Go and make disciples of all nations, baptizing them in the name of the Father and of the Son and of the Holy Spirit, and teaching them to obey everything I [Jesus] have commanded."[72] And, "How, then, can they call on the one they have not believed in? And how can they believe in the one of whom they have not heard? And how can they hear without someone preaching to them? And how can anyone preach unless they are sent?"[73]

In Jesus' parable that He told to the Pharisees (in response to their reaction after he healed on the Sabbath), Jesus tells us, "When you make a dinner or a supper, do not invite your friends, or your brothers, or your relatives, or rich neighbors, so that perhaps they may also return the favor and pay you back. But when you make a feast, invite the poor, the crippled, the lame, the blind, and you will be blessed, because they cannot repay you. Certainly, you will be repaid in the resurrection of the righteous."[74] This is a perfect reminder for us, because typical Church ministries all too often cater to those who are

---

72. Matthew 28:19-20 (NIV).
73. Romans 10:14-15 (NIV).
74. Luke 14:12b-14 (EHV).

already churched, those we identify with best, those who are well-to-do or well-behaved, and who can return the favor. But that is not our mission nor calling. Later in that passage, after various invitees gave excuses, Jesus says, "Then the master said to the servant, 'Go out into the highways and hedges, and urge them to come in, so that my house may be filled.'"[75] If the metaverse and virtual reality aren't byways and hedges, then I don't know what is!

In many ways, ministry in the metaverse is comparable to the apostle Paul's experience on Mars Hill in Athens, where he engaged an entirely new cultural space. Standing in the Areopagus, he engaged with Greek philosophers on their own terms in their own spaces. He quoted their poets, used their language, and met them where they were, on their turf, without compromising the truth of the Gospel. If Paul were alive today, would he not do the same with the metaverse…engaging people in virtual spaces just as he engaged those in physical marketplaces? If people are spending significant hours of their lives in virtual spaces, then it is not just an option but an imperative for the Church to bring the Gospel into those spaces. Missionaries have historically traveled to the edges of the known world to reach people groups untouched by the Gospel. Today, some of the most unreached cultures and people groups are not in distant foreign lands, but in digital spaces where the church has yet to fully engage.

4. Ordinances and Sacraments in the Metaverse

One of the biggest questions and challenges with ministry in the metaverse is how to handle ordinances like baptism and communion when you can't be physically present. After all, Baptism in the early church was a public declaration of faith and the Great Commission calls us to baptize people, too.[76] So, if people get saved in the metaverse, can they get baptized there, too? Or do they need to come to a physical building? Likewise, Jesus took the Passover observance and instituted a new ritual of communion based on it, telling us "Do this in remembrance of Me."[77] Paul also recounts Jesus' institution of the Lord's Supper, emphasizing remembrance.[78] So if a church meets in the metaverse and wants to be faithful to Jesus' and Paul's teachings, can they observe communion virtually, too? Or do they need to come to a physical building and partake of actual physical elements?

Unfortunately, space does not permit me to explore this issue as deeply as I would like. After all, I only have a chapter to focus on VR and the metaverse, so

---

75. Luke 14:23 (EHV).
76. Acts 2:38-41; Acts 8:26-40; Matthew 28:19-20.
77. Luke 22:1-23 (NASB).
78. 1 Corinthians 11:23-26.

I will only devote just a few paragraphs to this issue. And, regrettably, there are no easy solutions. In fact, the answers to this are as nuanced and complex as the number of denominations who wrestle with this question. Jason Poling delves into this to some extent, but one of the things I like about Jason's approach is that his is a true hybrid church…they have a physical church building in Yuba City, CA, and they have modeled their virtual campus in the metaverse to look a lot like it.[79] They have full-time pastoral staff at the physical campus, but also have a dedicated "Metaverse Pastor" (Michael "Goose" Uzdavines) who leads the virtual ministries, along with a team of volunteers who serve in both Horizon Worlds and VRchat. So when someone gets saved, they can encourage them to get baptized in actual water in real life, and if they're not from that geographic area, they encourage them to get connected to a real-world church.[80] But if you watched that NBC Today Show feature video I referenced earlier in this chapter,[81] you also saw that they do indeed offer virtual communion and baptism. In my mind, this is the best possible option (both modalities, as needed).

Jeff Reed devotes several pages to this issue in *VR & the Metaverse Church*;[82] for the most part, he takes a symbolic approach (as do I) to the sacraments, so has no qualms with churches doing virtual sacraments. Of course, it is clear that when Jesus instituted the Lord's Supper (communion), he was using actual, physical elements.[83] However, multiple passages where communion is described also seem to convey that it was a symbolic act. After all, Jesus is using metaphorical language ("in remembrance of" and "this is my body");[84] obviously, he is not physically dying again, nor is he saying the disciples are drinking his actual blood or eating his actual body (that would contradict Jewish prohibitions against consuming blood, as well as be illogical and improbable to hold his own body and blood),[85] so this has to be a case of strong symbolism. Furthermore, when Jesus said, "this is my body," the Greek word he used was ἐστιν (estin),[86] which is often used in Scripture to mean "represents" or "signifies."[87] Likewise, Jesus intention-

---

79. Cornerstone Church of Yuba City (n.d.), "About Us," accessed Mar. 5, 2025, https://cornerstoneyc.com/vr/
80. Jason Poling (2002), "A Theology of the Metaverse" [White paper], 6.
81. NBC Today Show, S2022, E183, "How the Metaverse is Changing the Way People Attend Church," https://bit.ly/MetaverseChurch-NBC
82. Jeff Reed (2022), *VR & the Metaverse Church*, 53-58.
83. Luke 22:14-20.
84. Luke 22:19, Matthew 26:26-28.
85. Leviticus 17:10-14.
86. Luke 22:19, Greek/interlinear.
87. ἐστιν (estin) is the third person singular present indicative active verb tense of εἰμί (eimi): "1510. eimi," *Bible-Hub Interlinear*, accessed Mar. 7, 2025, https://biblehub.com/greek/1510.htm. Examples of its use to mean "represents" or "signifies" can be found in Matthew 13:38 and Luke 8:11.

ally instituted the Lord's Supper during Passover, a highly symbolic observance, to draw clear reference to the multiple ways in which he fulfills it.

Similarly, baptism is a highly symbolic experience as well; by it, we signify being buried with Christ to walk in newness of life.[88] It functions as a public declaration of faith.[89] Many faith traditions (especially Wesleyan-Arminian, Reformed, and Baptist) hold to this symbolic view, explaining that these ordinances are outward signs of what has happened on the inside, not saving works themselves. If that is the case, then why wouldn't a symbolic declaration in a virtual world be every bit as "real" and relevant as physical elements or actual water? What should matter most is the act of faith and dedicated commitment on the part of the person making the decision, not the physical or virtual nature of the elements themselves. A virtual baptism, witnessed by a gathered body of believers, still serves the same symbolic function of identifying with Christ's death and resurrection. A virtual communion, where believers partake in elements from their physical locations while united in a shared virtual space, still honors the intent and command of Christ.

One of the areas of pushback I often find intriguing is when people who don't understand or embrace virtual or metaverse ministry question whether it's real. Ironically, these same people have no problem reading letters from the apostle Paul in the New Testament, which were written to believers when he could not be physically present with them. Likewise, if a missionary on furlough shows pictures or videos of their work overseas, we don't even question its validity, even though we are not physically present. In each case, we are experiencing the letters, images, or videos remotely…through media technology. Perhaps it is the simulated environment of metaverse platforms that trips people up? However, every avatar you see in virtual reality, and every screen name you see in online platforms, is a person with a soul who is deeply loved by God. So, if you're real, and they're real, and you're using a simulated environment to interact with each other, wouldn't any evangelism, counseling, prayer, preaching, teaching, and even sanctification you do there be just as real?

I will admit that the ordinances are a bit trickier to navigate. However, the key question should not be, "Is this real?" but rather, "Does this modality fulfill the purpose of the ordinance?" If the purpose of baptism is *declaration and identification*, and the purpose of communion is *remembrance and participation*, then there is no inherent reason those ordinances cannot take place in the metaverse… provided they are done with reverence, intentionality, and communal account-

---

88. Romans 6:3-4; Galatians 3:26-27.
89. Acts 2:38-41.

ability. Personally, my preference would be that new believers experience water baptism and believers experience communion with actual physical elements, but I see nothing in Scripture that would invalidate the observance being achieved virtually in metaverse spaces. In fact, some of the highlights of my ministry have been when I got to witness new believers who found Christ online, through a livestream, or in the metaverse be baptized and/or partake of communion while physically present among others. It's a beautiful thing that showcases the reality of the inward change.

Nevertheless, if you are from a theological tradition that believes in real presence – trans-substantiation or consubstantiation – or if your denomination would struggle with virtual elements (or if you just want to explore this issue in much more depth), I would highly recommend reading Chapter 7 of Bock & Armstrong's (2021) *Virtual Reality Church* where they discuss various approaches to communion and baptism from a variety of theological perspectives.[90] And if it's important to your church (or to the believer), you can offer those opportunities or recommend that they find a local church in their area to experience it in person.

NEXT STEPS: LEADING WITH WISDOM

The metaverse is neither a utopia nor a dystopia; it is simply a new virtual space where people gather, interact, and explore meaning. As with every cultural and technological shift, the church has a choice: Ignore it, reject it, or engage with it faithfully. While digital spaces lower barriers for connection, they also can make accountability and discipleship more challenging. Pastors and ministry leaders who explore metaverse ministry need to ensure they are not simply being "cool" or catering to preferences but instead genuinely meeting real people where they are, and working patiently with them over time to form real disciples who experience growth, mentorship, and accountability. The question is not whether God can work in digital spaces (of course He can, because He is present everywhere[91]); the question is whether His people will be there, too.

The Metaverse is not a passing fad. It is an emerging space where people are forming relationships, exploring ideas, and even seeking spiritual connection. If we, as the Church, ignore it simply because it is unfamiliar or unconventional, we risk missing an entire mission field – a field that is already popu-

---

90. Darrell L. Bock & Jonathan J. Armstrong (2021), *Virtual Reality Church: Pitfalls and Possibilities*, Chicago: Moody, 201-234.

91. Psalm 139:7-10

lated with spiritually curious but institutionally skeptical individuals. While the idea of worshiping, discipling, or evangelizing in a virtual space may feel foreign, it would be helpful to remember that every new technology and all of the major technological shifts in history have initially felt unnatural before it became integrated into normal life. The question is not whether God can work in digital spaces, but whether His people will be there to meet those He is already drawing.

A CALL TO PROACTIVE LEADERSHIP

This metaverse and VR storm has been forming for quite some time, and it's a big one. The role of the wise ministry leader is not to fear it, but to be prepared. While some may be tempted to dismiss or ignore the shifts taking place, history has shown that technological and cultural transformations rarely wait for the Church to catch up. What may seem like an experimental niche or passing fad today could be a dominant mode of engagement tomorrow, and since this one has been around and growing for considerable time, I think it's going to be a major paradigm shift (I suspect that we have all underestimated it).

That is why it is critical to pay attention now. I do not expect every pastor, leader, or church to run headlong into this space. But I do believe that understanding it, evaluating it, and discerning its opportunities and risks is essential to leading well in the years ahead. That is, after all, my primary purpose in this book – to provide an early warning system so that pastors and ministry leaders are not caught off guard by the rapid technological changes that are already shaping our culture. The goal is not reckless innovation, nor blind rejection, but thoughtful engagement that ensures the Church remains both faithful and effective in the midst of change.

PRACTICAL STEPS FOR IMPLEMENTATION

If you want to move forward with exploring the potential of virtual reality and the metaverse, discovering how you could utilize it in your ministry, I would recommend starting small, experimenting thoughtfully, and engaging with purpose. Rather than treat it like an all-or-nothing proposition, instead, be strategic. How one church might use it will likely be entirely different than how another church uses it in their context, and that is perfectly OK.

Here are a few ways to begin:

1. Identify Who in Your Church is Already Engaging in Digital Worlds

Chances are, you already have members – especially younger generations – who already spend significant time in virtual spaces like Roblox, Minecraft, VRChat, or Meta's Horizon Worlds. Instead of assuming that the metaverse is foreign to everyone in your congregation because it's unfamiliar to you, start by asking around to learn who else is using it. The same goes for Virtual Reality platforms. Changes are fairly good that a healthy percentage of your younger adults work in jobs where they have participated in training that was conducted using VR, or they bought VR headsets for their kids (or grandkids) recently, or they may be spending time in VR themselves.

You should engage in conversation with them. Ask them what it's like, what they enjoy, and what they think about the platform. Ask them what they think the future holds with this technology, and whether they – or their kids – have been wanting to explore VR or the metaverse further. Ask them about the people they meet in virtual worlds, how their faith informs the connections they make, and what kinds of church involvement or presence in these spaces might be meaningful or helpful. Consider forming a discussion group within your church to explore how digital engagement might play a role in discipleship, outreach, or even community building (but if you do, make sure you don't stack the deck with either naysayers or advocates, but bring together a healthy cross-section of your congregation; make sure you have some who are already active and using it regularly, some who are open to it and seeking possibilities, and some who may be apprehensive or uncertain).

2. Visit a Metaverse Church

The best way to understand the potential (and the challenges) of ministry in virtual spaces is to experience it firsthand. So why not visit a metaverse church service and observe how they worship, fellowship, and engage? In fact, I would recommend visiting several different churches, and hopefully visiting each more than once so that you're not basing your impressions solely on a one-time experience. Ideally, take the time to meet some people, whether that's by chatting with people who approach you, attending a discussion group, or wandering the space and greeting some avatars you meet. Avoid churchy language, and resist the urge to criticize or preach (remember, you are a guest); this subculture welcomes authentic engagement and genuine questions, but resists and distrust anyone who's pushy or comes across as self-righteous. Rather than visit metaverse spaces solo, I would recommend that you have several leaders from your ministry join you in these visits; spend some of that time together, but also explore independently. Then gather to debrief afterwards. You may even want to reach out to the pastor and schedule a meeting with them and/or their leadership team to follow up and better understand after you have made a series of visits. These can be very enlightening and insightful.

Some churches in the Metaverse I would recommend visiting include Lakeland Church,[92] Cornerstone Church – Yuba City,[93] VR MMO Church,[94] Oasis Church VR,[95] and ChurchOne Community Church.[96] I have visited all of these in the metaverse and know that their services are geared toward seekers and the curious; they are designed for those who have never stepped foot in a church building.

As you attend, ask yourself:

- What aspects of this experience feel familiar? What feels different?

- Why is that? (how much of your cognitive dissonance is simply because it's different than you're used to, and how much is because it's made for a different audience?)

- What kinds of people and personalities does this gathering attract?

- What are the common elements you recognize from your own church experience, and how is their expression different than you have experienced it? Why is it different?

- Why do you think this type of experience is attractive, experiential, and "real" to those who attend it?

If this seems too overwhelming to consider or too big of an investment at this stage in your ministry, you should at least visit their websites, read information about their VR/metaverse campuses, and watch any videos they provide about the experience (or search for them on YouTube).

3. Explore the Potential for Digital Discipleship

Beyond Sunday services, consider how discipleship and spiritual formation could take place in digital spaces. Many metaverse churches host small groups, Bible studies, prayer meetings, and even one-on-one discipleship and mentoring in virtual worlds. Could your church use VR spaces to connect with members who are homebound, deployed in military services, or living in

---

92. https://www.lakeland.church/vr - Currently meeting in Big Screen (previously in AltSpace VR)
93. https://cornerstoneyc.com/vr/ - Currently meeting in Horizon Worlds and VR Chat (previously in AltSpace VR and Rec Room)
94. https://www.vrchurch.org/guide - Currently meeting in Rec Room and VR Chat
95. https://oasischurchvr.org/about/ - Currently meeting in VR Chat (previously in AltSpace VR and Spatial.io)
96. https://visitonecc.com/metaverse/ - Currently meeting in Spatial.io

remote or closed locations where gathering together at a physical building isn't an option? Test the waters by creating an experimental group that meets virtually for discussions, teaching, or prayer. You could even host a small group or an event in a digital space…or volunteer to serve or help in a metaverse church.

If you're not ready to try this out in VR/metaverse spaces yet, or if you don't have (and aren't ready to borrow or invest in the equipment), you could just try connecting with people during the week using technology like Zoom, Teams, or other kinds of live videoconferencing. If you're ready to go a step further, consider hosting a small group, outreach event, or digital ministry gathering in a virtual world. Many VR platforms offer free, customizable spaces where groups can meet and interact. Alternatively, you could volunteer to serve in an existing metaverse church for a season (they will likely want you to attend for awhile before serving). Rather than launching something from scratch, offer to observe, participate, and assist with digital hospitality, prayer ministry, or small group leadership. These experiences will give you a clearer sense of the possibilities without requiring a long-term commitment up front.

RESOURCES FOR FURTHER EXPLORATION

Books & Articles

If you want to read more to better understand these possibilities, I would recommend:

- *VR & the Metaverse Church* (2022) by Jeff Read – it's short, and concise, and filled with tangible examples and firsthand testimony. Start with this.

- *Virtual Reality Church* (2021) by Bock & Anderson – Very helpful if you want to go deeper and learn more.

- *Experience on Demand* (2018) by Jeremy Bailenson – ideal for those who need more, such as the research evidence and rationale for VR experiences; it is a secular book on the power and impact of VR, but extremely useful for diving deeper.

- "Theology of the Metaverse" [white paper] (2022) by Jason Poling – very helpful for understanding the theological implications further than I have unpacked here (also, Bock & Anderson dive much deeper into the theological aspects, too).

- Digital Transformation of the Church Repository – Early in the COVID-19 pandemic, Seattle Pacific University hosted a virtual conference on this theme, and all of the presentations and papers presented were archived here. It is an open, growing collection of theological and technological resources supporting the digital transformation of churches. https://digitalcommons.spu.edu/churchdx/

Metaverse Ministry Networks & Communities:

- **TheChurch.Digital** – Founded by Jeff Reed, this platform provides training, networking, and discussions on digital ministry. TheChurch.Digital resources digital missionaries and pioneers to make disciples in digital spaces. www.thechurch.digital

- **Digital Missionary Conference** – An international gathering for pastors and digital missionaries, offered both online (Altar Live) and in virtual reality (Spatial.io), which explores. First debuted in April 2025, so hopefully it will continue in future years. www.thechurch.digital/conference

- **Digital Church Next** – Exponential's NEXT ministry initiative is the pioneering arm of Exponential that explores innovative models, methods, and approaches for church planting and multiplication. This one is led by Mark Lutz (who planted Lux Digital Church) and is focused on digital, virtual, & metaverse church planting. https://exponential.org/digital-church-next/

The Church has always been at its strongest when it engages new frontiers with wisdom, faith, and intentionality, and the emergence of virtual reality and metaverse possibilities is no different. It is a space where people are already gathering, searching, and forming relationships, and although it might feel strange or foreign to us, it isn't to chose who regularly spend time in these spaces and identify with this subculture. If we ignore it or resist it because it feels (and looks) so different than "church" looks to us, we risk missing an opportunity to meet people where they are…people who would never come to your physical church building, but might explore the possibilities of faith on their turf if it's presented in a familiar way. It is not only a wide open mission field, but a modern equivalent of what Paul did on Mars Hill at the Areopagus in Athens.

For those concerned about whether digital presence is "real" enough, we should remember that Jesus Himself redefined presence when He told the Samaritan woman in John 4 that worship was not about being in the right physical location, but about worshiping "in spirit and in truth." If presence is about engagement, connection, and participation in the body of Christ, then digital spaces can be meaningful extensions of real-world ministry. The storms of technological change are not something to be feared; rather, they are opportunities to lead with wisdom, adapt with discernment, and innovate for the sake of the Gospel. Those who prepare now will equip the next generation to navigate these spaces well. Those who wait will find themselves scrambling to catch up. The choice is ours.

Chapter 5

ON DEMAND & DRIVERLESS

Autonomous Transport & Delivery

The rapid growth of on-demand & subscription-based cloud services (streaming platforms over cable & broadcast, SaaS services, subscription models, & cloud hosting) was just the beginning of a massive paradigm shift in delivery expectations. Now rapidly emerging is the rise in distributed convenience delivery (like DoorDash & Grubhub, food & grocery delivery robots on university campuses, & Amazon drone delivery) and autonomous transport (driverless cars & passenger service).

This is no longer just sci-fi or theory, as actual devices and working models are already deployed on numerous campuses and in multiple cities where they are being perfected for large-scale rollout within the next few years. These disruptive changes will dramatically shift parishioners' expectations of church leaders and ministry involvement, how we order & obtain supplies, where & when we gather, and before long, even how the congregation arrives at Church.

Tesla's "We, Robot" unveiling in October 2024 creatively unveiled a future of driverless cabs. In this innovative and entrepreneurial showcase (one which was reminiscent of an Apple WWDC unveiling), Tesla, Inc's CEO was picked up and rode as a passenger in a sleek RoboTaxi.[1] These vehicles, also known as the Cybercab, are fully autonomous, two-seater electric vehicles designed for urban transportation; they feature a minimalist interior with no steering wheel, and thus rely entirely on Tesla's Full Self-Driving (FSD) system. The showcase event, which was broadcast live on X, featured 20 Cybercabs driving autonomously, taking attendees to various destinations around the Warner Brothers lot while dodging cyclists and bystanders.[2] Tesla fans in attendance were "pleasantly surprised" and impressed by how flawlessly they navigated

1. Tesla (2024, Oct. 10), "We, Robot." Tesla Live, Live Video Broadcast on X, Oct. 10, 2024, 10:58 pm, 53:00 - 1:18:00, accessed Nov. 9, 2024, https://x.com/i/broadcasts/1YqJDkbjazvGV
2. Tom Carter, (2024, Oct. 12), "A Tesla Fan Experiences the Cybercab for the First Time," *Business Insider*, accessed Nov. 13, 2024, https://www.businessinsider.com/tesla-elon-musk-fan-robotaxi-event-experiences-cybercab-2024-10

different paths and obstacles."[3] The event also debuted a fully autonomous 20-passenger RoboVan,[4] as well as robots for entertainment and service.

With approximately 1.1 million live viewers tuned in[5] (and millions more watching on demand later), it was by far one of the highest profile events for autonomous (self-driving) vehicles and many people's first awareness of the capability. Tesla's CEO proclaimed, "Our autonomous future is here."[6] However, the reality is that such technology has been in development for significantly longer and is very close to reaching maturity. Various attempts at driverless vehicles have been experimented with since as early as the 1920s, much of it spurred on by the U.S. military's need for a risk-free way to resupply troops.[7]

A major turning point occurred in 2004 when the Defense Advanced Research Projects Association (DARPA) developed a driverless car competition... the DARPA Grand Challenge. By a decade later, traditional automotive manufacturers like Mercedes, BMW, and Toyota were competing with tech giants like Apple, Google, Uber, and Tesla for market share, each experimenting with various designs and technologies as well as exploring the potential of neural networks for training data.[8]

Out of these, Waymo (Google's self-driving car spinoff) seems poised to dominate the market. Google's foray into self-driving technology began when Stanford computer science professor Sebastian Thrun (along with a team of 15 engineers on the Stanford Racing team) developed Stanley, which won the 2005 Grand Challenge (the vehicle is now on exhibit in the Smithsonian Institution's National Museum of American History) and Junior, which placed 2nd in the DARPA Urban Challenge in 2007. Thrun is the former director of the Stanford Artificial Intelligence Laboratory (SAIL), and in that role, he developed the AI which became the brains behind what was then known as the Google self-driving car project.[9]

Google promptly hired Thrun, and after almost two years of road testing with seven vehicles, they revealed to the world what they had been working on.[10] In 2018 they launched Waymo One in metro Phoenix, which opened

---

3. Ibid.
4. Tesla (2024, Oct. 10), "We, Robot." 1:10:00 - 1:11:30.
5. Simon Alvarez (2024, Oct. 10), "Live Blog: Tesla 10/10 'We, Robot' Robotaxi Unveiling Event," *Teslarati*, accessed Nov. 13, 2024, https://www.teslarati.com/tesla-10-10-we-robot-robotaxi-unveiling-event-live-blog
6. Ibid.
7. Peter H. Diamandis & Steven Kotler (2020), *The Future is Faster Than You Think: How Converging Technologies are Transforming Business, Industries, and Our Lives* (New York, NY: Simon & Schuster), 13.
8. Ibid.
9. Diamandis & Kotler (2020), *The Future is Faster Than You Think*, 13.
10. Sebastian Thrun (2010, Oct. 9), "What We're Driving At," Google Official Blog, accessed Nov. 13, 2024, https://googleblog.blogspot.com/2010/10/what-were-driving-at.html

up to the public as a ride-hailing service in 2020. In 2022, they expanded the service to San Francisco (and to the Phoenix Sky Harbor airport), and the following year they expanded the ride-hailing service to Los Angeles.[11] In 2026, they plan to launch the service in Washington, D.C.[12]

When the Learning eXperience Design team I served on at Indiana Wesleyan University traveled to Phoenix in 2023 to learn from some of the best examples of innovation & future-focused educational technology, my longtime technology innovator friend and colleague Rick Bartlett reminded me that this was one of the places Waymo operates. So, I was ecstatic at the opportunity to try out riding in a self-driving car myself using Waymo. One of my colleagues dropped me off at a Wal-Mart, and using the iPhone app, Waymo One picked me up and took me to the airport. It was by far one of the smoothest and safest drives I have ever been on, and I was very impressed with how it navigated multiple lanes of traffic, intersections, merges and lane changes, roundabouts, and more…and especially how it handled unexpected interruptions and challenges (such as other drivers not following the rules or behaving unpredictably) admirably. I was also encouraged by the presence and ready assistance of Rider Support (which reminded me a lot of OnStar, but even better).[13] I captured the experience in a video that I have posted to YouTube, so you can experience the drive along with me: https://bit.ly/WaymoRide-DS (or you can scan the QR code).

Waymo isn't the only one, either: Apple, Uber, General Motors, Tesla, and Google have all been working on developing autonomous (self-driving) vehicles. GM has invested several billion dollars into GM Cruise since 2018, ultimately shuttering their operation in 2023 after an unfortunate accident. Apple reportedly spent over $1 billion a year developing Project Titan (their electric and autonomous vehicle), but in early 2024 shifted their focus to generative AI. Tesla has been working on theirs, but hasn't shared much about it until their recent reveal. In a very interesting twist, Uber opted to stop working on developing their own self-driving cars, and is instead now partnering with Waymo, Cruise, and UK-based Wayve to bring autonomous ride-sharing through their well-established Uber ecosystem.

11. Waymo (n.d.), "Waymo Story," *Our History*, accessed Nov. 13, 2024, https://waymo.com/about/#story

12. Indeed, when my son and I visited D.C. in October 2025, we saw more than one Waymo vehicle doing test rides to navigate the city. https://waymo.com/blog/2025/03/next-stop-for-waymo-one-washingtondc

13. David Swisher as WildcatTech (2023, Jan. 20), "My First Ride in a Self-driving (Driverless) Vehicle!, YouTube video, 9:58, accessed Nov. 10, 2024, https://www.youtube.com/watch?v=xble_WPkIsc

However, Waymo is by far the furthest along: By October 2018, Waymo had logged over 10 million miles of actual driving in 6 states and 25 cities across the U.S. – as well as billions of miles (10+) in simulation driving.[14] By January 2020, they had logged over 20 million actual driverless miles. As I write this, they have now logged over 25 million actual driverless miles (and that number will likely be well over 250 million).[15] After all, with a fleet of 20,000 autonomous vehicles driving hundreds of thousands of rides a day, Waymo is now logging over a million miles of driverless driving *every single day*, all of which helps to train and improve its AI.[16] The more it drives, the more roads, intersections, signage, unique situations, challenges, and obstacles it will encounter, giving the AI (& their human overseers) more training data and opportunities to discuss how the vehicles should handle them.

Although many people I talk with are hesitant and unsure about whether they would be comfortable riding in a driverless car, I believe this is a temporary familiarity hangup that will quickly become a non-issue for most people once the technology becomes commonplace and normative. After all, most of us felt the same way about using a mouse instead of a keyboard, using remotes instead of buttons and knobs to control TVs and stereos, using the Internet, talking to Alexa and Siri, and using other computer software and AI-powered technology: It felt weird and awkward the first few times, but then you quickly got used to it, and it now feels as natural as using your own hands. It won't take long for us to get used to driverless vehicles, too (in fact, in the cities where it has been operating, drivers are already getting used to seeing driverless vehicles on the road, and more and more riders are trying out the service).

The savings and possibilities are incredible: As Diamandis & Kotler explain it, "the average roundtrip commute is 50.8 minutes of hair-pulling, mind-numbing drudgery."[17] Imagine if instead we could sleep, read, relax, or catch up on news or social media, arriving at our destination relaxed, prepared, and ready to go?! Imagine no longer have to spend 15-20+ minutes searching for parking spots, and not having to fill up with gas frequently (most of these autonomous vehicles are electric). In Tesla's reveal, Musk highlighted the cost savings, noting (for example), that the average cost to operate a city bus is

14. John Krafcik (2018, October 10), "Where the Next 10 Million Miles Will Take Us," *Company News.*, accessed Jan. 20, 2023, https://waymo.com/blog/2018/10/where-next-10-million-miles-will-take-us

15. Waymo (n.d.), "Our Safety Philosophy," Safety, accessed Nov. 13, 2024, https://waymo.com/safety.

16. David Swisher as WildcatTech (2023, Jan. 20), "My First Ride in a Self-driving (Driverless) Vehicle!, YouTube video, 9:58, accessed Nov. 10, 2024, https://youtu.be/xble_WPkIsc?si=EliQpIk_Gx6tZva6. 4:16 – 4:30

17. Diamandis & Kotler (2020), *The Future is Faster Than You Think*, 15.

about \$1/mile, while the cost to operate the CyberCab they plan to roll out will be about one-fifth of that cost.[18]

JUST THE BEGINNING

But self-driving cars are just one fascinating aspect of a myriad of disruptive technologies that have been growing at an exponential pace and will undoubtedly influence church contexts and practices in years to come. Most of them are centered in the rapid growth of on-demand & subscription-based cloud services, and these are completely reshaping consumer expectations. For example:

- Streaming platforms like Netflix, Hulu, Disney+, and HBO Max now dominate the market. Not only have these services allowed consumers to "cut the cable," eliminating their reliance on cable TV or satellite, but in an ever-increasing bid to compete for market share, these companies are aggressively developing their own content to grow their base, increase their profits, and maintain consumer loyalty.

- Subscription-based music streaming services like Spotify, Apple Music, Amazon Music, and more are changing the way consumers listen to music. The days of purchasing physical cassettes and CDs to listen to in your home are rapidly diminishing, and in its place is a whole new approach to music listening habits…one where everything is customizable and personalizable, but you don't technically "own" any of it.

- On the computing side of things, Software as a Service (SaaS) is rapidly becoming the dominant model for corporate and higher education software purchasing: Rarely do we actually purchase and install software that is housed on the school or company's servers anymore; now it is nearly always hosted in a cloud-based online platform and we just pay a licensing fee to use that software and host our data. In recent years, this shift has made its way into consumer software as well, from downloadable software to online platforms.

This is just the beginning of a massive paradigm shift in consumer expectations. I still remember when there was a Blockbuster Video store a block or

18. Tesla (2024, Oct. 10), "We, Robot." 1:02:00 - 1:03:00. Eric Stafford & Elana Scherr (Oct. 10, 2024), "Tesla Robotaxi Is a Driverless Car That Will Cost Under \$30,000," Car & Driver, accessed Dec. 7, 2024. https://www.caranddriver.com/news/a62567491/tesla-robotaxi-reveal

so away from where I lived, and we had a membership there. Remember when you had to fill out an application, present your identification, pay a membership fee, and sign a rental agreement just to be able to check out movies there? Now there's only one Blockbuster store left in the country[19] because everything has gone digital. With all the streaming providers, rarely do you need physical media anymore (and a growing number of households don't even have players that can play them). Instead, we find a movie or series we want to watch and just pay the access fee to subscribe to it. Sometimes it's digitally downloaded to your device, but far more frequently, you simply gain access to it when you subscribe or pay the upgrade fee.

The same is true of software as well: When was the last time you stopped by Staples, Walmart, or Best Buy and bought software that included a physical CD you installed on your computer in order to use? These days, it is far more common to buy a box off the shelf which contains the user manual, promotional materials, and an access code for you to use to download the software. You can still buy some software products on a physical CD, but that is rapidly becoming the exception rather than the norm. What we're rapidly moving toward is a future where very little of that is even downloaded to your machine anymore, but instead you sign up and pay for access via a subscription, and everything you want to use is available online.

SHIFTING EXPECTATIONS

Streaming platforms, subscription-based services, and cloud-based Software as a Service have also opened the door to convenience delivery services like DoorDash & Grubhub that offer a plethora of fast food and restaurant options delivered right to your door for a nominal upcharge, delivery fee, and/or monthly subscription. At first, these were novelty services offering a unique convenience at a premium. But with the COVID-19 pandemic, they became practically ubiquitous. With dining rooms closed due to lockdowns, and in-person counter sales restricted due to masking mandates and social distancing, most restaurants and fast-food providers struggled to stay in business. Those that remained viable did so primarily by bringing the food to the customer through services like DoorDash and GrubHub, which offered contactless pickup and delivery right to the customer.

19. The last remaining Blockbuster Video store in the world is located in Bend, Oregon. The story of the Blockbuster chain's decline and the last store's resilience is creatively told in: "The Last Blockbuster" (2020), The Internet Movie Database (IMDb), accessed December 7, 2024, https://www.imdb.com/title/tt8704802

In fact, this model has become so successful that many fast food franchises that have historically operated their own delivery services (Domino's, Taco Bell, etc.) have transitioned toward it as well: Rather than employ their own delivery drivers and maintain a fleet of vehicles and cover the liability insurance…and train dedicated staff to handle this high-impact role, many fast food chains (and a growing number of restaurants) have opted to outsource that convenience to such service providers.

You may also recall some grocery stores experimenting with curbside pickup and "personal shoppers." Wal-Mart was one of the first, but Dillons/ Kroger and Meijer soon followed. It wasn't immediately popular, and initially seemed to take off most in wealthier areas where the customer base had substantial disposable income and limited time. But again, the COVID-19 pandemic changed all that: With the mask mandates and social distancing (as well as related fears and concerns), many consumers found it safer and more expedient to order online and then just swing by the store to pick it up, while a personal shopper employed by the store walked the aisles, scanned the products, and bagged everything for you. Now this service is fairly commonplace, and the majority of grocery store chains offer it.[20] In fact, a growing number of other businesses offer some variation of it as well.

And it doesn't stop there, either. When my IWU team visited the Arizona State University campus for our innovation exploration field trip, I was impressed to see a number of delivery robots navigating the campus.[21] These mobile robotic carts carried fast food, meals, and groceries in an insulated compartment directly to their destination, navigating pedestrians and cyclists, parking lots, vehicles, crosswalks, and more, traveling at an average pedestrian's walking speed. Starship Technologies, the company who operates those food delivery robots in partnership with the university, has them deployed on 56 university campuses in 55 cities around the U.S. as well as 56 other locations in Europe.[22] It is also well known that Amazon not only utilizes robots extensively in its warehouses[23] (in fact, they have an entire division dedicated to

20. In the area where I live, prime sections of the parking lot are reserved just for curbside pickup customers.
21. Arizona State University (2020, Sept. 4), "Starship Technologies, Aramark Launch Contactless Robot Food-Delivery Service at ASU," ASU News, accessed Dec. 7, 2024, https://news.asu.edu/20200904-asu-news-starship-aramark-launch-contactless-robot-food-delivery
22. Starship Technologies (n.d.), "University Campuses," Our Solutions, accessed Dec. 7, 2024, https://www.starship.xyz/operations
23. Amazon (2023, Oct. 18), "Amazon Announces 2 New Ways It's Using Robots to Assist Employees and Deliver for Customers," About Amazon > News > Operations, accessed Jan. 11, 2025 from https://www.aboutamazon.com/news/operations/amazon-introduces-new-robotics-solutions

developing this technology),[24]but also has been perfecting delivery drones, and is already utilizing them in multiple test markets.[25]

Other delivery services, including pizza franchises, have been exploring the potential of delivery drones. Domino's Pizza became the first to successfully use a drone to deliver pizza over 8 years ago (2016) in New Zealand, and they began actively testing drone delivery services in select markets in 2022.[26] In the U.S., Jet's Pizza in Detroit and Seattle's Pagliacci Pizza have also announced plans to introduce drone delivery of pizza.[27] As of December 2024, DoorDash customers in the Dallas-Fort Worth metroplex can get orders delivered from about 50 merchants by drone through Alphabet's Wing Aviation subsidiary,[28] and other retailers like Wal-Mart are also partnering with Wing to expand their drone delivery services. In January 2025, Wal-Mart announced plans to offer drone delivery for about 75% of the Dallas-Fort Worth metroplex.[29] In December 2022, Amazon's Prime Air service began testing drone deliveries in select U.S. locations, including College Station, Texas, and areas in Arizona, and conducted its first successful drone delivery in Italy.[30]

This used to be the stuff of science fiction and movies, but now it is a very present reality. Although drone delivery certainly isn't nationwide (yet) nor normative, and progress has been slowed by regulatory approvals (as well as testing of methods and customer reactions), it's definitely coming...and most likely only a few years away for most of us. Unfortunately, most pastors I talk with about these technological developments have not really given much thought to how these trends are going to reshape their ministry approaches in years to come. After all, these are just small novelty innovations happening sporadically over time, right? Think again! As Amy Webb deftly explains,

24. Amazon (2024, Oct. 9), "Meet the 8 Robots Powering Your Amazon Package Deliveries," About Amazon > News > Operations, accessed Jan. 11, 2025 from https://www.aboutamazon.com/news/operations/amazon-robotics-robots-fulfillment-center

25. Amazon (2023, Oct. 18), "Amazon Announces 8 Innovations to Better Deliver for Customers, Support Employees, and Give Back to Communities Around the World," About Amazon > News > Operations, accessed Jan. 11, 2025 from https://www.aboutamazon.com/news/operations/amazon-delivering-the-future-2023-announcements

26. Skydrop (2023, July 14), "SkyDrop and Domino's Expand Drone Delivery," YouTube video, 1:21, accessed Feb. 22, 2025, https://www.youtube.com/watch?v=mSwEGUhLm1A

27. Adam Wahlberg (2024, April 22), "Panera and Jet's Pizza To Offer Drone Delivery in Select Markets," Food on Demand: The Intersection of Food, Technology, & Mobility, accessed Feb. 22, 2025: https://foodondemand.com/04222024/panera-and-jets-pizza-to-offer-drone-delivery-in-select-markets/

28. Jess Weatherbed (2024, Dec. 18), "Alphabet's Wing Will Deliver DoorDash by Drone in Dallas-Fort Worth," The Verge, accessed Feb. 22, 2025: https://www.theverge.com/2024/12/18/24324111/alphabet-wing-doordash-drone-deliveries-dallas-fort-worth

29. Walmart (2024, Jan. 9), "Sky High Ambitions: Walmart To Make Largest Drone Delivery Expansion of Any U.S. Retailer," Wal-Mart > News, accessed Feb. 22, 2025: https://corporate.walmart.com/news/2024/01/09/sky-high-ambitions-walmart-to-make-largest-drone-delivery-expansion-of-any-us-retailer

30. Umar Shakir (2024, Dec. 6), "Amazon Just Completed its First Delivery by Drone in Italy," The Verge, accessed Feb. 25, 2025: https://www.theverge.com/2024/12/6/24314789/amazon-drone-test-italy-prime-air-delivery

"Today's fringe is tomorrow's mainstream."[31] We tend to (mistakenly) presume that if it's not something I regularly use or need or experience, it doesn't affect me. But the reality with disruptive technology innovation is that it WILL impact you significantly as the idea catches on and more and more consumers seek it out or expect it, at which point more vendors will compete for market share. So, by the time most of us realize it's a trend, we will have already missed prime opportunities to embrace it, and we are then a late adopter.

Furthermore, these disruptive changes will dramatically shift parishioners' expectations of church leaders and ministry involvement, how we order & obtain supplies, where & when we gather, and before long, even how the congregation arrives at Church.

IMPLICATIONS FOR CHURCH MINISTRY

So what does this mean for your church or ministry? It means that, unless your parish is in an extremely rural area where very few of these services are available, the majority of your congregation is *already* taking advantage of these conveniences. They most likely already subscribe to multiple streaming services and entertainment platforms, do a lot of purchasing online, and get their groceries delivered to their home (or at least order it online and pick it up curbside). They most likely get all their apps and software on their phones, devices, and computers installed digitally, and probably use more than a few software services that are entirely cloud-based and solely exist online.

And yet, for the majority of churches, nearly all of the services we offer are ONLY available in person and on-site. That is a huge disconnect, and I believe it is one of the many reasons our culture increasingly considers the Church to be obsolete and irrelevant. If we want to change the world and convince people that we have a life-changing message, we really need to avoid resisting the very technologies that enable rapid dissemination of our message and instead embrace the potential of newer technology that's already transforming how businesses and organizations operate.

Let's consider a few specifics. You may livestream your services, use social media, and send out email newsletters, but what about the rest of the community life and discipleship at your church?

---

31. Amy Webb (2016), *The Signals Are Talking: Why Today's Fringe is Tomorrow's Mainstream* (New York, NY: Public Affairs). This is a key theme of the entire book (as evidenced by the subtitle), but for a good succinct synopsis, the Introduction (pages 1-15) develops it well and then each chapter explores it further. Chapter 4 "Finding the Fringe" (pages 94-132) especially lays out her framework for forecasting the future by analyzing today's fringe.

- Do you have a way for parishioners to give tithes and offerings electronically throughout the week, as income comes in and needs or opportunities arise? Or do you expect them to wait until Sunday and come to the service in person and drop an offering in the collection plate? *If the latter, that's a key reason your offerings have been decreasing and budgets are tight.*

- How do you distribute your follow-ups to the weekly teaching, whether that's a devotional or application of the pastor's message or parent tips to follow up on their kids' Sunday School or kids' church lessons? Do you have an app or easy-to-sign-up reminder service that delivers those devotions, applications, or lesson takeaways to them directly? Or do you expect them to pick them up at the church via handout, flyer, or other in-person methods? *If the latter, that's surely one of the reasons that so few are engaged in those discipleship learning opportunities.*

- Do you have a way for congregation members to digitally RSVP for events, outings, activities, classes, outreaches, etc.? Do you have all of the information about these resources readily available on your website (or through other online means) and make it easy for people to respond – while in the service or whenever they think of it? Or do you expect them to take notes during the service and physically visit a booth or table or bulletin board to sign up? *If the latter, that's a big reason why participation in these events is so low: You're making it hard for people to respond.*

These are just some of the most basic and fairly obvious examples that every church should *already* be embracing (after all, every one of these technologies I mention have been around for over a decade and are commonplace in most other contexts). On demand resources, cloud-based subscriptions, convenience-based delivery, autonomous shuttles and ride-hailing services, and more are already in the works and are all extremely likely to impact the way we do ministry within the next 3-5 years. Does this seem farfetched? Consider the following fairly plausible scenario.

PASTOR SANDRA'S JOURNEY WITH EMERGING TECHNOLOGIES

Pastor Sandra leads a vibrant and diverse congregation in a mid-sized city. As the senior pastor of Grace Community Church, she has always been passionate about leveraging technology to enhance ministry and outreach. Over the past few years, Pastor Sandra has embraced on-demand and subscription-based cloud services, convenience-based delivery, and ride-hailing services and autonomous delivery systems to serve her congregation more effectively.

Scene 1: Embracing On-Demand and Subscription-Based Cloud Services

Pastor Sandra sat at her desk, scrolling through the church's newly-launched digital platform. This platform, which was designed to mimic popular streaming services, allowed congregants to access sermons, Bible studies, and worship sessions on-demand. She clicked on the latest sermon series, "Hope in Times of Change," and smiled as she reviewed the engagement metrics – views were higher than ever.

"Pastor Sandra," her assistant called from the doorway, "we've received wonderful feedback on the new subscription-based Bible study materials. Families are thrilled with the personalized devotional plans they're receiving every month."

"That's fantastic, Erin," Pastor Sandra replied. "It's amazing how these services allow us to reach people in their homes, providing spiritual nourishment tailored to their needs. But I do wonder about the implications. Are we fostering genuine community, or are we encouraging isolation by making everything so easily accessible at home?"

Scene 2: Convenience-Based Delivery for Ministry Needs

A few days later, Pastor Sandra was organizing a community outreach event. The church had partnered with a local food pantry to deliver meals to families in need. Thanks to the convenience-based delivery services, she had arranged for groceries and essential items to be delivered directly to the homes of those who couldn't make it to the church.

As she coordinated with the delivery service, Pastor Sandra received a notification on her phone. The autonomous delivery robot was en route to drop off supplies at the church for the event.

Pastor Sandra watched as the sleek, wheeled robot navigated the church parking lot and came to a stop at the entrance. "Technology is incredible," she thought. "We're able to serve more people efficiently. But I also worry. Are we losing the personal touch that's so crucial to ministry?"

Scene 3: Utilizing Ride-Hailing and Autonomous Transport

Later that evening, Pastor Sandra was preparing for a leadership meeting. She had arranged for several elderly members of the leadership team to be picked up by an autonomous shuttle service. It was a new initiative to ensure that all members could participate, regardless of their ability to drive, and if it went well, they planned to add the app to the church's website and recommended participation tools.

As she greeted the arriving members, she spoke with Mr. Thompson, an 85-year-old deacon. "How was your ride, Mr. Thompson?" she asked. "It was smooth and convenient," he replied. "I appreciate not having to drive at night anymore. But it's still weird to me not having a driver. I sure do miss the days when we'd all carpool and chat on the way to church."

Pastor Sandra nodded, understanding the sentiment. "These technologies make things easier, but they also change how we connect. It's a balance we need to find."

Scene 4: Theological Reflections

That night, after the meeting, Pastor Sandra sat in her study, reflecting on the day's events. She opened her journal and began to write:

"Today, I saw firsthand how technology can transform ministry in multiple ways. On-demand services keep our congregation spiritually fed, delivery services allow us to serve efficiently, and autonomous transport makes church accessible to all. Yet, I feel a tension. Are we losing the personal, relational aspect of our faith community? How do we ensure that our technological advancements don't replace genuine human connection?" She knew that the key somehow lay in the way they communicated and stewarded the opportunities that technology provides.

She paused, looking at the cross hanging on the wall. "Lord, guide us as we navigate these changes. Help us use technology to enhance, not replace, our sense of community and connection."

All of the technologies I describe in this vignette currently exist, and businesses regularly utilize the first two of these technologies, and some are exploring the third. Furthermore, there are churches which are employing both of the first two technological innovations in various ways (but as far as I am aware, no church has implemented all 3 of them…yet). But it certainly won't be long before all of these technologies are commonplace, and I hope your congregation embraces the opportunities they provide.

POTENTIAL APPLICATIONS FOR CHURCHES & MINISTRIES

Opportunities abound for church leaders to take advantage of convenience-based delivery services, cloud-based platforms, ride-hailing and autonomous transport services, and other emerging models of distributed, yet hyperconnected, consumer interaction. Here are a few possibilities using technology that already exists and is readily available to churches today:

- **Subscription-based Services:** Many online vendors (such as Walmart, Church Supply Warehouse, Christian Book Distributors, and Amazon) offer some form of automated reordering systems or subscriptions to have frequently-recurring purchases made and automatically shipped, and charged to a payment method on file.

This can be very useful for re-ordering office supplies, bulletins, communion elements, seasonal candles and decorations, and other essential items that a church frequently orders.

- **Online Quick Delivery Providers:** Several online companies (Amazon in particular) offer efficient online ordering and quick delivery of study resources, books, Bibles, and other resources that you may need for sermons, classes, or church events, reducing the need for pastoral staff to spend precious time physically visiting stores to shop. In fact, if you set up an Amazon Business account,[32] you can actually order books for multiple individuals and have them drop shipped so that each one is individually delivered to specific members (this is perfect for timely ordering and delivery of discipleship training resources).

- **Ride-Sharing and Carpooling:** Promoting such services among members and using apps and platforms to coordinate transportation can not only reduce parking needs on-site, but also foster community connections during transit. Similarly, providing church vans or buses for members who lack transportation can support the engagement of elderly or disabled congregants. Routes can be optimized through delivery and logistics software.

In addition, here are a few possibilities that are currently being explored and are likely to become available in many markets within the next few years:

- **Delivery Drones & Robots:** Although the most obvious (and most likely soon) potential would be for handling the delivery of goods and fast food from major retailers, I think there are significant opportunities coming for churches and ministries in the near future:
  - Delivery drones could distribute weekly devotionals, bulletins, communion elements, or other resources – even personalized greetings – to elderly or disabled members who cannot attend in person. Imagine a care package arriving from your church for someone who wants to be there, but can't.
  - Churches that operate food pantries, community kitchens, or gardens could use delivery robots to transport groceries and hot meals to those in need, especially those without reliable transportation.
  - Churches engaged in disaster relief efforts could deploy drones to transport emergency supplies such as food, water,

---

32. See details here: https://tinyurl.com/AmazonBusinessPro.

blankets, and first aid supplies to areas that are inaccessible by vehicles…and can distribute care packages or hygiene kits to displaced families in shelters.

- On the mission field, drones could deliver Bibles, study materials, and print resources or care packages to remote or underserved areas where physical distribution is difficult. They can also be used to deliver supplies to local pastors in isolated, treacherous, island, or mountainous regions.

- Youth and children's ministries could incorporate drone-based scavenger hunts, robot-assisted games, or other technology-driven interactive experiences to engage children and teens.

- Larger churches with multiple campuses could use drones to rapidly deliver resources between sites (everything from essential tech to misplaced notes or equipment, even AEDs, EpiPens, etc.), patrol parking lots and event spaces, monitor offices and less-frequented spaces for suspicious activity during services, or even assist with distribution of resources.

- **Autonomous Transport Services:** Partnering with autonomous vehicle services to offer (or arrange) rides to and from the church can provide a safe and convenient option for members – especially the elderly, disabled, young mothers, teens, and low income patrons – while promoting environmentally friendly transportation options. Within a few years, driverless multi-passenger transport options will also become available.

The integration of these emerging models and consumer expectations into church practices can significantly enhance the efficiency, accessibility, and inclusivity of church operations and community engagement. By leveraging technology and innovative delivery models, churches can better meet the needs of their members while maintaining a strong sense of community and spiritual growth.

INSIGHTS FROM CHURCH HISTORY

Although most of this technology seems futuristic and unprecedented, we actually have a great example from church history of a Christian leader who successfully navigated these kinds of innovative and entrepreneurial opportunities: Martin Luther and his utilization of Gutenberg's printing press.

The early 16th century was a time of profound political, social, and religious upheaval. The Holy Roman Empire was in turmoil, with shifting allegiances among European rulers, growing dissatisfaction with the Church's financial and political power, and increasing calls for reform. The Renaissance had spurred intellectual curiosity and the questioning of long-held assumptions.[33] It was in this environment that Martin Luther emerged – a German monk and theology professor who would, through his writings and actions, become one of the most significant catalysts of the Protestant Reformation.

A TIME OF UPHEAVAL AND OPPORTUNITY

Luther's world was in flux. The Catholic Church wielded enormous power, not only as a religious institution but also as a political force.[34] The sale of indulgences—a system in which the Church granted remission of sins in exchange for financial contributions—had become a major source of contention, with many viewing it as corruption.[35] At the same time, economic and political shifts were decentralizing authority, creating an environment in which radical ideas could gain traction.[36]

The printing press, developed by Johannes Gutenberg in the mid-15th century, became the tool that accelerated these debates and allowed ideas to reach the masses in ways never before possible. Unlike handwritten manuscripts, which were expensive and labor-intensive, the printing press enabled the rapid reproduction of texts at a fraction of the cost. This lowered the barriers to entry for new ideas and voices, allowing reformers like Luther to reach a far broader audience than previous generations of scholars and theologians.

LUTHER'S STRUGGLE TO BALANCE REACH AND CONTROL

Luther's use of the printing press was not without its challenges.[37] While he recognized its power as a tool for spreading his message, he also grappled

---

33. Desiderius Erasmus (1511), "Moriae Encomium" (The Praise of Folly).

34. Joshua J. Mark (2022, July 18), "The Printing Press & the Protestant Reformation," *World History Encyclopedia*, accessed Feb. 23, 2025: https://www.worldhistory.org/article/2039/the-printing-press--the-protestant-reformation

35. Bruce L. Shelley (2008), *Church History in Plain Language*, 3rd, Nashville: Thomas Nelson, 240; Martin Luther (1517), "Disputatio pro declaratione virtutis indulgentiarum" (Ninety-Five Theses).

36. Jeff Jarvis (2013), *Gutenberg the Geek:* History's First Technology Entrepreneur and Silicon Valley's Patron Saint, Seattle: Amazon Digital Publishing / Audible Studios: https://amzn.to/3CZPOEl

37. Both Jarvis and Schultze explore this in depth: Jeff Jarvis (2013), *Gutenberg the Geek:* History's First Technology Entrepreneur and Silicon Valley's Patron Saint (Seattle: Amazon Digital Publishing / Audible Studios): https://amzn.to/3CZPOEl; Quentin Schultze (2012), *Gutenberg, God, and the Devil's Plug-In: Lessons about Digital Publishing from the Famous Printer's Failed Killer App* (Grand Rapids, MI: Edenridge Press LLC): https://amzn.to/3D5P3cK.

with how to balance reach and control. His early works, including his *95 Theses* (1517), were intended to spark academic debate, but once they were printed and widely distributed – without his direct oversight – they took on a life of their own. Unauthorized reprints, distortions of his arguments, and pamphlets published under his name but without his approval became widespread.[38]

This mirrors many of the challenges faced today by churches navigating digital platforms and subscription-based content distribution. The ability to reach larger audiences is unprecedented, but so is the loss of control over how messages are consumed, interpreted, rehaped, and re-shared. Luther's experience underscores the importance of strategic engagement: Utilizing technology effectively while maintaining theological and doctrinal integrity.

ENTREPRENEURIAL STRATEGY AND MISSION-DRIVEN INNOVATION

Luther was not merely a theologian; he was an innovator who understood the necessity of leveraging emerging tools for mission.[39] He recognized that the printing press could be used not just for scholarly debate but also for engaging the broader public. By writing his works and translating the Bible into German (the common language) rather than Latin (understood only by the clergy), he made sure that ordinary people could read the Bible for themselves. No longer did the Bible require explanations from the rich and powerful religious elites who controlled interpretations.[40] In doing so, he bypassed the traditional, clerical channels of communication, limiting (if not disarming) their power and authority.[41]

Luther also published short-form pamphlets and sermons alongside his longer theological works, much like many ministries today use both long-form teaching and bite-sized digital content to engage different audiences. His strategic use of printing also extended to hymnbooks, catechisms, and illustrated materials, anticipating modern trends in multimedia ministry. Just as subscription-based platforms today curate and deliver personalized content to users,

38. Euan Cameron, et. al. (n.d.), "Wild Boar in the Vineyard: Martin Luther at the Birth of the Modern World," *Columbia University Libraries Online Exhibitions*, accessed February 25, 2025, https://exhibitions.library.columbia.edu/exhibits/show/martin-luther/flug

39. David Bagchi (2016, Aug. 31), "Printing, Propaganda, and Public Opinion in the Age of Martin Luther," *Oxford Research Encyclopedia of Religion*, Accessed Feb. 24, 2025: https://oxfordre.com/religion/view/10.1093/acrefore/9780199340378.001.0001/acrefore-9780199340378-e-269

40. Musée virtuel du Protestantisme (n.d.), "Martin Luther, His Written Works," *Musée Protestant*, accessed February 24, 2025, https://museeprotestant.org/en/notice/martin-luther-his-written-works/

41. Barry Waugh (Oct. 30, 2017), "The Printing Press and the Protestant Reformation," Reformation21, Alliance of Confessing Evangelicals, accessed Oct. 13, 2025, https://reformation21.org/the-printing-press-and-the-protestant-reformation-php-2/

Luther structured his publications in ways that made theological education and devotional material more accessible to the masses.

The printing press was not a "Christian" technology; it was an economic and commercial innovation. Printers were businesspeople, not missionaries, and they sought to print whatever would sell or had a market.[42] Luther understood this and worked closely with printers to ensure the quality and accuracy of his works. He did not see secular involvement as a barrier but rather as an opportunity. Today, churches face similar decisions when engaging with convenience-based services, ride-hailing, and digital distribution platforms. Much like Luther's partnership with printers, modern ministry leaders must navigate relationships with technology providers whose primary motives are financial, not spiritual. The lesson from Luther is that engagement with these platforms is not inherently compromising; rather, it is an opportunity to advance the mission by using the tools effectively and ethically.

Luther's success with the printing press was not incidental—it was the result of intentional strategy, adaptability, and a willingness to embrace new tools while staying true to his mission. His experience offers several key lessons:

- First, disruptive technology often emerges during times of social and institutional instability. Just as the printing press thrived in an era of decentralization and upheaval, today's digital and on-demand technologies are reshaping expectations about accessibility, convenience, and engagement. Churches must recognize that these shifts are not temporary trends but fundamental changes in how people interact with content and community.

- Second, new technologies can amplify a message, but they also create challenges in maintaining control and consistency. Luther struggled with unauthorized reproductions and misinterpretations of his work, just as churches today face the challenge of balancing broad digital reach with theological clarity. This underscores the need for thoughtful strategies that ensure faithfulness to core beliefs while embracing the opportunities that technology provides.

- Third, mission-driven innovation requires both accessibility and intentionality. Luther's use of German rather than Latin, his publication of short-form works, and his embrace of varied formats illustrate the importance of meeting people where they are. Churches today should consider how best to structure their use of subscription-based platforms, digital resources, and autonomous delivery methods to serve their communities effectively.

---

42. Jeff Jarvis (2013), *Gutenberg the Geek*.

143

- Finally, partnership with secular entities does not automatically mean compromising the Gospel. Luther's collaboration with printers was not about endorsing their commercial motives but about ensuring that the message of the Reformation reached those who needed to hear it. Similarly, churches today must navigate relationships with technology companies, service providers, and content platforms with discernment, ensuring that these partnerships serve the mission rather than dictate it.

Just as today's disruptive technologies – on-demand subscriptions, convenience-based delivery services, cloud-based platforms, and autonomous transport – are reshaping consumer behavior and challenging traditional models of ministry, the printing press in Luther's time upended the established order of information distribution. Luther's ability to utilize this emerging technology to spread his message, despite numerous challenges, provides valuable insights for church leaders today.

CONCLUSION: THE CHURCH'S ROLE IN NAVIGATING DISRUPTIVE CHANGE

The printing press was one of the most transformative innovations in history, not because it changed theology, but because it changed how theology was communicated.[43] By leveraging a technology whose underlying innovations (movable metal type, oil-based ink, and mechanical pressing) had been perfected in Gutenberg's workshop, Luther was able to spark a revolution in religious thought and practice. Today's technologies are similarly transforming the way people connect, learn, and engage.

Luther's example shows that the Church need not fear technological change. Instead, it must ask: How can these tools be leveraged missionally, ethically, and effectively? Just as Luther seized the opportunities of his day, church leaders today should approach emerging technologies with wisdom and boldness, ensuring that these tools serve the mission rather than dictate it. The Church's role is not to resist innovation, but to harness it for the advancement of the Gospel in a world that is more connected – and yet more fragmented – than ever before.

---

43. David Bagchi (2016, Aug. 31), "Printing, Propaganda, and Public Opinion in the Age of Martin Luther."

BENEFITS AND OPPORTUNITIES FOR CHURCHES & MINISTRIES

The growth and popularity of convenience-based delivery services will most certainly have an impact on Churches. To explore that, let's consider first how these disruptive technology innovations may be shaping church members' expectations.

1. Shaping Church Members' Expectations

First, parishioners are growing accustomed to accessibility and convenience. They will likely expect a range of delivery and modality options for church communications tools like newsletters, bulletins, Bible Study guides, sermon notes, or devotionals. Making those available on the church's website and/or via a church app would be a great start, and for anything that's hosted online, it is very convenient and affordable to generate QR codes that make it easy to download them to phones and devices, whether on-site or connecting via livestream. While this does represent a change, it can also yield a tremendous savings over time as congregation members grow accustomed to digital options: You could continue providing printed bulletins, newsletters, and other resources for the time being and simply offer the QR codes as an additional method for those who prefer to access them digitally, but over time, as more and more people access (and even prefer them digitally), you may be able to drop the physical (& costly) printing and mailing of those communication tools altogether.

Similarly, people will likely begin to expect delivery of church materials directly to their homes, whether that is Sunday School curriculum, special event kits for livestream participation in Easter and Christmas celebrations, or communion elements for use when participating online. If it's important to the life and ministry of the church, consider making it easy for parishioners to either pick up on their way out from a service (or to swing by and pick up "curbside") or, better yet, arrange for them to receive them at home. Perhaps not everyone needs – or wants – that convenience yet, but imagine how your shut-ins, those who are sick or in the hospital, and those whose work schedules don't permit Sunday morning attendance will appreciate being intentionally included in those vital participation opportunities. It sends a powerful message regarding how much you value them.

Secondly, people are growing accustomed to instant access. Of course, one of the easiest ways to achieve this is through livestreaming and recording your services, making them available whenever members are able to view and participate, wherever they are. But this could also mean providing convenient ways for parishioners to submit prayer requests and inquire about pastoral care… or making it easy to schedule an appointment with a pastor…or providing a means for real-time notifications and updates regarding church events and activities. For example, are you using a texting service (like Text in Church)? Those services make it easy for attendees to respond to event announcements (RSVP or sign up), submit prayer requests, request communication tools like newsletters, personalize messaging, and build relationships…even if attendees aren't comfortable giving you their phone number yet.[44]

Third, the growing prevalence of personalization and customization will inevitably impact churches, too. On demand printing and easy online generation of custom products will undoubtedly begin to shape parishioners' expectations over the next few years. They will likely begin to expect personalized spiritual growth plans and customized Bible reading plans and devotional materials; while that may seem daunting or difficult to do, it actually is very easy with some AI tools and some basic software resources. They may begin to expect customized reminders and notifications based on their family's personal profile, just like email providers, grocery stores, and pharmacies tailor their options. They may even want to receive tailored worship playlists or prayer guides. Again, this would be fairly easy to do with some AI tools and a basic Church Management Software (ChMS) platform.[45]

2. Rethinking Delivery Models & Assumptions

Although most parishioners have internet and mobile devices, it is not a given that everyone does. Not everyone lives in areas with high-bandwidth Internet and not everyone can afford the high cost of smartphone/wireless plans – particularly retirees, those in nursing and retirement homes, and anyone on a fixed income. In fact, one of the challenges that the growth of such technologies creates is a widening access gap between those who have easy and affordable access and those who don't. Admittedly, this won't apply in all areas (it tends to be a non-issue in most metro areas, but a very present reality in rural regions, and some poverty-stricken areas of inner cities also face this challenge. So, if your community is one with such economic or technological disparity, this can be one way the church can shine by modeling Jesus' desire to serve all, not just those that can afford it or show up.

---

44. See https://textinchurch.com/messaging for more information

45. At my church, we use Church Community Builder (CCB), and I've been a part of other congregations that used ACS, Servant Keeper, Shelby, PowerChurch Plus, or Planning Center's suite. You can learn more about these and explore links and descriptions at https://www.g2.com/categories/church-management

Some examples of ways that your congregation can rethink delivery models in such circumstances would be to:

1. Implement a system for delivering printed sermon transcripts and/or study materials to members without Internet access.

2. Create a subscription service for regular delivery of family devotion kits and/or children's ministry resources.

3. Offer home delivery of care packages for those dealing with food insecurity or in need of basic hygiene or other such resources.

4. Establish a church-run delivery service for distributing books, DVDs, and other media resources from the church's library.

5. Partner with local businesses to deliver welcome kits to new members or attendees.

On-demand pastoral care could be another approach. Some examples for doing this, inspired by the convenience-based delivery models, could include:

1. Provide on-request video or phone-based pastoral counseling sessions…in the same way that doctor's offices and clinic providers often offer telehealth.

2. Deliver pastoral care materials such as grief counseling booklets or recovery program guides to those who have recently lost loved ones or who struggle with addictions and related challenges.

3. Create a virtual chaplain service where members can request prayer or spiritual support at any time.

4. Partner with a hotline for immediate pastoral support and crisis intervention, ideally with local referrals as appropriate.

5. Set up a mobile app (or text-based service) for scheduling and receiving pastoral care.

Community support services are yet another possible approach. Some examples for this include:

1. Partner with local grocery stores or food banks to deliver food to elderly or homebound members…perhaps even a shopping concierge.

2. Coordinate with local pharmacies to deliver medications to members who can't get out.

3. Organize volunteer drivers to deliver meals to families with new babies, recent surgeries, or those recovering from an illness.

147

4. Set up a service to deliver essential supplies during emergenices or natural disasters.

5. Create a network of volunteers to deliver holiday meals and gifts to those in need.

3. Innovating Outreach & Enhancing Engagement

Another opportunity these developments encourage is the potential to innovate in terms of outreach, and even (hopefully) to enhance engagement. For example, churches can explore what flexible outreach and engagement could look like. It might involve organizing home deliveries of church newsletters, devotional guides, prayer cards, or other such resources to keep members connected. It might involve using delivery services to distribute event materials for a virtual Vacation Bible School or summer camps. It could mean facilitating hybrid events where participants can join online or in person, and those who connect remotely can easily receive event materials delivered to their homes or made available digitally. Those are opportunities that almost any church could do with little technological investment. However, within the next few years, there will be opportunities to utilize drones or delivery robots to deliver materials as well as driverless vehicle pickup services. If you're open to what God can do through such technologies, you may want to begin praying and discussing now how you church could utilize such services once they become more readily available and affordable.

4. Efficient Administration

Additional opportunities inspired by the rise of convenience-based delivery services involve efficiency gains that be achieved in church administration practices. For example, there are cloud-based platforms (like Planning Center)[46] for scheduling volunteers and church leadership teams. There are cloud-based e-delivery services available for distributing financial reports, annual meeting materials, and other such documents; in fact, many (if not most) ChMS systems can handle this if you've organized your congregation with a variety of distribution groups. Services like Text in Church,[47] Tithely,[48] and similar platforms enable convenient online donations, as well as facilitate the sending of donation acknowledgements, thank you notes, and similar. There are even companies that are designed to handle on-demand printing of books

46. Planning Center info: https://www.planningcenter.com/services
47. Text in Church info: https://textinchurch.com
48. Tithely info: https://get.tithe.ly

and printed materials, t-shirts, and branded resources featuring your church's name & logo or messaging. The opportunities are numerous.

RISKS AND CHALLENGES FOR CHURCHES & MINISTRIES

Although the growth and popularity of convenience-based delivery services and its inherent assumptions can have a positive impact on churches, there are definite risks and challenges involved with the shift to distributed yet hyperconnected platforms.

1. Loss of Personal Interaction

Reducing the opportunities for in-person face-to-face interactions may weaken community bonds and cause further isolation rather than fostering personal relationships. There is also a risk of members feeling disconnected from the church body and/or leadership as more opportunities for engagement are facilitated remotely or through various forms of technology. Only limited research has been done on this so far, but the impact of personal hand-held technology (especially coupled with social media and generational factors) seems to have a negative impact overall on individuals' ability to communicate and avoid loneliness.

Also, as we saw during the COVID-19 pandemic and the shift to remote work, the increasing use of technology to facilitate meetings and conduct business can have a negative impact as well: There is the potential loss of opportunities for spontaneous interactions and personalized as-needed ministry and personal engagement (although they can certainly happen via Zoom, Facetime, Teams, or other technologies, those on-the-fly interactions with one another certainly come much easier when you're physically present and chatting freely). There are also challenges associated with maintaining accountability and discipleship relationships. Again, these can certainly happen and be facilitated via technology, too, but you have to be a bit more intentional about it (it's much easier to pick up on someone's mood, struggles, or distractions when you're sitting across the table with them, and it isn't always easy to detect via technology).

There is also a risk that some members will prefer digital interaction over physical fellowship. This isn't necessarily a problem (I, for one, am an extreme introvert and I definitely prefer written, text-based, or digital forms of communication, and I'm married to a partner who feels the same), but sometimes when this is the dominant paradigm for communication, it can be challenging to get someone who's struggling or introverted to engage any other way. If you're seeing this communication pattern evolve, you need to be especially attuned to subtle hints when communicating in digital spaces.

2. Technology Dependence

Another challenge that can arise stems from the risk of technology dependence. Over-reliance on technology can lead to issues when systems fail or services are disrupted. For example, if you experience a power or network outage, will you be able to quickly adapt and switch to physical instruments and non-electronic resources? Do you have backup options and people who know how to use them? Or would that shut down your service entirely? A related challenge is the growing need for tech-savvy volunteers and readily available tech support. Anyone who has hosted their livestream using Facebook Live or used technology platforms like SlingStudio that were discontinued knows firsthand what this can mean: Things don't work like expected when unannounced changes happen, and when nobody is available to contact for support, your tech team and volunteers are left struggling to figure out how to fix it in short order without resources or understanding.

Likewise, dependence on third-party products or cloud-based services can be problematic if there is a network outage or the vendor goes out of business, and this can introduce logistical challenges. Although people tend to be understanding when such issues arise (especially when it's a widespread and well-known outage), it still wreaks havoc and causes a lot of extra work on volunteers who often have minimal expertise and/or budget. There are also risks involved with the increased costs for maintaining and upgrading technology infrastructure. After all, technology adoption almost never involves a single one-time purchase; it typically requires an investment over time, with periodic upgrades and continual maintenance. And lastly, there is a risk of alienating members who are technology-averse, not tech-savvy, or simply lack reliable Internet service.

3. Data Security & Privacy

There are also risks and challenges associated with data security and privacy. After all, the church's ministry and its potential hinges on trust and involves a lot of confidential information – everything from personal spiritual growth to mental health issues like chemical dependencies, additions, and behavioral struggles to financial and counseling records. Although technology can enable secure and efficient management of such critical records, great care should be taken in selecting providers who offer exceptional privacy and security functions and who have solid policies for role-based access as well as a stellar track record of never divulging or experiencing breaches of privacy. In the current divisive (and sometimes anti-Christian) climate of our culture, churches and church leaders are increasingly becoming targets for those seeking to expose Christians and conservatives for perceived hypocrisy, and the last thing your church needs is a data breach that exposes the private lives, financial records, or struggles of your members.

Furthermore, certain types of records and transactions (such as financial, payment card transactions, etc.) have compliance regulations associated with them, so it is important that you choose providers who understand and fully comply with those laws…and who can certify their compliance. Cybersecurity is a relevant concern, too, and this means everything from guarding (& vetting) who has access to sensitive data, training those who do on what can be used and how, and insisting on cautious use and disclosure of passwords for important systems. Sadly, many churches – in their understandable eagerness to utilize volunteers and make it easy to use and share church systems – make it all too easy for a rogue user or hacker to exploit this trust and cause problems. This doesn't just pertain to pastoral staff, either: Volunteers who handle any sensitive data need to be trained in proper handling and safeguards, members who have leadership roles need to be educated in data security practices, and everyone who uses the systems needs to be reminded regularly of not only appropriate uses, but also of what should never be disclosed, too.

By understanding and addressing these factors, churches can effectively integrate convenience-based delivery and cloud-based services to enhance their ministry while being mindful of potential challenges. It is important that you ensure these services align with your church's mission and values; that will be an essential key for successfully leveraging these tools without experiencing grief or embarrassment in your attempts to utilize technology. The integration of convenience-based delivery models and autonomous transport into church practices offers exciting possibilities for enhancing accessibility, outreach, and efficiency. However, it also brings significant theological, ethical, and practical considerations that must be thoughtfully addressed. By proactively engaging with these issues, churches can leverage autonomous technology to enrich their ministry while upholding their core values and mission.

BIBLICAL VALUES & THEOLOGICAL IMPLICATIONS

As we consider the impact of autonomous transport and on-demand delivery models, it is important for us to reflect on their theological implications and evaluate them in light of Biblical values. These emerging models and consumer expectations have the potential to reshape church ecclesiology significantly. The Church has always adapted to technological shifts, yet with each innovation comes a need for discernment. How do these changes align with Biblical values? What theological concerns should ministry leaders keep in mind as we seek to steward these advancements wisely? Here are a few key areas that I think are essential for these topics.

Theology of Presence and Embodiment

The incarnation of Christ – God taking on human flesh and dwelling among us (John 1:14) – demonstrates the profound importance of presence. Christian community thrives on personal relationships, shared experiences, and embodied worship. As hybrid worship experiences, virtual reality, and convenience-based delivery services make remote and extended participation in church life easier, we need to wrestle with the proper balance between accessibility/convenience and physical presence.

The author of Hebrews reminds us that we should "Consider how we may spur one another on toward love and good deeds, not giving up meeting together, as some are in the habit of doing, but encouraging one another."[49] Sometimes this verse gets wrongly thrown around to repudiate any form of gathering other than physically, but it is important to understand the verse in its historical context: That passage is rooted in the early church's struggle to preserve its identity and cohesion in a challenging environment in the face of Roman persecution of Jewish believers. Often it was unsafe to gather. And when they did gather, it certainly didn't look like our large-group worship services today; these were gatherings in living rooms and over the dinner table, often because they couldn't gather in the synagogue.[50]

Since its earliest days, the Church has adapted and found ways to gather even while geographically dispersed, while undergoing systematic persecution, and the New Testament is filled with such examples (many of those books were encyclicals written by the apostle Paul while he was in prison to churches who couldn't gather publicly). So, it is important to read verses (and letters) like that with an innovation and creativity mindset: Not gathering is simply not an option, but how we do it is, of course, quite flexible. While digital and distributed models enable engagement, they should supplement, not replace, embodied community in whatever form that takes. Churches should be inten-

---

49. Hebrews 10:24-25 (NIV).
50. For a fascinating historically accurate narrative that provides practical context, I highly recommend reading Robert Banks' (2011) *Going to Church in the First Century* (Beaumont, TX: Seedsowers): https://amzn.to/4hQIKsS

tional about fostering deep relationships, ensuring that convenience does not erode the richness of face-to-face fellowship.

Stewardship and Sustainability

Scripture calls us to be good stewards of the resources entrusted to us.[51] The rise of on-demand subscriptions, convenience-based delivery services, and autonomous vehicles and transport presents an opportunity for churches to reconsider not only the efficiency of our presumed practices but also its environmental impact. Should churches invest in electric shuttles to transport members efficiently? Should we utilize technology to optimize supply chains and reduce waste?

At the same time, there is a financial stewardship aspect to consider. The cost of implementing high-tech solutions needs to be weighed against the benefits. Just because a technological innovation exists does not necessarily mean it is the wisest investment for every congregation. Churches should evaluate how these tools serve their mission and whether they align with their calling to love and serve their communities.

Hospitality and Outreach in a Changing World

Hospitality is a central biblical theme that appears throughout both the Old and New Testaments. In the Old Testament, we see it exemplified in Abraham's example with the three visitors, in Lot's encounter with unexpected guests, as well as in the Law's mandate, which emphasized that caring for strangers is both a duty and a reflection of God's character.[52] In the New Testament, we see practical exhortations in multiple places,[53] it's listed among the qualities desired of leaders,[54] and Jesus Himself advocated for it in the parable of the Good Samaritan.[55] Throughout the Bible, it's not merely about offering a meal or a place to rest; it's an expression of love, respect, and care toward strangers and the needy, an attitude and a form of generosity and character that reflects God's own graciousness as well as His heart for the stranger among us.

This Biblical theme of hospitality reminds us that the Church is called to be a welcoming community. Autonomous transport and delivery services do indeed offer new ways to extend hospitality, whether that is by ensuring the elderly or disabled have accessible transport to services or by using delivery models to bring meals, communion, or discipleship materials to those

---

51. Genesis 2:15; Matthew 25:14-30.
52. Genesis 18 & 19, Leviticus 19:34.
53. Romans 12:13; Hebrews 13:2; 1 Peter 4:9; etc.
54. 1 Timothy 3:2 and Titus 1:8.
55. Luke 10:25-37.

who cannot physically attend. However, at the same time we need to also ask whether these innovations may unintentionally diminish the personal touch of ministry: A robot delivering a meal lacks the warmth of a personal visit. A livestreamed service does not replace the experience of being physically present in worship, and although you can see and connect "face-to-face" via screens, you can't hug, embrace, or easily eat together. A timely drone delivery to a distant or difficult-to-access member can make a valuable connection, but a sacrificial effort to connect in person is even more powerful. So, it's a balancing act. Church leaders should explore ways to integrate these tools and utilize them effectively without sacrificing personal connection.

Trust, Dependency, and Ethics

Proverbs exhorts us to "trust in the Lord with all your heart and lean not on your own understanding."[56] As we embrace AI-driven transportation and delivery systems, we need to be mindful of what we place our trust in. While technology can enhance efficiency, an over-reliance on automated systems could lead to vulnerabilities, whether that involves data security risks, system failures, or unintended consequences of algorithmic decision-making. Moreover, the shift toward automation can also raise ethical concerns, such as the displacement of workers. What happens to those whose livelihoods depend on driving? How should the Church respond to job loss in sectors impacted by AI? The early Church modeled radical generosity and care for the displaced,[57] and to serve well in that light, churches today need to consider how to advocate for and support those affected by technological shifts.

Expanding the Boundaries of the Church

One of the most exciting possibilities of autonomous transport and delivery is the expansion of the Church's geographic reach. No longer bound by proximity, congregations can engage with members and seekers in a broader radius. Before his ascension, Jesus commissioned His followers to be His witnesses "to the ends of the earth."[58] In that same light, John Wesley famously said the world was his parish.[59] Technology now makes this possible in far more ways than ever possible before, enabling churches to extend their ministry. However, while technology can enable and even enhance access, it cannot easily (yet) replace the depth of in-person relationships and discipleship.

---

56. Proverbs 3:5-6.
57. Acts 2:41-46.
58. Acts 1:8.
59. John Wesley (1739, March 20), "To James Harvey," The Letters of John Wesley, *Wesley Center Online*, accessed Feb. 24, 2025: https://wesley.nnu.edu/john-wesley/the-letters-of-john-wesley/wesleys-letters-1739/

Yet, this expanded reach also challenges traditional models of church participation and raises new questions: Does a church member who only attends digitally or interacts with a mobile outreach unit experience the fullness of Christian community? Are they every bit as integral to the body life as those who attend in person, or are they an afterthought (out of sight, out of mind)? Are all of the church's resources equally available to everyone, regardless of the modality by which they participate? Or are there some things they must show up for in person (communion, baptism, classes, luncheons, business meetings, etc.)? If yes, why is that a necessity? There are no easy answers here, and church leaders must navigate these waters carefully, ensuring not only that expanded ministry opportunities do not lead to a fragmented body nor pander to a consumer-driven faith, but also ensuring that we don't unintentionally send messages of exclusion to those whose health, location, or circumstances limit their physical presence.

LOOKING AHEAD

As we stand on the threshold of some amazing technological advancements, the Church has an opportunity to respond not with fear, but with wisdom and confidence. Rather than viewing these changes as threats to tradition, we can embrace them as tools that, when used with discernment, serve the mission of Christ well. By remaining anchored in Biblical truth and focused on the needs of our communities, we can integrate innovation in ways that enhance connection, expand outreach, and strengthen discipleship.

The road ahead will require thoughtful leadership, intentional application, and a steadfast commitment to fostering authentic Christian community. As we move forward, we are called to navigate this transformation with faith, ensuring that new technologies do not replace what is essential, but instead create new avenues for ministry. In the next section, we will explore practical steps and resources for leading with hope and peace in an era of rapid change.

NEXT STEPS: LEADING WITH WISDOM

So, how should churches respond practically to these emerging technologies? What steps can ministry leaders take to lead with wisdom, adaptability, and faith? Rather than reacting out of fear or uncertainty, churches should engage thoughtfully and strategically. The following steps provide a framework for assessing, discussing, and preparing for change in a way that remains mission-driven, theologically sound, and community-focused.

1. Assess the Opportunities & Challenges in Your Context

Before making any decisions about how your church might engage with autonomous transport, delivery services, or subscription-based platforms, start by assessing your congregation members' current engagement with these technologies. Conduct informal conversations or structured surveys to understand how people in your church already use streaming subscriptions, grocery delivery or pickup, ride-sharing services like Uber or Lyft, and digital engagement tools. Conversations about the likelihood of autonomous vehicles and ride-hailing services in the future can be insightful, too. By identifying existing habits and thoughts, you can gauge the level of receptivity to new applications in ministry.

Beyond individual usage, consider **accessibility barriers** that your current attenders and members may currently be experiencing. Are there elderly members, individuals with disabilities, or families without reliable transportation who struggle to attend in-person services or events? Are there ministry volunteers or staff members who spend excessive time handling logistical needs – such as distributing printed materials, preparing communion, or managing outreach events – when more efficient solutions could free them to focus on spiritual formation and community engagement? These realities will shape how technology can serve, rather than distract from, your church's mission.

Another key area to evaluate is your current **ministry logistics** – the ways in which your church currently distributes resources, organizes outreach, and facilitates participation. Could delivery services help get discipleship materials, event supplies, or pastoral care resources to those who need them most? Would automation or ride-sharing services enable greater engagement from those who face transportation challenges? By assessing these factors, you can lay the groundwork for informed decision-making that meets needs and improves your current situation.

2. Discuss & Explore Possible Applications

Once you have a clearer picture of your church's current landscape, the next vital step is conversation: Bring together key ministry leaders, volunteers, and trusted voices within your congregation to discuss the potential applications of convenience-based on-demand services and autonomous transport. These discussions should be framed not simply as technology adoption, but as ministry innovation: How do these tools align with your church's mission to serve, disciple, and engage your community? Meeting needs, caring better for members, addressing barriers, addressing inequities, and solving problems is a far better approach than just thinking about technology because it's available…and such innovations will last, too.

A key part of these conversations will be identifying relevant concerns and priorities. Privacy, surveillance, and data security are increasingly important in a digital age, and church leaders must be proactive in understanding the ethical implications of integrating automated services. Additionally, while technology can enhance accessibility, it also risks eroding personal connection if not implemented thoughtfully. As you explore these innovations, consider the relational impact: How can these tools enhance community rather than replace meaningful relationships, embodied presence, and personal discipleship?

To ensure balanced and informed decision-making, it would be prudent to take time to evaluate local and global trends. You should research how churches in urban, suburban, and rural contexts are leveraging delivery services, ride-sharing, and automation. Are there larger churches in your denomination or whose model and impact you respect? Find out what they're doing and how they're approaching these future technologies. Connect with ministry networks, universities, or business leaders who are already engaged in these spaces (you probably even have some of them in your congregation). Businesses and higher education often innovate at a faster pace than churches, and they have probably already been discussing and exploring options. Understanding the successes and challenges faced by others will help you make informed choices that align with both your theological convictions and your practical realities.

3. Prepare & Experiment with Practical Applications

With a firm foundation of assessment and discussion, your church can then strategically experiment with small-scale applications that align with its mission and needs. Start with low-risk, high-impact initiatives that provide real benefits without requiring major overhauls. For example, if accessibility is a concern, consider partnering with existing ride-sharing services or autonomous transport providers to help elderly or disabled members attend worship and events (that would have a high impact with a low cost and risk factor). If distribution of ministry resources is a challenge, explore digital or physical delivery methods for Bible study guides, discipleship materials, or pastoral care resources. If volunteer burnout is an issue, identify areas where automation or outsourced services could reduce logistical burdens and allow leaders to focus more on people rather than processes.

Alongside these experiments, develop strategic partnerships with local businesses, universities, and technology providers to explore long-term possibilities. Many industries are actively integrating autonomous and on-demand solutions, and forming connections with early adopters can open doors for collaborative ministry opportunities. Notice how none of the product providers (other than Amazon) are directly developing their own drone-based delivery services, but are instead partnering with companies that specialize in that? That's a wise approach we can learn a lot from. Churches that engage proactively rather than reactively will be better positioned to influence how these technologies are used within their communities.

At the same time, maintain a long-term vision for how these innovations may evolve. Not every new technology needs to be adopted immediately, but understanding emerging trends allows church leaders to prepare for shifts in congregational expectations and engagement patterns. Perhaps it's too soon for your church, or maybe these technologies haven't made their way into your region yet. If so, keep your eyes and ears open, because it's coming, sooner or later. Knowing what is possible and paying attention to the opportunities will help you lead confidently and wisely, knowing when your congregation will be in a good position to explore new possibilities. By keeping a flexible mindset and an openness to experimentation, you can test what is effective, adapt as needed, and position your church to serve faithfully in a changing world.

4. Lead with Wisdom in Times of Disruption

The rapid pace of technological change can feel overwhelming, but ministry leaders are not called to fear the future; we are called to shepherd God's people with wisdom and faith. Remember the Sons of Isaachar (men who understood the times and knew what Israel should do)?[60] Every generation of the Church has faced disruptive technology innovations, and that is the kind of leadership our churches need to lead confidently and explore possibilities with hope and peace. The mission remains unchanged: To proclaim the gospel, make disciples, and build up the body of Christ. But the *methods* of how we accomplish that will be ever-changing.

Rather than resisting change or rushing into adoption, church leaders should lead with discernment and trust in God. The same God who used Roman roads, the printing press, and TV & radio to spread His message in the

---

60. 1 Chronicles 12:32 (NIV).

past is at work today, equipping His Church with new tools to reach people in new ways. When evaluated through the lens of mission and ministry, these technologies present not just challenges but opportunities.

By staying informed, fostering dialogue, and engaging with technology wisely, as a ministry leader you can guide your church into the future with confidence, clarity, and a commitment to Biblical values. The goal is not to chase every trend but to ensure that every decision – whether to adopt, adapt, or refrain – is rooted in a desire to love, serve, and disciple in the best way possible for your local context. As the Church continues to navigate these shifts, the most important truth remains unchanged: Our hope is not in technology, but in Christ. But technology, used wisely, can be a powerful too for achieving the mission. Let that confidence shape how you lead, innovate, and shepherd your congregation through the ever-changing landscape of ministry.

Conclusion

WHERE DO WE GO FROM HERE?

When I first envisioned this book, I conceived of it as a textbook that mirrored the topic flow of the "Technology for Ministry" class I developed for a Christian college and taught for several years. I also thought it might make a great updated edition of *Wired Church 2.0,* a book which had been so influential in my own ministry. Thankfully, my publisher and friend Len Wilson wisely coached me, guiding me toward something that would be far more useful to a wider audience…and the result is what you have been reading. A key turning point was when Lori Wagner, one of Invite Press' best-loved editors – who edited and helped shape many books and D.Min dissertations, as well as Leonard Sweet's voluminous writings over the years – helped me to focus on five distinct chapters, each representing a significant technology disruption that is likely to impact pastors in the coming 3-5 years.

In doing this, I took some cues from the Horizon Report, an annual report for higher education leaders that "profiles key trends and emerging technologies and practices shaping the future of higher education,"[1] produced by the New Media Consortium and Educause. It's called the "horizon" report because it focuses on disruptive technology innovations that are currently on the horizon, and which are likely to impact higher education institutions over one, three, and five-year timeframes. Having followed that report for two decades in my educational technology roles, it has been a primary way I have stayed attuned to emerging trends, enabling me to advise our academic leaders and decision-makers on how best to focus our technology and training efforts strategically. However, I realized that no such resource existed for the Church, and that is something I hope to have achieved through this book.

---

1.   Educause (2025, Jan. 7), "Horizon Reports," The Educause Horizon Report, accessed Feb. 7, 2025, https://library.educause.edu/resources/2021/2/horizon-reports

THE ELUSIVE ART OF FORECASTING FUTURE TECH TRENDS

In a sense, that's what the Sons of Isaachar do.[2] It's what Leonard Sweet's doctoral progam in "Semiotics & Future Studies" at Portland Seminary taught us to do well. And there are many wise and astute leaders who've done it before. But I didn't have a Delphi study or a team of several dozen scholars and ministry leaders scanning the horizon, developing research, and analyzing trends. I only had access to my own research and experience with how technology innovation cycles work. Most of these technologies I have studied and followed for many years now, and I've experimented with them to see and experience firsthand what's possible. I also read voraciously to discern what's coming.

But technology is constantly evolving, and it changes *rapidly*. In *The Future is Faster Than You Think*, Diamandis & Kotler included spoken updates in the audiobook after each chapter, detailing what had changed since printing. In many cases, market leaders had lost their status to new competitors in just nine months![3] The pace of technological innovation and disruption is astounding and accelerating.

So, admittedly, there is a very real likelihood that I could be wrong in some of my assumptions or predictions about emerging technology and its likely impact. There could be surprises and new developments I haven't anticipated that hit the market or technology leaders I have featured who drop out of the picture after we go to press. After all, forecasting is an inexact science. However, I have been doing this long enough – and successfully enough – that I'm pretty comfortable putting these disruptive technology innovations out there despite what may come. Plus, my information and expertise comes from multiple different fields and perspectives, so it is well diversified. I am fairly confident that what I have identified is what's *inevitable*: If you haven't already felt the impact of these technologies in your congregation, you WILL within the next few years. They're coming.

So, how can we realistically prepare for an uncertain future when so much can change so quickly? Well, this is the same challenge I faced when I developed that first course on Technology for Ministry. I had to focus on timeless principles, overarching guidance, and broader categories of technology, rather than on specific products, vendors, or editions (and that is a similar approach

2.   1 Chronicles 12:32.
3.   Peter H. Diamandis & Steven Kotler (2020), *The Future is Faster Than You Think: How Converging Technologies are Transforming Business, Industries, and Our Lives,* narrated by the authors (New York: Simon & Schuster, 2020), MP3 audiobook, 9 hr. 53 min., www.audible.com: Chapter 1: Convergence at 51:30.

to what I have taken in this book). In the technology sector, change is a constant, and you have to keep up with developments to remain viable. It's also the same challenge that my colleague and friend Tiffany Snyder faced when she developed a course on "Current Issues for the Virtuous Organization" which included quite a bit of work not only demystifying AI, but researching and staying atop of the latest news and developments.[4]

How do you develop and teach a high-quality course on a topic that is changing weekly if not *daily*?? She had to focus on timeless principles as well, and for the specific use cases and technology research and experimentation, she led students through a Problem-Based Learning approach to keep the learning focus constantly up-to-date with student needs as well as current and emerging technologies.[5] It's also the same challenge the Church has wrestled with through the ages, whether we're talking about the Sons of Isaachar studying the times to know what Israel should do or the disciples working through a very practical logistical problem involving the care of widows and orphans.[6]

SHIFTING OUR FOCUS

I see a very powerful depiction of this in the way Moses handled the fiery serpents that the Israelites struggled with during their wilderness wanderings.[7] It's a fascinating account that foreshadows Christ, and Jesus himself specifically mentioned it as the essential context for what has become the most famous verse in Scripture (John 3:16).

The context for the incident was a significant detour and delay, as the Edomites refused to allow them passage through their territory,[8] which meant that the Israelites had to journey a significant distance, going the long way *around* an entire region (likely several weeks' travel), by foot. Understandably, they grumbled and complained, speaking out against both God and their leader, Moses, however, their complaints were considerably harsh and accusatory: "Why have you brought us up from Egypt to die in the wilderness? For there is no food and no water, and we are disgusted with this miserable food" (v. 5). Keep in mind that this was only a short time after God had miraculously

---

4.   Rubya Ahmed, et. al (2024). "Exploring Generative AI through Problem-Based Learning and Student-Driven Inquiry." *C2C Digital Magazine*, 1 (21), article 2. Colleague2Colleague. https://scalar.usc.edu/works/c2c-digital-magazine-spring---summer-2024/exploring-generative-ai-through-problem-based-learning-and-student-driven-inquiry

5.   Ibid.

6.   1 Chronicles 12:32 (NASB); Acts 6:1-7.

7.   Numbers 21:4-9.

8.   Numbers 20:14-21.

provided water from a rock, and the "food" they are complaining about is *manna*, which God also miraculously provided to sustain them.[9]

So, God "sent fiery [venomous] serpents among the people and they bit the people, so that many people of Israel died" (v. 6). The "wilderness" of Zin is the kind of arid Middle Eastern environment where poisonous snakes naturally inhabit.[10] The use of the word "sent" makes it seem like God created or drove the snakes there, but the reality is that these venomous serpents were there all along; God had simply provided a hedge of protection to keep them from harming the Israelites (until they complained, at which point He removed the hedge, thus "sending" the serpents).[11]

The Israelites realized their attitudes and their sin, and repented, asking Moses to intercede for them (v. 7). And then, as we always do (as is human nature), they asked God to remove the serpents from among them…they asked God to take away their problem. But that isn't how God chose to answer them. The solution God gave Moses was very unique, specific, and prophetic: "And the Lord said to Moses, 'Make a fiery serpent, and set it on a pole; and every one who is bitten, when he sees it, shall live.' So Moses made a bronze serpent, and set it on a pole; and if a serpent bit any man, he would look at the bronze serpent and live."[12]

At first glance, this seems like a highly improbable and very ineffective solution: After all, if fiery serpents are the problem, why on earth would I want to look at another fiery serpent, hung upon a pole? The practical reality is that the serpents on the ground are biting and causing people to die. Furthermore, didn't God curse the serpent in Genesis?[13] And hadn't God said in Deuteronomy "anyone who is hung on a pole is under God's curse"?[14] So God is asking the Israelites to look at a cursed thing that is under a curse in order to obtain healing and live. Focusing solely on the circumstances, from a human point of view, this makes no sense whatsoever; it seems unreasonable at best, if not outright preposterous: Why should I look upon a serpent on a pole if the ones on the ground are my problem?

9. David Swisher (2009, Aug. 1), "Look & Live," Sermon, Hall Wesleyan Church (Delphos, KS). Available on YouTube at: https://www.youtube.com/watch?v=f3znxbBSbK8 (Part 1: 6:48 – 7:58).

10. Some examples of venomous snakes which inhabit the region include the desert horned viper, Palestine viper, and Israeli mole viper. For more information and pictures, see Arik Haglili (n.d.), "The Deadliest Snakes in Israel," Fauna of the Holy Land, APT Private Tours of Israel, accessed Mar. 1, 2025, https://private-tours-in-israel.com/the-deadliest-snakes-in-israel

11. David Swisher (2009, Aug. 1), "Look & Live," Sermon, Hall Wesleyan Church (Delphos, KS). Available on YouTube at: https://www.youtube.com/watch?v=xvFv52ttNN8 (Part 2: 1:04 – 3:44)

12. Numbers 21:8-9 (RSV).

13. Genesis 3 (especially vv. 14-15).

14. Deuteronomy 21:23.

It's actually a brilliant solution, however. What this forced them to do was (1) take their eyes off the problem, and instead (2) look to God as the source of their healing and deliverance. That is a huge act of faith! If they wanted to redeem the situation, they had to look to the symbol of their suffering to live. It also painted a powerful picture for them…a prophetic one, because one day Jesus would take our curse upon Himself, becoming the very symbol of our suffering and shame, to take away <u>our</u> sins.[15] In the collective narrative of the people of Israel, this event had powerful semiotic implications that stuck with the people…so much so that Jesus could directly mention it to explain his own work of redemption: " 'Just as Moses lifted up the snake in the wilderness, so the Son of Man [Jesus] must be lifted up, that everyone who believes may have eternal life in him.' For God so loved the world that he gave his one and only Son, that whoever believes in him shall not perish but have eternal life."[16]

RETHINKING OUR PERSPECTIVE

So what does this have to do with disruptive technology innovations? A lot! Most of the time, our default reaction to any new technology is to treat it with suspicion, fear, concern, or even outright rejection. We often see technology as the problem, and when we do, we want to rid ourselves of the perceived threat we see (of the technology we don't understand). But asking God to remove the problems we're facing is rarely effective, and with technology, it simply won't change anything. Criticizing, demeaning, or even condemning the technology won't take it away, nor will it make its influence any less significant. So, instead, what we need to be doing is asking God to show us what He is doing through that technology…asking Him to help us understand it…or even asking God to show us how He can work through it, wisely discerning how we can best utilize the technology to accomplish his purposes.

One of the things I find most fascinating – as well as humorous – about new technology innovations is how we tend to frame (or even name) the new technology using the language and paradigms of its predecessor. For example, when automobiles first came out, they were known as "horseless carriages" because their predecessor was horse-drawn carriages. However, the technology behind them is substantially different: Not only were no animals necessary to power it, they also provided the ability to travel farther and faster, and it re-

---

15. For a more in-depth analysis of this "suffering servant" (symbol) imagery, see Matt Smethurst (2012, April 5), "The Suffering Servant and Isaiah 53: A Conversation with Darrell Bock," The Gospel Coalition, accessed Feb. 27, 2025, https://www.thegospelcoalition.org/article/the-suffering-servant-and-isaiah-53-a-conversation-with-darrell-bock/

16. John 3:14-16 (NIV)

quires much different infrastructure (paved roadways and refueling stations). Also, automobiles enable entirely different opportunities than a "horseless carriage," but that was the dominant paradigm we were familiar with, so the new technology was introduced and explained using familiar concepts, even though it only nominally applied.

The same was true of electric lights, which were referred to as "artificial candles." However, they aren't candles in any way, shape, or form (and only in recent years have we manufactured lights to imitate candles). They do not burn fuel directly, but instead can be turned on instantly, and they last longer without requiring refueling or relighting. Furthermore, electric lights enable businesses to stay open 24/7, power brightly lit cities and signage, and even paved the way for light-based communication and data transmittal. They also enable vastly creative lighting displays at holiday times, as well as creative messaging and gameplay. Electric lights are SO much more than "artificial candles," but that was the dominant paradigm people were familiar and comfortable with when they first emerged.

The same was true of radio, which was referred to as "wireless telegraphy," and movies (motion pictures), which were known as "moving photographs." Television was seen as "radio with pictures," while computers were often hailed as "electronic brains." Even today we still call electronic messaging "email" (short for electronic mail), even though the technologies and protocols that make it possible have very little in common with the physical delivery of postal mail. Satellite television was often referred to as "cutting the cable" and often marketed as an improvement over cable, but it was really an entirely different technology. Cloud computing has often been explained or pitched as "online hard drives," and cryptocurrency is often described as "digital money."

Although these later examples do provide closer parallels in functionality, our tendency to view and understand new technologies through the paradigms they replace instead of their potential can sometimes be quite problematic. A worst-case example of this is when newspapers and magazines began using websites and online platforms to publish digital or "e-replica" versions of their periodicals: Rather than utilize the new capabilities of the new medium (such as hyperlinking, interactivity, the inclusion of multimedia, the advantage of unlimited space, and the capability of instant updating), they essentially made exact replicas of their print equivalents in digital form…and in so doing, completely missed the point and value of the new technology.

The first online newspapers in 1980 were simply a plain text version of the exact same content, delivered via computer terminals without any images,

165

ads, or formatting (this was in the days before graphical user interfaces became normative).[17] It took a full decade and a half (until the mid 1990s) before we began seeing digital editions of traditional newspapers, but these were nothing more than digital replicas of their print counterparts.[18] And then, it wasn't until the mid-2000s (25 years later) that traditional news and media publishers *finally* began to embrace the unique advantages of digital media, transforming their content to engage readers in new and innovative ways...and reaching entirely new markets. And people wonder why newspapers and traditional news media are dying?

Even today, the vast majority of news outlets simply offer online articles with greater searchability and tagging, and minimal inclusion of mixed media...and much of that they put behind a paywall (i.e., limited to only paid subscribers). They are completely missing the opportunity the new mediums provide. As a consumer, why would I want to pay extra to read what I can find online via other sources for free? Admittedly, if I was already a subscriber and they simply wanted to retain me, giving me electronic access might seem like a value add. But for the rest of us – those who never were print subscribers and never will be, those who grew up on digital media? This seems like a complete waste of money. If I were to pay for news, I would want it to offer something I cannot get any other way – such as fully immersive, multimedia content...or live conversation about events as they're happening....or localized and global perspectives in real-time, etc. There is a lesson for the Church in this: If we can't adapt, innovate, & keep pace with changing technologies, we become increasingly irrelevant and useless...bringing upon ourselves our own demise.

In *Gutenberg, God, and the Devil's Plug-In*, church communication specialist Quentin Schultze makes a compelling case that this was precisely the mistake Johannes Gutenberg made.[19] Although his invention revolutionized multiple industries, paved the way for the Protestant Reformation, and lasted for well over 600 years (an impressive record in terms of technology), he also struggled to make ends meet, spent far too long trying to perfect his process, and was sued by his initial startup investor who called in his loan.[20] The result was that

---

17. David Shedden (2014, Sept. 24), "Today in Media History: CompuServe and the First Online Newspapers," The Poynter Institute, accessed Feb. 28, 2025, https://www.poynter.org/reporting-editing/2014/today-in-media-history-compuserve-and-the-first-online-newspapers/

18. Rick Edmonds (2020, June 23), "E-replica Editions, the Ugly Ducklings of Digital News, Have Suddenly Become Strategic," The Poynter Institute, accessed Feb. 28, 2025, https://www.poynter.org/locally/2020/e-replica-editions-the-ugly-ducklings-of-digital-news-have-suddenly-become-strategic

19. Quentin Schultze (2012), *Gutenberg, God, and the Devil's Plug-In: Lessons about Digital Publishing from the Famous Printer's Failed Killer App* (Grand Rapids, MI: Edenridge Press LLC), Kindle edition, Loc. 48 of 605: https://amzn.to/3D5P3cK

20. Jeff Jarvis (2013), Gutenberg the Geek: History's First Technology Entrepreneur and Silicon Valley's Patron Saint, Seattle: Amazon Digital Publishing / Audible Studios: https://amzn.to/3CZPOEl.

his investor repossessed his equipment and then became his biggest competitor (even hiring his chief press operator and completing the project, the first Gutenberg Bible).

Schultze argues, quite convincingly, that Gutenberg's problem wasn't his invention nor his cash flow, but his failure to recognize the potential of what he had developed.[21] Consequently, "Gutenberg's financial expenditures fed attorneys, irritated his staff, and worsened his struggles to find more investors."[22] Why? He was focusing all of his efforts on the high-end printing of religious books that were modeled after traditional illuminated manuscripts, even though there was already a considerable (and profitable) market for printing indulgences, calendars, dictionaries, and the like.[23] His competitors found that market; Gutenberg didn't. Gutenberg's investor, Johann Fust, eventually called in his loan and successfully sued him in 1455, repossessing Gutenberg's printing workshop and equipment. He even partnered with Peter Schöffer, Gutenberg's former apprentice and press operator.

How is this possible with such a skillful technological innovator? Although Gutenberg had figured out how to mass reproduce what took most monks a year and a half to produce by hand, and had perfected the process, devising the optimal paper thickness, a very effective custom ink, and the ideal number of lines per page for maximum efficiency,[24] he simply couldn't see past the traditional paradigm: He kept envisioning his press as enabling the creation of beautiful artisan designs that closely replicated the illuminated manuscripts of his day, and all of his processes and decision-making (from the way he developed his moveable type designs to the size, format, and framing of his press pages) were centered around that former paradigm…finding a faster way to mass produce the same thing. Not only did he model the typefaces of his letter molds on the actual script characters lettered by scribes,[25] but he even experimented with single-plate copper engravings of beasts of prey, birds, flowers, and deer (apparently attempting to re-create the illuminations which were often inset in traditional manuscripts).[26]

After all, religious books in his day "were well illustrated to make reading more interesting, informative, and inspiring" and their design reflected a theological premise that the Bible was worth all of the time and effort or careful and

21. Quentin Schultze (2012), *Gutenberg, God, and the Devil's Plug-In*, Loc. 48 of 605.
22. Ibid., Loc. 296 of 605.
23. Ibid., Loc. 179 of 605.
24. Jarvis (2013), *Gutenberg the Geek*.
25. Schultze (2012), *Gutenberg, God, and the Devil's Plug-In*, Kindle, Loc. 179 of 605.
26. Ibid., Loc. 354 of 605.

creative adornment.[27] But that didn't pay the bills, and Gutenberg spent most of his time and profits chasing the "killer app" that people weren't asking for instead of producing what would have made his investment not only a financial success but a game-changer for innovation.[28] His competitors found it, but Gutenberg missed it.

Fust and Schöffer completed the first Gutenberg Bible and focused on profitable publications like calendars, dictionaries, and indulgences – the market opportunity that Gutenberg had missed. Despite the legal and financial setbacks, Gutenberg did finally manage to rebuild and resume his printing activities, but on a much smaller scale and with limited influence. He spent his last days destitute and blind, relying on a government-provided stipend to survive. Sadly, what he failed to realize was that he had developed an entirely new medium which could do so much more than the traditional manuscripts he kept trying to imitate.

REFRAMING WHAT WE OFFER

Unfortunately, churches have often fallen into this same presumption trap, too: We offer – and even promote – on Sunday morning (only) what the average person can already easily find online 24/7 through Wikipedia, online articles, and YouTube. In our current information age, someone who's going through difficult life challenges (marital struggles, job loss, depression, anxiety, issues with their kids, addictions, etc.) or asking questions about the existence of God or His relevance to their life, or about Jesus, the gospels, or the Bible can do a quick Google search to find dozens of articles and videos to answer their questions. And emerging generations are growing up with this continual availability of such resources, and YouTube is their default norm for finding out whatever they want to know. Today, generative AI leverages those vast quantities of freely available online content and can even conversationally respond to inquiries, rendering the competent help of pastors, youth leaders, and church ministries seemingly unnecessary.

So, what does the Church offer that they can't already find? Biblical community. Genuine compassion. Insight contextualized for their specific challenges. Caring ministries with connections to real people who can walk through life's struggles with them, people who have been there and understand. THAT is what people today desperately need and crave, but sadly, we rarely promote

27. Ibid., Loc. 263 of 605.
28. Ibid., Loc. 296 of 605.

this. What most churches say they offer instead is *information*…the one thing people already have too much of. Unfortunately, most churches tend to cater to those who are already members, and they pitch their "relevance" in terms of commitment ("join us," "come see," "visit," etc.). And we wonder why church attendance is declining nationwide? We are selling what people don't want or need, while simultaneously ignoring what they do need and desire most.

I believe one of the key takeaways for pastors and ministry leaders in this is that we should look at new technologies not as a simple replacement or update of what we already have, but as entirely new opportunities to spread the gospel and serve our churches and communities well. Instead of merely doing what we've always done but with a new tool, we should instead be asking ourselves what new and incredibly innovative things we can do with the new tool *that could never be done previously*. THAT is the power and potential of innovative technology! After all, doing the same thing we've always done in a new format simply perpetuates the status quo with diminishing returns. That doesn't reflect the creative impulse of God, nor is it an effective strategy; it's just a lazy response to oversimplify whatever seems new or challenging. Considering the genius and abundant examples of our creative God who sits at the helm, churches and ministries should be the ones driving creativity and innovation, not merely adopting it a decade or two after a new innovation or technology has gone mainstream. We should be in the driver's seat of innovation, not in the backseat.

MCLUHAN'S FOUR LAWS OF MEDIA

A great paradigm for understanding and evaluating new technologies and their impact was developed by Marshall McLuhan (1911–1980). He was a Canadian philosopher and media theorist whose ideas were groundbreaking in the study of media and culture, and his insights had a significant influence in fields like media studies, communication theory, and digital culture (an impact which remains to this day). He is best known for his work on media, communication, and technology, and is famous for the phrase "the medium is the message." However, as Frost & Hirsch note, it is important to understand that "When McLuhan used the word 'media,' he is actually using it as a synonym for what we might call technology and technique, not media in the narrow sense of the word."[29] The idea behind this phrase is that the medium (the technology) we choose to deliver a message IS the message…the choice to

---

29. Michael Frost & Alan Hirsch (2003), *The Shaping of Things to Come: Innovation and Mission for the 21st-Century Church* (Grand Rapids, MI: Baker Books).

use that particular medium, and the way it delivers and frames the content is far more important and impactful than the content of the message itself.. That can offer both intriguing insight into our media/technology choices as well as some discomfort and questioning as we discuss Biblical messaging using communication media.

However, his tetrad of media effects (often referred to as his "four laws of media") is a set of questions to ask of any new technology,[30] and it is a very useful tool for analyzing the impact and effects of that technology. I have taught it in all of my Technology for Ministry classes, and I think it is well worth considering here. McLuhan can be a bit enigmatic and challenging to understand for those not already deeply immersed in media effects and communication research, but Shane Hipps does an incredible job of explaining it in terms that are useful for pastors and ministry leaders.

Here are the questions to ask, along with Hipps' synopsis explanation and a few examples I have gathered:

- **What does the medium (technology) <u>extend</u>?** McLuhan believed that every new medium enhances, amplifies, or extends some human capacity:[31] A megaphone amplifies a human's voice, a hammer extends the power of our hand, vehicles extend walking ability, and glasses enhance our vision. We create technology to help us do things we can already do so that we can do it better, stronger, or more efficiently. So, *asking what human capacity that technology extends helps us better understand its **purpose** and its **potential**.*

- **What does the medium (technology) make <u>obsolete</u>?** Every new technology replaces another technology, and usually makes it obsolete. That doesn't necessarily mean that the former technology has disappeared or is no longer relevant, but that its function has changed.[32] For example, automobiles replaced horse & buggy, making that mode of transportation obsolete. They still exist, but their function now is primarily for quaint entertainment and romance. Podcasts have essentially replaced radio broadcasts; they do still exist, but their function has been relegated to news, talk shows, and political commentary, without the level of influence and support that podcasts now have. *Asking this question helps us to understand **what the new technology replaces**.*

- **What does the medium (technology) <u>reverse</u> into?** When pushed to an extreme, every medium will reverse into its opposite inten-

---

30. Shane Hipps (2005), *The Hidden Power of Electronic Culture: How Media Shapes Faith, the Gospel, and* Church (Grand Rapids, MI: Zondervan).

31. Hipps, *Hidden Power*, 41.

32. Ibid.

tions.[33] For example, a hammer can be a very powerful tool for construction, but when pushed to an extreme, it can also be used destructively. Online technology can great facilitate communication and enable publication, but those same capabilities, when pushed to an extreme, can also spread hate and pornography, or be used to manipulate and deceive. Although social media was intended to connect people, it can also lead to isolation and information overload, or even misperceptions of worth or identity by seeing carefully curated posts and pics from others divorced from reality. *Asking this question can help us discern the **dangers and risks** of any new technology.*

- **What does the medium (technology) <u>retrieve</u>?** Intriguingly, every new technology or medium also retrieves some ancient experience or medium from the past (or another way to look at it is that there is no such thing as an entirely new technology).[34] For example, the medium of email retrieves the earlier technology of a telegraph. Movies retrieve the medium of campfire storytelling or play-acting. *Asking this question helps us clarify those dangers but also understand its implications and any far-reaching effects.*

For example, if we want to evaluate the potential future dangers and risks of email, we can look at what often went wrong with communication by telegraph – delayed communication, absence of context, misunderstanding through brevity and word choices, etc.

So, as we consider each of the disruptive technology innovations we have reviewed thus far, it would be very helpful to evaluate them according to McLuhan's four laws. This will give us insight into their (1) purpose and potential, (2) what it replaces, (3) the dangers and risks, and (4) the implications and far-reaching effects. As newer technologies emerge that I haven't covered in this book, you can use these same questions to evaluate them as well.

WHAT LIES AHEAD FOR THE CHURCH

There's a scene in *The Matrix* (1999)[35] that always causes me to chuckle, but which I think is profoundly prophetic, too. In that scene, the protagonist Neo (aka Thomas Anderson) is a computer programmer and hacker, and he is being rescued by Morpheus (leader of the rebel group) and Trinity (a key leader in the resistance). After Neo takes the red pill, he experiences a series of

---

33. Ibid.
34. Ibid.
35. *The Matrix* (1999), directed by Lana Wachowski and Lilly Wachowski, produced by Joel Silver (Warner Brothers Pictures, 1999), DVD (Warner Home Video, 1999).

unsettling sensations. Morpheus explains that the pill is part of a trace program designed to disrupt Neo's input/output carrier signal, which will enable them to locate and extract him from the Matrix. Confused, Neo asks, "What does that mean?"

Cypher, a technical operations specialist, responds with, "It means buckle your seatbelt, Dorothy, 'cause Kansas is going bye-bye."[36] This indicates that Neo is about to experience a reality-altering event. That moment signifies Neo's transition from the fabricated simulation world of the Matrix to the harsh reality of human existence under machine control. In Cypher's role as "operator," he facilitated the crew members' connections into the matrix, helping them enter and exit the simulation safely. Because Cypher oversaw their digital presence while they engaged in missions inside the Matrix, he could be joking and flippant about it with crew members because he had seen lots of first-timers' reactions to this jarring transition between perceived realities. But having never been aware of the Matrix simulation previously, it was a confusing and enigmatic moment for Neo.[37]

Pastors and ministry leaders today are facing a similar moment. The cultural and technological landscape is shifting so rapidly that the familiar models of ministry and church engagement are being completely upended. What once seemed stable and reasonably predictable – large-group gatherings for worship around a sermon, traditional church attendance patterns, centralized authority structures, and predictable methods and modalities of discipleship – is now entirely in flux. Successful navigation of the next decade of ministry will require leaders to let go of outdated assumptions and embrace new paradigms to effectively engage their congregations and communities. This transition will not be easy, but just as Neo discovers his true purpose beyond the illusion of the matrix, the Church has an opportunity to step into a future that is both challenging and full of promise, too.

To lead confidently with hope and peace into this uncharted territory, church leaders need to not only understand the specific *technologies* involved (as I have provided guidance with in the preceding chapters), but to also recognize the larger movements that are shaping faith, community, and engagement in this new landscape today.[38] Based on insights gleaned from a variety

---

36. "Synopsis for The Matrix (1999)," The Internet Movie Database (IMDb), accessed March 3, 2025, https://www.imdb.com/title/tt0133093/plotsummary/?ref_=tt_stry_pl#synopsis. Scene: https://www.youtube.com/watch?v=0-JJuHpfN5g

37. Ibid.

38. If this prospect (of leading people into uncharted territory) excites you, but you want guidance and insight in how to do it beyond what I share in this book, I highly recommend reading Todd Bolsinger's (2018) *Canoeing the Mountains: Christian Leadership in Uncharted Territory* (Downer's Grove, IL: InterVarsity Press).

of sources, including Barna Research & Gloo,[39] CRC Research,[40] and Carey Nieuwhof,[41] I believe the following five overarching trends will shape the future of the Church over the next few years.

1. The Blurring of Physical and Digital Spaces

The line between in-person and online engagement continues to blur, and digital presence is no longer an optional extension but will need to become an integral part of your ministry. This reflects a cultural trend toward seamless integration across physical and digital environments, one that is already happening and which is well-documented in the business world.[42] This is why I focused not only on online and livestream ministry, but post-pandemic experiences and trends in the first chapter, and it is also why we explored metaverse and VR models of ministry in the fourth chapter. In fact, there is a new term that has emerged specifically to describe this blending of physical and digital worlds: "phygital." This is the reality that will become normative as we approach 2030.

So, what does this mean for pastors and ministry leaders? Churches will need to embrace hybrid models that go *beyond* livestreaming, integrating digital discipleship, virtual community building, and immersive worship experiences. Decades ago, you needed a Yellow Pages listing to be considered viable, as well as for people to find you. Then it was a website; without that, potential visitors wouldn't find you and check your church out. More recently, a social media presence was essential; people would check your social media presence to decide whether to visit. Now, it's your phygital presence: In the coming years, a presence in both physical and virtual spaces will become normative and assumed, and those which don't have a well-established and quality online and livestream ministry will not be taken seriously.

Congregants will expect seamless interaction across physical and digital environments, from online prayer meetings to pastoral care. In the church I attend, whenever I – or any of my family members – post pics, news, or updates on social media, our church family knows about it and asks about it the next

39. Gloo (2025, Feb. 3), "Gloo and Barna Launch New State of the Church 2025 Event Series," Religion News Service, https://religionnews.com/2025/02/03/gloo-and-barna-launch-new-state-of-the-church-2025-event-series/.

40. Tracy Munsil (2025, Jan. 22), "Barna, CRC Research Reveal 12 Trends that Will Shape Faith and Culture in 2025," Arizona Christian University, https://www.arizonachristian.edu/2025/02/18/barna_crc_research_reveal_12_trends_that_will_shape_faith_and_culture_in_2025-copy/

41. Carey Nieuwhof (2025, Jan. 2), "5 Disruptive Church Trends That Will Rule 2025, YouTube video, 23:53, Carey Nieuwhof Leadership Podcast, accessed March 3, 2025, https://www.youtube.com/watch?v=4PKOHKEqhf4

42. An excellent example of this (among many), and a great study full of leadership insights by industry experts is Geoffrey G. Parker, Marshall W. Van Alstyne, & Sangeet Paul Choudary (2017), *Platform Revolution: How Networked Markets Are Transforming the Economy—and How to Make Them Work for You* (New York: W. W. Norton & Company).

time we're together. This isn't a strategic or investigative move, and nobody's paid to do this; it's simply the natural interaction of an authentic Biblical community in today's culture (they know me in both physical and digital reality, and my Church's presence transcends those barriers).

Similarly, metaverse and VR spaces will continue to evolve and become increasingly important. At this point, I am not convinced that every church needs to have a virtual campus in the metaverse yet (but that day may come), but I do think that any pastor or ministry leader needs to be fully aware of the reality and potential of metaverse ministry and at least be supportive of those who engage in it. You will likely have congregation members who spend a lot of time in the metaverse or using VR, either on the job, in training, or for recreation, and it's a modality of experience that you definitely need to become familiar with. Some of them may even want to become digital missionaries, and don't be surprised if your youth leader wants to offer hangouts in virtual spaces...or if you walk in on them wearing a VR headset. If you don't personally see yourself donning VR gear and heading into the metaverse, at least take the time to talk with those who do to better understand their work, their opportunities, and the possibilities for ministry down the road.

2. Decentralization of Authority and Community

There is no question that in today's world, trust is shifting away from well-established institutions rapidly, and size and history/legacy is no longer a significant factor of influence. Scandals and abuse, along with a variety of other problems, have riddled long-time established institutions and denominations (as well as religious groups), and people no longer grant trust nor presume authority based on such factors. It doesn't matter if your church or denomination was one that abused people's trust or experienced such a scandal; ALL are now suspect (it's guilt by association). The prevailing mindset in today's culture is one of distrust, and if you serve in any kind of institution or established role, people will assume you have an agenda and that you inevitably bias your communication and message based on it. Many actively seek to expose it, and that hostility toward people of faith is likely to continue growing in years to come. Whether that's fair or deserved is irrelevant; it's simply the reality of the world that we now minister in.

Instead, peer networks are forming, and they are rapidly re-shaping the way people experience community and interpret authority. This is why I focused so heavily on Bitcoin, cryptocurrency, and DAOs in the third chapter, as those are all signs of what's clearly changing. It is a growing undercurrent that we need to pay close attention to. In business, the days of "this came down from higher ups" and "management has decided" are ending, but with it, so are expressions and assumptions like, "the Bible says," as well as "Because I'm the pastor and I said so," or "that's what our denomination believes." In its place, people are placing value and trust in the authenticity of relationships, and they're looking to those who will serve and lead without obvious bias or agendas. I suspect that the growing emergence and use of AI will also contribute to this perceived distrust, and it is likely that congregations which disclose their use of generative AI and have community-authored AI policies in place will have greater opportunities for influence and lasting change over those who don't.

Along with this, new models of church governance and accountability will emerge, emphasizing transparency and communal decision-making over top-down authority. If you still have closed business meetings or don't publish your minutes or financial reports, you're going to struggle to maintain trust in future years. You might keep your long-time members, but you will struggle to keep anyone under 30. Simply put, there is a growing distrust of ALL forms of institutional authority. Congregants are seeking more participatory roles in shaping church decision-making, and this mirrors trends in decentralized finance (blockchain/DAOs) as well as online communities: As digital platforms begin to enable decentralized models of governance and engagement, traditional hierarchical structures will be challenged, too. This will force churches to rethink how we establish credibility, gain trust, and cultivate leadership. In terms of advance warning systems for threatening storms, it will be far better to be on the leading edge of this shift than doing damage control afterwards. Consider yourself warned.

3. The Rise of Personalized Spiritual Formation

Driven by digital tools and platforms that allow for customized and on-demand publishing, video, and tailoring of pathways and products, faith development is becoming increasingly individualized, too. On-demand content consumption in our culture will shape church engagement, from worship experiences to how we utilize sermons, Bible studies, and other teaching content. Expect more and more people to access these asynchronously (after the fact) rather than in real-time (live). This is one of the reasons I emphasized on-demand and subscription-based models – along with autonomous delivery services – in the fifth chapter, as well as the capabilities and ease of use of generative AI in the second chapter. The changing consumer practices and cultural assumptions related to both of these innovation trends drives the need and explains the rationale. Fortunately, AI makes that kind of customization and personalization entirely possible without sacrificing your time and budget, and without requiring more staff and volunteers than you already have.

Decades ago, it would have been simply unheard of to preach a sermon and then generate tailored study questions for the senior adults, youth group, and women's group, then turn around and post snippets of the message to social media or draft an article or blog post to the church's website or podcast. That would have taken more time and expertise than most pastors and churches had, and only megachurches with multi-staff congregations could do it. But now, AI tools make this quite easy for any pastor and church of any size to do weekly. Furthermore, in multi-cultural communities, you could even take those sermon segments and generate foreign-language versions and posts to distribute more widely in Spanish, French, Hindi, or Creole...or whatever language people in your community speak at home.[43] In the coming years, tailoring your messaging and customizing content through AI will not be seen as pandering to consumer expectations, but a default expectation for any credible ministry.

This multiculturalism and diversity, along with significant trends amongst younger generations, also means that young people are seeking spiritual but non-traditional paths. It is simply not a given anymore that the teens and children of members will be enrolled in Sunday School, or taking catechism classes, or pursuing other types of faith formation. It is also not an automatic anymore that Sundays (or Wednesday nights) will be reserved for church. In fact, more and more communities are realizing that churchgoing families are now the minority, not the norm, and so schools and sports programs (and jobs) regularly schedule events on what many of us used to call "church days." So, if young families and/or students do come, it will most likely be more sporadically, making it harder to provide a consistent and cohesive plan for faith development...unless you provide it in tailored consumer-friendly ways that make it easy to stay connected and up to date despite life, work, and sports commitments.

Likewise, the rise of the "nones"[44] along with the increasing diversity and cultural presumptions means that these younger generations will not necessarily share the same assumptions we have, but will instead approach faith from the angle of pragmatics and authenticity:

43. The AI tool that I love to use for this is HeyGen. You can try it out with this referral link: https://tinyurl.com/HeyGenPromote

44. This is a term for the religiously unaffiliated...which today is the fastest-growing church affiliation group in America. If this is a new concept (or concern) for you, you may want to read Ryan P. Burge (2021), *The Nones: Where They Came From, Who They Are, and Where They are Going* (Minneapolis: Fortress Press).

- Can I trust this person?
- How can I know if this is true?
- Does this actually work? Or is this just hype or sales pitch?

This shift isn't anything to fear, however; it is a tremendous opportunity to lead people to Jesus <u>if</u> we approach it with hope and faith and engage with people authentically. These shifting preferences should prompt churches to offer more flexible, interactive, and exploratory approaches to faith...rather than assume that everyone was raised in a churched context and shares the same presumptions. It would also be prudent to begin shifting teaching and discipleship materials toward the questions people ask and the issues and uncertainties surrounding practical realities that we often just assume in church culture.[45]

4. The Church as a Hub for Mental and Emotional Well-Being

As stress, anxiety, and loneliness rise in our society, the Church also has a unique opportunity to become a central pillar for holistic well-being. That's a good thing. However, it does require a bit of a reframing as well as some rethinking about how we can best engage in these areas. For most of the first part of this century, the Church in the West has been a pillar of society and a foundation of our culture. But in recent decades, our influence and presumptive authority has waned dramatically, and that pace of decline has been steadily accelerating over the last decade and a half. There are lots of contributing factors to this which would require other books to explore fully, but it is definitely worth noting that at the same time, church attendance is at an all-time low and the vast majority of churches and denominations are plateaued or declining. Of course there is a significant correlation here.

But not all churches and denominations are plateaued or declining! The ones which aren't have managed to successfully offer a holistic message that balances love with truth...theology with patient application. They live what they teach and walk it out in very practical ways. Sadly, it is all too common for churches to either preach **love without truth** (lots of social justice themes, inclusive love without consequences, and minimal doctrinal clarity) OR preach **truth without love** (right doctrine, biblical discipleship, and clear convictions, but with a heavy dose of judgmentalism and little or no compassion). When a church properly balances <u>both</u>, it not only reflects the character and lifestyle of Jesus, but it is VERY attractive. People want that, and churches and denominations that do that well inevitably grow.

---

45. For example, my congregation has twice now offered the Alpha class, a group-led video-based study developed in the U.K. for post-Christian culture that is geared toward unchurched and de-churched people who have minimal faith background. It provides a safe context for asking questions. https://alphausa.org/about/

This has a few dramatic implications for pastors and ministry leaders: (1) Mental health support will be expected as an integral part of pastoral care, with churches offering counseling, coaching, and trauma-informed ministry. (2) The Church's role as a relational community will be vital in countering isolation, providing spaces for belonging and deep connection. (3) Ironically, although technology is undoubtedly one of the culprits for the rise in stress, anxiety, and loneliness, technology can also play a valuable role in assisting parishioners and inquirers with emotional and spiritual well-being: There are a variety of apps and tools, as well as digital surveys, AI chatbots, virtual therapy, and pastoral care options that can supplement traditional forms of pastoral ministry. Knowing what's available and exploring how they work can give you a useful leg up when you meet people to help start the conversations and explore possibilities for mental health and spiritual support with those who come to you or inquire.

If you're not professionally trained as a counselor (and realistically, most pastors and ministry leaders aren't), you will likely want to partner with Christian counseling organizations and professionals who do have that training so that you can offer that support alongside your regular ministry or as a referral when those needs arise. The more connected support options your church can provide or refer people to, the better: Support ministries such as DivorceCare, Celebrate Recovery, Prevail, crisis care, mental health support, etc. are essential. You don't have to be experts in all of that, and you don't have to provide all of it yourself, but you do need to know where and how seekers and inquirers can get the mental health support they need, and establish partnerships or connections with these kinds of services so that you can seamlessly refer or engage people to them (or even accept referrals from them, too, when they encourage struggling and hurting people to find a church community).

5. New Economic and Workforce Realities Will Reshape Church Engagement

Numerous economic shifts, automation, and changing workforce patterns will influence how people engage with church and ministry. As governmental and corporate entities downsize and restructure, you can expect that many who attend your church will be laid off. As AI use increases, many entry-level roles will be replaced (not necessarily by AI, but by people who know how to skillfully use AI in the emerging workforce). The gig economy was booming prior to the pandemic, took a huge hit, but is beginning to recover, although in intriguingly new, yet smaller, ways. Remote work existed prior to the pandemic, but became a prevalent norm as we recovered from it. These factors have led to multiple effects, one of which is a growing expectation among employees and job seekers that remote work and working from home is now fairly normative and beneficial. At the same time, there is also a big pushback from employers to try to get remote workers back into the office; some do, while others find new jobs that let them work remotely. As a result, the way we conduct meetings, travel, consult, and meet with people is also dramatically changing.

So, what does this mean for your church? Well, for one thing, on-demand work and non-traditional career paths (gig economy, consulting, AI-empowered, etc.) will lead to fluctuating attendance patterns, requiring more flexible ministry schedules and engagement strategies. You simply cannot expect everyone to come to a single service on Sunday morning, nor to devote one or more nights a week to discipleship and education activities. That pattern of engagement is no longer practical nor sustainable. The new reality is that people are going to need more options for participation, including watching video or connecting online and following up later (DVR'ing of services, or viewing highlights). You may need more than one service time, or a way for those who couldn't attend on Sunday morning to watch and engage in follow-up later. You may need to offer some classes that are done online or through Zoom, or offer some small groups ("life groups") that are embedded in workplaces or conducted entirely via technology. Your prayer gatherings can't simply be in person, either, but need to allow for a variety of modes of participation – both online and time-shifted.

These shifts are also going to challenge financial sustainability, forcing churches to explore new revenue streams beyond traditional tithes and offerings. If the only time or way parishioners can give to your ministry is through the offering plate on Sunday morning, you're going to struggle to stay afloat, because many who would consider giving simply won't be there. It will be important in the coming years to offer digital or text-based giving options, as well as multiple options for contributing (not just tithes, but missions, need-based, outreaches, etc., including the ability to drop off goods for campaigns or offer their services).

There will also be a growing need and opportunity – perhaps even an expectation – for the church to provide tangible community impact through responses to felt needs like job training, financial literacy programs, tutoring, helping people navigate AI, workplace change, etc., or even to embrace and encourage entrepreneurship. You don't have to do it all, or figure it out yourself; just partner with existing ministries and programs that are meeting those needs (and if none exist in your community, then you've found an ideal opportunity). You may not be aware of this, but the majority of effective church plants that are growing or matured in recent decades did so, at least initially, by meeting one or more specific felt needs like this in their community...needs which existing churches weren't meeting.

The more that technology and disruptive innovation reshapes the workforce and job market, the more it's going to become imperative for churches to not only be aware of and perceptive to that need, but responsive in practical, tangible ways. After all, a church that preaches truth and holds people to high standards is one thing (and a good thing), but if the messaging and services that the church provides don't provide meaningful and relevant guidance and support through the challenges and changes of life, it isn't going to last in the long run, and it's not going to result in transformed lives.

A CALL TO ADAPTIVE AND INNOVATIVE LEADERSHIP

For centuries, church leadership has functioned like navigation, relying on trusted maps that were passed down from one generation to the next. But what happens when the map no longer reflects reality? What if the familiar landmarks disappear? What do we do when we reach the end of the map and have to figure out a new way forward?

Two of my favorite movies depict this moment vividly:

- *The Truman Show*, when Truman Burbank reaches the literal edge of his world and must choose whether to step into the unknown.

- *The Thirteenth Floor*, when Douglas Hall sets out to find the truth about his world, only to discover that his world is a simulation that simply ceases to exist at its edges.

Many church leaders today find themselves in a similar position. The frameworks they've relied on no longer extend to where people actually live, work, and engage. The coming years will require adaptive leadership that embraces innovation while staying rooted in the unchanging mission of Christ. In his book *Canoeing the Mountains*, Todd Bolsinger tells the story of Lewis and Clark, who expected to find a water route to the Pacific, only to encounter the daunting peaks of the Rocky Mountains instead. Their well-planned strategies became useless, and they had to adapt. As church leaders, we are no longer paddling through familiar waters; we are entering uncharted territory. The question is not whether we will face disruption, but how we will respond. Will we cling to outdated maps, or will we *boldly go where no one has gone before*, navigating with faith, wisdom, and an unwavering mission?

Today, pastors and ministry leaders are confronting a technological landscape that bears little resemblance to the world in which our leadership models were formed. The disruptive technology innovations we have explored in this book challenge our paradigms and assumptions about presence, discipleship, authority, and influence. Leaders who insist on paddling through these mountains – clinging to outdated structures and resisting adaptation – will find that their trusty canoes are completely useless in the new landscape. The familiar boundaries of ministry have been redefined, not by theological drift, but by significant technological and cultural upheaval. Consequently, relying on past solutions will no longer be enough. Bolsinger argues that ***adaptive leadership*** is the only viable path forward: The willingness to leave behind ineffective tools, embrace uncertainty, and develop new competencies for an unfamiliar world. I agree wholeheartedly.

As we face the impact and uncertainties caused by disruptive technology innovations, we don't need to fear what's coming, but we do need to adapt our strategies to lead effectively. This is where the storm chaser metaphor comes full circle. Storm chasers don't fear storms; they pursue them, analyze them, and learn from them…providing early warnings that help others prepare. Similarly, wise ministry leaders will not resist technological change but will seek to understand it, engage with it, and leverage it.

The future belongs to those who see disruption not as a threat, but as an opportunity to reimagine how the timeless truths of the Gospel can be shared and lived out in this new era. The churches that thrive in the coming decades will be led by pastors who are willing to step beyond the old maps, embrace the uncertainty, and boldly chart a new course. This is not reckless—it is faithful. It is the posture of leaders who trust that God is already at work beyond the boundaries of what we can see, ask, or imagine. For those willing to pursue the horizon—to chase the storm, not avoid it—there is profound hope. Because both Biblical and church history has always belonged to those willing to venture just beyond the known, into what once seemed impossible.

> "The only way of discovering the limits of the possible is
> to venture a little way past them into the impossible."
> — *Arthur C. Clarke, Profiles of the Future (1962)*

181

Now to him, who is able, according to the power that is
*at work within us, to do **infinitely more than we can ask or imagine**,*
to him be the glory in the church and in Christ Jesus
throughout all generations, forever and ever! Amen.

— Ephesians 3:20–21 (EHV)

BIBLIOGRAPHY

ActivePlayer.io (n.d.). "Minecraft Live Player Count and Statistics." Minecraft. Accessed Mar. 4, 2025. https://activeplayer.io/minecraft

Ahmed, Rubya, Lovette Coston, Linsey A. Hollingshead, Johnny H. Manson Jr., Charles F. Swingle, Johngerlyn Young, and Tiffany R. Snyder (2024). "Exploring Generative AI through Problem-Based Learning and Student-Driven Inquiry." *C2C Digital Magazine*, 1 (21), article 2. Colleague2Colleague. https://scalar.usc.edu/works/c2c-digital-magazine-spring---summer-2024/exploring-generative-ai-through-problem-based-learning-and-student-driven-inquiry

Al Bustani, Hareth (n.d.). "Templar Banking: How to Go From Donated Rags to Vast Riches." Medievalists.net. https://www.medievalists.net/2021/08/templar-banking

Alvarez, Simon (2024, Oct. 10). "Live Blog: Tesla 10/10 'We, Robot' Robotaxi Unveiling Event." *Teslarati*. Accessed Nov. 13, 2024. https://www.teslarati.com/tesla-10-10-we-robot-robotaxi-unveiling-event-live-blog

Amazon (2023, Oct. 18). "Amazon Announces 2 New Ways It's Using Robots to Assist Employees and Deliver for Customers." About Amazon > News > Operations. Accessed Jan. 11, 2025. https://www.aboutamazon.com/news/operations/amazon-introduces-new-robotics-solutions

Amazon (2023, Oct. 18). "Amazon Announces 8 Innovations to Better Deliver for Customers, Support Employees, and Give Back to Communities Around the World." About Amazon > News > Operations. Accessed Jan. 11, 2025. https://www.aboutamazon.com/news/operations/amazon-delivering-the-future-2023-announcements

Amazon (2024, Oct. 9). "Meet the 8 Robots Powering Your Amazon Package Deliveries." About Amazon > News > Operations. Accessed Jan. 11, 2025. https://www.aboutamazon.com/news/operations/amazon-robotics-robots-fulfillment-center

Amazon Web Services (n.d.), "What is LLM (Large Language Model)?," https://aws.amazon.com/what-is/large-language-model/

American Bullion, Inc. (2023, April 28). "Why Do Modern Coins Have Ridges?" *American Bullion*. Retrieved from https://www.americanbullion.com/why-do-modern-coins-have-ridges/

Ammous, Saifedean (2018). *The Bitcoin Standard: The Decentralized Alternative to Central Banking*. Hoboken, NJ: Wiley.

Anderson, Alex (2021). *DAO - Decentralized Autonomous Organizations for Beginners: The Ultimate Beginner's Guide*. Independently published.

Aquino, Jerome (2022). *DAO Explained: Comprehensive Guide on Decentralized Autonomous Organizations (DAO)*. Independently published.

Arizona State University (2020, Sept. 4). "Starship Technologies, Aramark Launch Contactless Robot Food-Delivery Service at ASU." ASU News. Accessed Dec. 7, 2024. https://news.asu.edu/20200904-asu-news-starship-aramark-launch-contactless-robot-food-delivery

ASU Online (2022, May 2). "Take a Virtual Field Trip to the Alien Zoo with Dreamscape Learn." Arizona State University. YouTube video. Accessed March 4, 2025, https://www.youtube.com/watch?v=m-T1z8Lx6r4

Backlinko Team (2025, Feb. 25). "Roblox User and Growth Stats You Need to Know." Accessed Mar. 3, 2025. https://backlinko.com/roblox-users

Bagchi, David (2016, Aug. 31). "Printing, Propaganda, and Public Opinion in the Age of Martin Luther." *Oxford Research Encyclopedia of Religion*. Accessed Feb. 24, 2025. https://oxfordre.com/religion/view/10.1093/acrefore/9780199340378.001.0001/acrefore-9780199340378-e-269.

Bailensen, Jeremy (2018). *Experience On Demand: What Virtual Reality Is, How It Works, and What it Can Do*. New York: Norton.

Bailenson, Jeremy and Lesher, Molly (2024). Chapter 4: "Virtual Reality and its Opportunities and Risks." In OECD (2024). *OECD Digital Economy Outlook 2024* (Volume 1): Embracing the Technology Frontier. OECD Publishing. Paris. https://doi.org/10.1787/a1689dc5-en, 119-139

Baker, Frank, ed. (1980). *The Works of John Wesley*. Bicentennial ed. Vol. 25, Letters. Nashville, TN: Abingdon.

Banks, Robert (2011). *Going to Church in the First Century*. Beaumont, TX: Seedsowers.

Bar-Am, Aviva & Shmuel Bar-Am (2016, 25 January). "Get to the Roots of Israel's Historic Trees." *Times of Israel*. Accessed Feb. 24, 2018. https://www.timesofisrael.com/get-to-the-roots-of-israels-historic-trees/

Birken, Emily Guy (2024, June 25). "Robinhood Review 2024." Advisor > Investing. Accessed Sept. 2, 2024. https://www.forbes.com/advisor/investing/robinhood-review/#how_does_robinhood_work_section

Bitcoin Depot, "Bitcoin History: A Journey Through Memorable Transactions" (2024, June 12), accessed Mar. 16, 2025, https://bitcoindepot.com/bitcoin-atm-info/a-history-of-memorable-bitcoin-transactions

Board of Governors of the Federal Reserve System (2020, July 21). "Is it Legal for a business in the United States to Refuse Cash as a Form of Payment?" FAQs. Accessed Mar. 16, 2025. https://www.federalreserve.gov/faqs/currency_12772.htm

Bock, Darrell L. & Armstrong, Jonathan J. (2021). *Virtual Reality Church: Pitfalls and Possibilities*. Chicago: Moody.

Bolen, Todd (n.d.). "Cedar of Lebanon." BiblePlaces.com. Accessed Feb. 24, 2018. https://www.bibleplaces.com/cedar-of-lebanon/

Burge, Ryan P. (2021). *The Nones: Where They Came From, Who They Are, and Where They are Going*. Minneapolis: Fortress Press.

Bolsinger, Todd (2018). *Canoeing the Mountains: Christian Leadership in Uncharted Territory*. Downer's Grove, IL: InterVarsity Press.

Cameron, Euan, et. al. (n.d.). "Wild Boar in the Vineyard: Martin Luther at the Birth of the Modern World." *Columbia University Libraries Online Exhibitions*. Accessed February 25, 2025. https://exhibitions.library.columbia.edu/exhibits/show/martin-luther/flug

Carter, Tom (2024, Oct. 12). "A Tesla Fan Experiences the Cybercab for the First Time." *Business Insider*. Accessed Nov. 13, 2024. https://www.businessinsider.com/tesla-elon-musk-fan-robotaxi-event-experiences-cybercab-2024-10

Casey, Michael J. & Paul Vigna (2018). *The Truth Machine: The Blockchain and the Future of Everything*. New York, NY: Picador (Macmillan).

Castr (2024, Jan. 12). "The History of Live Streaming: A Look into its Past, Present, and Future." Castr Live Streaming, Inc. Accessed Sept. 28, 2024. https://castr.com/blog/history-of-live-streaming

CFI Team (n.d.). "Hawala." Corporate Finance Institute. Accessed August 26, 2024. https://corporatefinanceinstitute.com/resources/wealth-management/hawala/

ChainAnalysis Team (2024, Jan. 24). "Funds Stolen from Crypto Platforms Fall More Than 50% in 2023, but Hacking Remains a Significant Threat as Number of Incidents Rises." ChainAnalysis > Crime. Accessed Sept. 2, 2024. https://www.chainalysis.com/blog/crypto-hacking-stolen-funds-2024/

ChainAnalysis Team (2023, April 7). "Introduction to Decentralized Autonomous Organizations (DAOs)." Crypto Basics. Accessed Sept. 2, 2024, https://www.chainalysis.com/blog/introduction-to-decentralized-autonomous-organizations-daos/

Chimelu, Gloria Chinemerem (2024, July 18). "Coinbase Review." Buying & Selling > Crypto Exchanges. Accessed Sept. 2, 2024. https://www.investopedia.com/tech/coinbase-what-it-and-how-do-you-use-it/

Cloudflare (n.d.). "What does buffering mean? | Buffering in video streaming." Cloudflare. Accessed Sept. 28, 2024. https://www.cloudflare.com/learning/video/what-is-buffering/

CoinMarketCap, "Bitcoin," Cryptocurrencies, accessed Mar. 16, 2025, https://coinmarketcap.com/currencies/bitcoin

CoinMarketCap (2024, Aug. 31). "Today's Cryptocurrency Prices by Market Cap." Cryptocurrencies. Accessed August 31, 2024. https://coinmarketcap.com

Collins, Kenneth J. (1999). *A Real Christian: The Life of John Wesley*. Nashville, TN: Abingdon.

Cornerstone Church of Yuba City (n.d.), "About Us," accessed Mar. 5, 2025, https://cornerstoneyc.com/vr/.

Costello, Katie (2019, June 3). "Gartner Predicts 90% of Current Enterprise Blockchain Platform Implementations Will Require Replacement by 2021." Gartner, Inc.. Newsroom > Press Releases. Accessed Sept. 4, 2024. https://www.gartner.com/en/newsroom/press-releases/2019-07-03-gartner-predicts-90--of-current-enterprise-blockchain

Coxe, Charles (Ed.). (2025). *Artificial Intelligence: The Second Wave* [Special issue]. A360 Media.

Creatonics, Mr. (2022, Dec. 16). "A List Of Merchants Accepting Ethereum In 2024." CoinSutra. Retrieved from https://coinsutra.com/who-accepts-ethereum/

Daye, Jason (July 28, 2021). "DJ Soto: Why Virtual Reality Church Is Just As Legitimate As Gathering in Person." *Church Leaders*. Accessed Mar. 4, 2025. https://churchleaders.com/402303-dj-soto-virtual-reality-church-legitimate.html

Diamandis, Peter H. & Steven Kotler (2020). *The Future is Faster Than You Think: How Converging Technologies are Transforming Business, Industries, and Our Lives*. New York, NY: Simon & Schuster.

Edmonds, Rick (2020, June 23). "E-replica Editions, the Ugly Ducklings of Digital News, Have Suddenly Become Strategic." The Poynter Institute. Accessed Feb. 28, 2025. https://www.poynter.org/locally/2020/e-replica-editions-the-ugly-ducklings-of-digital-news-have-suddenly-become-strategic

Educause (2025, Jan. 7). "Horizon Reports." The Educause Horizon Report. Accessed Feb. 7, 2025. https://library.educause.edu/resources/2021/2/horizon-reports

Edwards, John (2024, May 26). "Bitcoin's Price History." Investopedia. Cryptocurrency > Bitcoin. Accessed August 30, 2024. https://www.investopedia.com/articles/forex/121815/bitcoins-price-history.asp

Els, Annie, Jones, Michael, & Swisher, David (2022, December). "Q&A About Extended Realities and Gamification: The Future of Work, Training, and Education," live virtual panel discussion. Alumni Association, Indiana Wesleyan University, Marion, IN. http://www.kaltura.com/tiny/2t9u3

Els, Annie, Jones, Michael, & Swisher, David (2022, August). "Modalities & Experiences: Unlocking the Gamified Metaversity." Fall Convocation, National & Global campus, Indiana Wesleyan University, Marion, IN.

Els, Annie, Jones, Michael, & Swisher, David (2023). Modalities & Experiences: Unlocking the Gamified Metaversity. *C2C Digital Magazine*, 1 (18), 22, article 2. Colleague2Colleague. https://scalar.usc.edu/works/c2c-digital-magazine-fall-2022---winter-2023/gamified-metaversity

Elwell, Craig K. (2011, June 23). "Brief History of the Gold Standard in the United States." Congressional Research Service. Accessed Sept. 1, 2024. https://crsreports.congress.gov/product/pdf/R/R41887/2

Erasmus, Desiderius (1511). "Moriae Encomium" (The Praise of Folly).

European Central Bank (2024, June 19). "What is Money?" Explainers. Accessed Sept. 1, 2024. https://www.ecb.europa.eu/ecb-and-you/explainers/tell-me-more/html/what_is_money.en.html

EWTN Vatican (2023, Feb. 12), "Vatican Radio: 92 Years of Broadcasting for the Catholic Church," Fondazione EWTN News (Rome, Italy), accessed Mar. 15, 2025, https://www.ewtnvatican.com/articles/vatican-radio-92-years-of-broadcasting-for-the-catholic-church-505

Fletcher, Elizabeth (n.d.). "Nazareth: Jesus' Home Town." *Life of Jesus Christ: Buildings Jesus Knew.* Accessed Feb. 24, 2018, http://www.jesus-story.net/buildings_NT.htm

Fitzpatrick, Daniel, Fox, Amanda, & Weinstein, Brad (2023), *The AI Classroom: The Ultimate Guide to Artificial Intelligence in Education,* The Hitchhiker's Guide for Educators Series. Beech Grove, IN: TeacherGoals Publishing.

Foggy Melson's Breakdown (2023, Feb. 1). "The Columbus Dispatch Becomes the First Newspaper to go Online (July 2, 1980)." YouTube video, 1:32. Accessed Mar. 1, 2025. https://youtu.be/nrcTOgxBAfY

Frost, Michael & Hirsch, Alan (2003). *The Shaping of Things to Come: Innovation and Mission for the 21st-Century Church.* Grand Rapids, MI: Baker Books.

Frow, Alan (2020, July 29). "These Precedented Times: Lessons from the Church's Response to the Spanish Flu in 1918.," Roots & Wings: From the Southland to the Nations [blog]. Accessed Sept. 28, 2024. https://alanfrow.blogspot.com/2020/07/these-precedented-times-lessons-from.html

Funk II, Kenneth H. (n.d.). "Definitions of Technology." Technology and Christian 'Values.' Oregon State University. Accessed Feb. 26, 2018. http://web.engr.oregonstate.edu/~funkk/Technology/technology.html

Galli, Mark (2020). "When a Third of the World Died: During the Catastrophic Black Plague, How Did Christians Respond?" Special issue. Plagues & Epidemics (2020): 17-19. *Christian History.* Accessed Sept. 29, 2024. https://christianhistoryinstitute.org/uploaded/ch135s.pdf

Georgia Straight Team (2024, June 15). "Detailed Guide: Companies That Accept Ethereum in 2024." Accessed Sept. 1, 2024. https://www.straight.com/guides/finance/crypto/companies-that-accept-ethereum/

Gloo (2025, Feb. 3). "Gloo and Barna Launch New State of the Church 2025 Event Series." Religion News Service. https://religionnews.com/2025/02/03/gloo-and-barna-launch-new-state-of-the-church-2025-event-series/

Gornold-Smith, Christopher (2020, Aug. 4). "Cyprian of Carthage: Finding Purpose in the Plague." International Media Ministries. Accessed Sept. 28, 2024. https://imm.edu/blog/cyprian-of-carthage-finding-purpose-in-the-plague

Hariname, Nikita (2023, Feb. 21). "Most Popular Roblox Games (February 2023)." GamerTweak. Accessed Mar. 4, 2025. https://gamertweak.com/most-popular-game-roblox

Haglili, Arik (n.d.). "The Deadliest Snakes in Israel." Fauna of the Holy Land. APT Private Tours of Israel. Accessed Mar. 1, 2025. https://private-tours-in-israel.com/the-deadliest-snakes-in-israel

Harvard University (2011, Sept. 29). "Experiences Build Brain Architecture." Excerpt from Part 1 of "Three Core Concepts in Early Development" Series. Center on the Developing Child. Harvard University. Accessed March 18, 2023. https://youtu.be/VNNsN9IJkws

Herron, Daniel (2018, Dec. 11). "Daniel Herron: Lessons from The Robloxian Christians Online Church." *Faith & Leadership*. Accessed Mar. 3, 2025. https://faithandleadership.com/ daniel-herron-lessons-the-robloxian-christians-online-church

Hipps, Shane (2005). *The Hidden Power of Electronic Culture: How Media Shapes Faith, the Gospel, and* Church. Grand Rapids, MI: Zondervan.

Hoffman, Rotem (2023, Oct. 21). "Trees of the Holy Land." *BibleWalks.com*. First accessed Feb. 24, 2018, https://www.biblewalks.com/trees/ (rechecked & updated Feb. 1, 2025)

Holy Trinity Church (n.d.). "History of HT." Holy Trinity Church Cambridge. Accessed Sept. 29, 2024. https://www.htcambridge.org.uk/our-story

Hordijk, Wim (2014, Nov. 8), "From Salt To Salary: Linguists Take A Page From Science," NPR > Cosmos & Culture. Accessed Sept. 1, 2024. https://www.npr.org/sections/13.7/2014/11/08/362478685/from-salt-to-salary-linguists-take-a-page-from-science

InterWorking Labs (2012, Dec. 26). "History of the Internet - Severe Tire Damage, The Internet's First Live Band." Vimeo. Accessed Sept. 28, 2024. https://vimeo.com/56349011

Israel National Parks Authority (n.d.). "Sepphoris." *See the Holy Land.* Accessed Feb. 26, 2018. http://www.seetheholyland.net/sepphoris/

Jahng, Kenny (2023, Feb. 17). "AI for Church Leaders & Pastors: ChatGPT, Claude, Gemini Prompts & more" Facebook group. https://www.facebook.com/groups/1230366870910779

Jarvis, Jeff (2013). *Gutenberg the Geek:* History's First Technology Entrepreneur and Silicon Valley's Patron Saint. Seattle: Amazon Digital Publishing / Audible Studios.

Jones, Dan (2017). *The Templars: The Rise and Spectacular Fall of God's Holy Warriors.* New York, NY: Viking.

Katerberg, William (2020, March 13). "The Flu Epidemic of 1918-1919 and 'Churchless Sunday'." *Origins Online.* Calvin University > Heritage Hall. Accessed Sept. 28, 2020. https://origins.calvin.edu/2020/03/13/the-flu-epidemic-of-1918-1919-and-churchless-sunday/

Krafcik, John (2018, October 10). "Where the Next 10 Million Miles Will Take Us." *Company News.* Accessed Jan. 20, 2023. https://waymo.com/blog/2018/10/where-next-10-million-miles-will-take-us

Krings, Emily (2024, Oct. 16). "What is Live Streaming Technology and How Does it Work?" The Video Experts Blog, DaCast. Accessed Dec. 30, 2024: https://www.dacast.com/blog/what-is-live-streaming

Kulevska, Angela (2024, February 9). "How Many People Play Roblox?" CyberCrew. https://cybercrew.uk/blog/how-many-people-play-roblox

"The Last Blockbuster" (2020). The Internet Movie Database (IMDb). Accessed December 7, 2024. https://www.imdb.com/title/tt8704802

Lewis, Antony (2021). *The Basics of Bitcoins and Blockchains: An Introduction to Cryptocurrencies and the Technology that Powers Them.* Coral Gables, FL: Mango Publishing.

Luther, Martin (1517). "Disputatio pro declaratione virtutis indulgentiarum" (Ninety-Five Theses).

Mark, Joshua J. (2020, April 16). "Religious Responses to the Black Death," *World History Encyclopedia.* Accessed Sept. 28, 2024. https://www.worldhistory.org/article/1541/religious-responses-to-the-black-death/

Mark, Joshua J. (2022, July 18). "The Printing Press & the Protestant Reformation." *World History Encyclopedia*. Accessed Feb. 23, 2025. https://www.worldhistory.org/article/2039/the-printing-press--the-protestant-reformation

The Matrix (1999). Directed by Lana Wachowski and Lilly Wachowski. Produced by Joel Silver. Warner Brothers Pictures, 1999. DVD (Warner Home Video, 1999).

McDowell Josh (1986). *More Than a Carpenter*. Living Books.

McLellan, Paul (2018, 3 April). "Deep Blue, AlphaGo, and AlphaZero." Cadence. Community > Breakfast Bytes. https://community.cadence.com/cadence_blogs_8/b/breakfast-bytes/posts/alpha-go-and-alpha-go-zero

Meisfjord, Tom (2018, April 23). "The Not-So-Ancient History of Live Streaming," Switchboard > Technology. Accessed Sept. 28, 2024. https://switchboard.live/blog/live-streaming-history

Milewski, Dennis (2020, Jan. 15). "HSB Survey Finds One-Third of Small Businesses Accept Cryptocurrency." *Business Wire*. Accessed Sept. 1, 2024. https://www.businesswire.com/news/home/20200115005482/en/HSB-Survey-Finds-One-Third-Small-Businesses-Accept

Moore, Jason (2022). *Both/And: Maximizing Hybrid Worship Experiences for In-Person and Online Engagement*. Plano, TX: Invite Press.

Moore, Jason (2024), *AI & the Church: A Clear Guide for the Curious and Courageous*. Plano, TX: Invite Press.

Mounce, Bill (n.d.). "τέκτων." *Greek Dictionary*. Accessed Feb. 24, 2018. https://www.billmounce.com/greek-dictionary/tekton

Museum of the Bible (July 25-26, 2024). "Generating Wisdom: Artificial Intelligence and the Bible" conference. https://www.museumofthebible.org/events/generating-wisdom-ai-and-the-bible-conference

Musée virtuel du Protestantisme (n.d.), "Martin Luther, His Written Works." *Musée Protestant*. Accessed February 24, 2025. https://museeprotestant.org/en/notice/martin-luther-his-written-works/

Nakamoto, Satoshi (2008, Oct. 31). "Bitcoin: A Peer-to-Peer Electronic Cash System." Satoshi Nakamoto Institute > Library. Accessed August 30, 2024. https://nakamotoinstitute.org/library/bitcoin

Nakamoto, Satoshi (2008, Oct. 31), "Bitcoin P2P e-cash Paper," email message to The Cryptography Mailing List, accessed August 30, 2024, https://satoshi.nakamotoinstitute.org/emails/cryptography/1

NBC Today Show, S2022, E183. "How the Metaverse is Changing the Way People Attend Church." Produced by Erin Farley. Directed by Lee Miller. Featuring Jason Poling and Cornerstone Church of Yuba City. Aired Aug. 3, 2022 on NBC. 2022. Accessed Mar. 2, 2025. https://www.today.com/video/how-the-metaverse-is-changing-the-way-people-attend-church-145390661832

O'Malley, Timothy (2021, Nov. 19). "How Did the Church Fare During the Black Death and 400 Years of the Plague?," *Church Life Journal*, University of Notre Dame. Accessed Sept. 28, 2024. https://churchlifejournal.nd.edu/articles/how-did-the-church-fare-during-the-black-death-and-400-years-of-the-plague/

Pace, Lisha (July 24, 2023). "The History of Leonardo da Vinci's Automata." History-Computer.com. https://history-computer.com/leonardo-da-vincis-automata

Pete, Kelly (2017, Oct. 25). "Hughes de Payens & the Birth of the Knights Templar." HistoryTime UK. YouTube video. Accessed Sept. 1, 2024. https://youtu.be/0DAUN6V4brA

Poling, Jason (2022). "A Theology of the Metaverse" [White paper]. Cornerstone Church of Yuba City. Accessed March 4, 2025. https://bit.ly/TheologyOfTheMetaverse

Portnoy, Gary (1982). "Where Everybody Knows Your Name." The Cheers Theme: Music. Accessed Mar. 3, 2025. https://www.garyportnoy.com/cds-cheers-theme

Ramsey, Dave (2023, Sept. 22), "Get Ready for a Digital Currency? The Ramsey Show Highlights, YouTube video, 1:44. Accessed August 30, 2024. https://youtu.be/mUywzuPY7xY

Ramsey Solutions (2024, April 5). "Are We Really Headed for a Cashless Society?" Budgeting > Spending. Accessed August 30, 2024. https://www.ramseysolutions.com/budgeting/cashless-society

Reed, Alexander (2024, Aug. 7). "Who Accepts Bitcoin as Payment?" 99Bitcoins. Accessed Sept. 1, 2024. https://99bitcoins.com/bitcoin/who-accepts/

Reed, Jeff (2022). *VR & the Metaverse Church: How God is Moving in This Virtual, Yet Quite Real, Reality.* Dallas, TX: Leadership Network.

Restream Team (2021, Feb. 2). "The History of Live Streaming," Restream. io. Accessed Sept. 28, 2024. https://restream.io/blog/history-of-live-streaming

Robie, Jonathan (Jan. 3, 2024). "Artificial Intelligence and Bible Translation" *Biblical Archaeology.* Accessed July 26, 2024. https://www.biblicalarchaeology.org/daily/artificial-intelligence-and-bible-translation

Robles, Stephen (2024, July 16). "What Is Live Streaming & How Does It Work? | Full Guide." Riverside FM. Accessed Sept. 28, 2024. https://riverside.fm/blog/what-is-live-streaming

Schultze, Quentin (2012). *Gutenberg, God, and the Devil's Plug-In: Lessons about Digital Publishing from the Famous Printer's Failed Killer App.* Grand Rapids, MI: Edenridge Press LLC.

Sharma, Rakesh (2024, June 12). "Non-Fungible Token (NFT): What It Means and How It Works," Investopedia. Accessed Sept. 4, 2024. https://www.investopedia.com/non-fungible-tokens-nft-5115211

Shakir, Umar (2024, Dec. 6). "Amazon Just Completed its First Delivery by Drone in Italy." The Verge. Accessed Feb. 25, 2025. https://www.theverge.com/2024/12/6/24314789/amazon-drone-test-italy-prime-air-delivery

Shedden, David (2014, Sept. 24). "Today in Media History: CompuServe and the First Online Newspapers." The Poynter Institute. Accessed Feb. 28, 2025. https://www.poynter.org/reporting-editing/2014/today-in-media-history-compuserve-and-the-first-online-newspapers

Shelley, Bruce L. (2008). *Church History in Plain Language*, 3rd. Nashville: Thomas Nelson, 240.

Shubham, Nena (2023, December 27). "How Many Games Are in Roblox? (2023)." GamerTweak. Accessed Mar. 3, 2025. https://gamertweak.com/how-many-games-roblox/#how-many-roblox-games-are-there-in-total-2023

Skydrop (2023, July 14). "SkyDrop and Domino's Expand Drone Delivery." YouTube video, 1:21. Accessed Feb. 22, 2025. https://www.youtube.com/watch?v=mSwEGUhLm1A

Smethurst, Matt (2012, April 5). "The Suffering Servant and Isaiah 53: A Conversation with Darrell Bock." The Gospel Coalition. Accessed Feb. 27, 2025, https://www.thegospelcoalition.org/article/the-suffering-servant-and-isaiah-53-a-conversation-with-darrell-bock

Snyder, Howard (2014). *The Radical Wesley: The Patterns and Practices of a Movement Maker*. Franklin, TN: Seedbed.

Stafford, Eric & Scherr, Elana (Oct. 10, 2024), "Tesla Robotaxi Is a Driverless Car That Will Cost Under $30,000." *Car & Driver*. Accessed Dec. 7, 2024. https://www.caranddriver.com/news/a62567491/tesla-robotaxi-reveal

Starship Technologies (n.d.). "University Campuses." Our Solutions. Accessed Dec. 7, 2024. https://www.starship.xyz/operations

Suleyman, Mustafa (2023). *The Coming Wave: Technology, Power, and the 21st Century's Greatest Dilemma*. New York: Crown.

Sunshine, Glenn (2020, July 01). "The Church's Response to Pandemics Throughout History and the Lessons for Today." *Mission Frontiers Magazine*. Accessed Sept. 28, 2024. https://www.missionfrontiers.org/issue/article/the-churchs-response-to-pandemics-throughout-history-and-the-lessons-for-to

Swisher, David (2024, August 15). "The Current State of AI." AI Advisory Committee Kickoff. The Wesleyan Church, Fishers, IN.

Swisher, David (2024, June). "Doing the Right Thing with AI: AI Ethics for Educators and Nonprofit Leaders." AI Fusion Conference 2024, Carmel, IN. Hosted by Blaizing Academy & Indiana Wesleyan University.

Swisher, David (2024), "Ethical Standards Framework," AI Fusion Conference, https://tinyurl.com/EthicalStandardsFramework

Swisher, David (2024, April 22). "Inconceivable! Field Preaching, Digital Church, & the Metaverse: Embracing John Wesley's Legacy of Innovation to Inform the Virtual Ministry of Tomorrow." *Didache: Faithful Teaching*, 24:1 (Spring 2024). ISSN: 15360156 https://didache.nazarene.org/index.php/volume-24-number-1

Swisher, D. (2024, April 17). "AI & Preaching." Guest speaker for REL 665 - Advanced Homiletics course. Pastoral Ministries (Kern) Program, graduate. Indiana Wesleyan University, Marion, IN.

Swisher, David (2023, August 22). "Research-Based Best Practices for Developing Effective Presentations," Indiana Wesleyan University (Marion, IN): http://www.kaltura.com/tiny/hk31z

Swisher, David (2023, August). "Academic Integrity in an Era of Generative AI." Fall Faculty Professional Development emphasis on "Generative AI and Adult Education" (Faculty Enrichment, National & Global Campus). Indiana Wesleyan University, Marion, IN.

Swisher, David (2023, March). "Inconceivable! Field Preaching, Digital Church, & the Metaverse: Embracing John Wesley's Legacy of Innovation to Inform the Virtual Ministry of Tomorrow." Annual meeting of the Wesleyan Theological Society, Asbury Theological Seminary, Wilmore, KY.

Swisher, David (2018, March). "Not Necessarily a Carpenter: Bridging the Technology Gap by Reconsidering Jesus' Role as τέκτων." Inaugural address. Society for the Study of the Integration of Technology with Wesleyan Theology & Praxis (SSITWTP). Joint session of the Wesleyan Theological Society and the Society for Pentecostal Studies. Lee University (Cleveland, TN).

Swisher, David (2009, Aug. 1). "Look & Live." Sermon. Hall Wesleyan Church (Delphos, KS). Available on YouTube at: https://www.youtube.com/watch?v=f3znxbBSbK8 (Parts 1 & 2)

Swisher, David & Els, Annie (2024). Rethinking Assessment in Light of Generative AI. *C2C Digital Magazine*, 1 (20), article 3. Colleague-2Colleague. https://scalar.usc.edu/works/c2c-digital-magazine-fall-2023--winter-2024/rethinking-assessment-in-light-of-generative-ai

Swisher, David & Snyder, Tiffany (2023, August 24). "Preparing Your Classroom for the World of AI." CAS Faculty Retreat (College of Arts & Sciences), Indiana Wesleyan University; held at Eastview Wesleyan Church, Gas City, IN.

Swisher, David & Teoh, Jase (2023, January). "Bakhtin, Vygotsky, & the Metaverse: Why Learning Flourishes in Virtual Reality." Colleague2Colleague Professional Development Workshop, Overland Park, KS. https://tinyurl.com/BakhtinVygotskyMV-C2C

Swisher, David & Teoh, Jase. (2022, August). "Bakhtin, Vygotsky, & the Metaverse: Why Learning Flourishes in Virtual Reality." Summer Institute for Distance Learning & Instructional Technology (SIDLIT) Conference, Johnson County Community College, Overland Park, KS.

Swisher, David as WildcatTech (2023, Jan. 20), "My First Ride in a Self-driving (Driverless) Vehicle!, YouTube video, 9:58, accessed Nov. 10, 2024, https://www.youtube.com/watch?v=xble_WPkIsc

Tesla (2024, Oct. 10). "We, Robot." Tesla Live. Live Video Broadcast on X. Oct. 10, 2024, 10:58 pm, 53:00 - 1:18:00 https://x.com/i/broadcasts/1YqJDkbjazvGV

Thorne, David (2024, Nov. 8), "AI for Churches" Facebook group, https://www.facebook.com/groups/aiforchurches

Thrun, Sebastian (2010, Oct. 9). "What We're Driving At." *Google Official Blog*. Accessed Nov. 13, 2024. https://googleblog.blogspot.com/2010/10/what-were-driving-at.html

Trithemius, Johannes. *In Praise of Scribes*. Translated by Roland Behrendt. Lawrence, KS: Coronado Press, 1974. https://archive.org/details/inpraiseofscribe0000trit/page/56/mode/2up

Turner, Jordan (2022, March 22). "A CFO's Quick Guide to Cryptocurrency," Gartner, Inc. Insights > Finance. Accessed Sept. 4, 2024. https://www.gartner.com/en/articles/a-cfo-s-quick-guide-to-cryptocurrency

Van der Laan, Ray (n.d.). "The Language of Culture." *That the World May Know*. Accessed Feb. 25, 2018. https://www.thattheworldmayknow.com/language-of-culture-article

VR Church (n.d.), "VR Church in the Metaverse," accessed Mar. 3, 2025, https://www.vrchurch.org

Wahlberg, Adam (2024, April 22). "Panera and Jet's Pizza To Offer Drone Delivery in Select Markets." Food on Demand: The Intersection of Food, Technology, & Mobility. Accessed Feb. 22, 2025. https://foodondemand.com/04222024/panera-and-jets-pizza-to-offer-drone-delivery-in-select-markets/

Walmart (2024, Jan. 9). "Sky High Ambitions: Walmart To Make Largest Drone Delivery Expansion of Any U.S. Retailer. Wal-Mart > News. Accessed Feb. 22, 2025. https://corporate.walmart.com/news/2024/01/09/sky-high-ambitions-walmart-to-make-largest-drone-delivery-expansion-of-any-us-retailer

Ward, Reginald W. & Heitzenrater, Richard P., eds. (1988). The Works of John Wesley. Bicentennial ed. Vol. 18, *Journals and Diaries*. Nashville: Abingdon.

Waugh, Barry (2017, Oct. 30). "The Printing Press and the Protestant Reformation." Reformation21. Alliance of Confessing Evangelicals. Accessed Oct. 13, 2025. https://reformation21.org/the-printing-press-and-the-protestant-reformation-php-2/

Waymo (n.d.). "Waymo Story." *Our History.* Accessed Nov. 13, 2024. https://waymo.com/about/#story

Waymo (n.d.), "Our Safety Philosophy," Safety, accessed Nov. 13, 2024, https://waymo.com/safety

waymonho (2023, Dec. 5). "What is a File Hash?" KC7 Foundation. Accessed Sept. 2, 2024. https://kc7cyber.com/blog/what-is-a-file-hash

Weatherbed, Jess (2024, Dec. 18). "Alphabet's Wing Will Deliver DoorDash by Drone in Dallas-Fort Worth." The Verge. Accessed Feb. 22, 2025. https://www.theverge.com/2024/12/18/24324111/alphabet-wing-door-dash-drone-deliveries-dallas-fort-worth

Webb, Amy (2016). *The Signals Are Talking: Why Today's Fringe is Tomorrow's Mainstream.* New York, NY: Public Affairs.

Webb, Amy (2019). *The Big Nine: How the Tech Titans & Their Thinking Machines Could Warp Humanity.* New York, NY: Public Affairs.

Wesley, John (1739, March 20). "To James Harvey." The Letters of John Wesley. *Wesley Center Online.* Accessed Feb. 24, 2025. https://wesley.nnu.edu/john-wesley/the-letters-of-john-wesley/wesleys-letters-1739/

Wesley, John (1739). *Journal of John Wesley.* Ed. By Percy Livingstone Parker. Christian Classics Ethereal Library. https://www.ccel.org/ccel/wesley/journal.vi.iii.i.html

Wolfram, Stephen (2023). *What Is ChatGPT Doing ... and Why Does It Work?* Champaign, IL: Champaign, IL.

Author Biography

ABOUT
DAVID J. SWISHER

David J. Swisher is an AI Trainer & Consultant and ordained Wesleyan minister with almost four decades of bivocational ministry experience, nearly all of it utilizing technology and multimedia to communicate the gospel effectively. Recently, he trained thousands of T-Mobile employees nationwide on Enterprise ChatGPT and has also done AI training workshops for district and denominational groups. He is currently serving as the Director of Online Services at Kingswood University and teaches adjunct at several universities.

Swisher previously served as Senior Learning Experience Designer and Technology Integration Specialist at Indiana Wesleyan University, and for nearly a decade was the Director of Learning Management Technologies at Tabor College. With more than 24 years in leadership roles involving educational technology, innovation, and online learning, he has helped multiple institutions and ministries adopt cutting-edge tools with strategic intentionality, including major online learning and LMS platform transitions.

Swisher earned his Doctor of Ministry (DMin) in "Semiotics, Church, & Culture" from Portland Seminary at George Fox University, where he studied under author and futurist Leonard Sweet. He also holds a Master's in Instructional Design & Technology, a Bachelor's in Christian Ministries, and a certificate in Practical Theology. He is a past chair and active leader in College2Colleague, a regional professional association equipping educators to navigate the challenges of instructional technology and distance learning.

A practitioner as well as a scholar, Swisher developed and taught a first-of-its-kind *Technology for Ministry* course at Tabor College and founded a focus group for the Wesleyan Theological Society on technology and ministry. He researches and implements strategies for the effective use of generative AI, virtual reality & metaverse platforms, and multimedia learning in ministry and education, and he regularly collaborates with innovators and pioneers in these fields.

Swisher's published research, "Top Writer" designation on Quora (where his answers have drawn over 4.7 million views), and extensive training experience all highlight his ability to convey complex technology concepts with clarity. He has successfully guided multiple organizations through major technology transitions and continues to help pastors and ministry leaders face technological disruption with wisdom, clarity, and strategic insight.

SCAN HERE to learn more about
Invite Ministries—created to invite people to a deeper
faith and living relationship with Jesus Christ